ESSENTIALS

of Intellectual Property

Second Edition

ESSENTIALS SERIES

The Essentials Series was created for busy business advisory and corporate professionals. The books in this series were designed so that these busy professionals can quickly acquire knowledge and skills in core business areas.

Each book provides need-to-have fundamentals for those professionals who must:

- Get up to speed quickly, because they have been promoted to a new position or have broadened their responsibility scope
- Manage a new functional area
- Brush up on new developments in their area of responsibility
- Add more value to their company or clients

For more information on any of the above titles, please visit www.wiley.com.

ESSENTIALS
of Intellectual Property
Law, Economics, and Strategy

Second Edition

Alexander I. Poltorak

Paul J. Lerner

WILEY

John Wiley & Sons, Inc.

Published by John Wiley & Sons, Inc., Hoboken, New Jersey.
Published simultaneously in Canada.

Library of Congress Cataloging-in-Publication Data

Poltorak, Alexander (Alexander I.)
    Essentials of intellectual property / Alexander I. Poltorak, Paul J. Lerner.—2nd ed.
        p. cm.—(Essentials series)
    Includes bibliographical references and index.
    ISBN 978-0-470-88850-6 (pbk.)
    1.   Intellectual property—United States.   I. Lerner, Paul (Paul J.)   II. Title.
    KF2980.P65 2011
    346.7304'8—dc22

                                                                        2010039904

10 9 8 7 6 5 4 3 2 1

Contents

Foreword to the Second Edition

The three most important developments in world history, according to Abraham Lincoln, were the perfection of printing, the discovery of America, and the introduction of patent laws.

Printing allowed the widespread communication of ideas across time and space. The discovery of America unveiled a vast continent of resources and had produced a unique form of government where, for the first time in world history, people governed themselves. "The patent system," Lincoln said, "added the fuel of interest to the fire of genius."

Lincoln's appreciation of patent laws reflected that of George Washington and the other founding fathers of the United States. The framers of the Constitution, of which Washington was the most prominent, put into that document a simple 32-word provision that has been the foundation of U.S. progress for more than two centuries:

> The Congress shall have power to promote the progress of science and useful arts, by securing for limited times to authors and inventors the exclusive right to their respective writings and discoveries.

This is the only place in the body of the Constitution where the word *right* exists. The rights to engage in free speech, own a gun, petition the government, and not incriminate yourself, among others, were enacted later as constitutional amendments.

In Washington's first State of the Union message (January 1790), he asked the first Congress to enact patent and copyright laws.

On April 10, 1790, the sixth law enacted in the United States was the Patent Act. The eighth law, enacted on May 31, 1790, was the Copyright Act. With that, the first Congress established a national development policy based on stimulating innovation, creativity, investment, and the sharing of knowledge that patents and copyrights facilitate.

The genius of Article I, Section 8, is that in authorizing Congress to write the laws on intellectual property (IP) rights, it also encouraged it to change those laws to accommodate the needs of a growing nation. As anticipated, Congress has altered those laws, often wisely but sometimes not.

The intellectual property rights of the American people represent a golden covenant between society and creative individuals that encourages the sharing of their knowledge in exchange for a publicly granted right of exclusive use for a set time. This covenant is the foundation of the American economy.

Despite the fundamental importance of these intellectual property rights, most Americans—including corporate leaders, academics, businesspeople, members of Congress, and even most inventors—have only a vague awareness of what those rights are and how they are applied.

Alexander I. Poltorak and Paul J. Lerner published, in 2002, a book that set out to clarify what they termed the *Essentials of Intellectual Property*. Almost immediately, their book became the standard for anyone wishing to understand what intellectual property is and how best to protect and advance one's IP rights.

Poltorak was a prodigy physicist who earned his doctorate at age 22. He emigrated to the United States from the former USSR in 1982, became an inventor, and formed General Patent Corporation (GPC), which helps inventors and companies protect their intellectual property.

Lerner is an aeronautical engineer who holds an MBA and a law degree. Prior to becoming the senior vice president and general counsel of GPC, he led the IP departments at Olin Corporation, Black & Decker Corporation, and other major national companies.

This update of their original book also includes new chapters on how the courts are changing the patent law via reinterpretation of rules and practices long thought settled, and it gives an up-to-the-minute analysis of the patent reform legislation that, fortunately for inventors and most companies, Congress has refused to enact during the 109th, 110th, and 111th sessions.

This revised edition of *Essentials of Intellectual Property* is a well-written, jargon-free compendium of information about IP, coupled with shrewd advice, which I recommend highly to all interested in invention, innovation, intellectual property rights, and national development.

Pat Choate

Washington, Virginia

September 3, 2010

Foreword to the First Edition

As I write this, the U.S. Patent and Trademark Office (USPTO) has just released its annual report of the top 10 private-sector organizations receiving patents in the prior year. A comparison of the listing for 2001 to those of past years reveals that the number of patents required to rank first (as IBM has done since 1993) has more than tripled in the past decade; the total number of U.S. patents issued annually has gone up nearly 65 percent; and the proportion garnered by the top 10—all well-known electronics companies—has increased from 7.5 percent to nearly 10 percent of all patents issued in 2001.

Fascinating statistics, but what's behind them? Simply put, it's money. Dollars, yen, euros—billions of them, collected in the form of royalties every year by companies and individuals (the late Jerome Lemelson, for example) with valuable intellectual property, principally patents. IBM alone will have received nearly $2 billion during 2001 in IP-related payments, most of it cash, and nearly all of it pure profit. Canon, Hitachi, Lucent, and many other top patent holders enjoy significant returns on their R&D investments. And then there are the software companies—Oracle, Microsoft, and, yes, IBM again—whose products *are* intellectual property, protected globally by copyrights and earning billions in sales.

No wonder companies of all sizes throughout the world (8 of the USPTO's top 10 are non-U.S. companies) are paying close attention to acquiring and leveraging patents, copyrights, trademarks, and other intellectual property. What was once the province of the patent department, all too often a corporate backwater, now has the full attention of most CFOs and many CEOs. As IP is seldom taught outside of law schools, and then only to those focused on this niche of jurisprudence, where can the business executive turn for a clear, concise, and useful briefing on this new phenomenon? Most legal tomes cover in dreary prose, and at great length, every aspect of IP law but none of the exciting potential of their subject matter. *Essentials of Intellectual Property*, by Alexander Poltorak and Paul Lerner, admirably fills this vacuum.

The authors—who are the principals of General Patent Corporation (GPC), an imaginative and successful intellectual property management and licensing firm—not only know the subject matter, they explore the nuances and expose the pitfalls in a thorough and refreshingly readable fashion. They resort to plain English to guide us to a clear understanding of this "currency of the New Economy" by systematically explaining the essential legal elements and business value of each type of IP, with useful suggestions on how to acquire, protect, and deploy these fruits of creativity.

It is well realized that most IP, particularly that held by corporations, is undervalued and unappreciated. As IP is usually not reflected on the balance sheet (there is currently a groundswell of proposals to change this), it is widely ignored by those charged with providing a return on investment, as represented by assets. Nevertheless, the returns are extremely generous once these valuable assets are recognized and tapped for their potential. The authors provide comprehensive and useful insight and guidance for an effective process of protection, recognition, valuation, and exploitation of what a recent book on the subject referred to as "Rembrandts in the attic."[1]

---

[1] Kevin G. Rivette and David Kline, *Rembrandts in the Attic* (Boston: Harvard Business School Press, 2000).

A chapter addressing the prospect of liability to corporate executives and directors for mismanaging intellectual property makes sobering reading and, if nothing else will, should be a wake-up call to many who have approved large sums to acquire IP without having a clue of what to do with it and why. If this were not sufficient, Chapter 10, "The Patent Portfolio and Its Effect on Stock Price," should arouse the most somnolent of corporate custodians.

Poltorak and Lerner have provided a clear and useful road map for the non-lawyer business executive, without stinting on necessary detail—and, surprisingly for the genre, they have done so with much grace and good humor. Moreover, the appendixes include very usable sample forms that address everything from applying for a patent to a model license agreement.

I can think of no more sincere tribute to Alex and Paul than to say, "This is the book I wish I had written."

Emmett J. Murtha
Stamford, CT
January 25, 2002

Preface:
Intellectual Property:
The Currency of the
New Economy

Intellectual property, also known simply as IP, has become one of the most talked about topics in business today, yet it is still one of the least understood. Simply stated, intellectual property consists of products of the human mind and creativity that are protected by law. It is an intangible, lacking physical substance. It has neither length nor width nor height. It has no weight and casts no shadow. It is colorless, odorless, and tasteless.

Like tangible property, intellectual property can be bought, sold, and rented. Also like tangible property, it can be lost or destroyed through carelessness or neglect. It is insurable and could be used as collateral. It may be the result of a momentary flash of inspiration or years of diligent and painstaking labor. It may be lost in a moment or continue in perpetuity.

Whatever its other characteristics, however, intellectual property *does* have economic value—often great economic value, although this value is often overlooked, underestimated, and underreported. In business, it may constitute either an opportunity or a threat, depending (in large part) on who owns it.

It has often been said that "knowledge is power." Although unsaid, knowledge is also wealth. Indeed, in today's knowledge-based economy, intellectual property is often the single most important asset of an enterprise. As of 2009, intangible assets represented 81 percent of the total market value of the S&P 500 companies—more than double what it was 20 years ago.

Those companies that fail to accord intellectual property a position at the top of the corporate agenda are now, at best, doomed to lose competitive advantage; at worst, they may face ruin. It is for this reason that businesspeople should have a basic understanding of the nature and uses of intellectual property.

Intellectual property presents different opportunities (and different challenges) as an enterprise or an industry moves through the normal business life cycle. It may constitute the basis for a start-up company or even a new industry. It may offer new products or services to growing enterprises; in mature industries, it may establish the competitive advantage that spells the difference between prosperity and decline, leading to ultimate demise.

Until recently, it was thought that intellectual property was of concern only to a rare few engineers and scientists (and, of course, to the patent attorneys). This belief, never correct, is now largely discredited. In actuality, intellectual property is, or properly should be, of concern to marketing and product planning staffs, engineers and product designers, and product promotion and advertising personnel. Needless to say, intellectual property must be well understood and be of foremost concern to corporate boards, chief executive officers (CEOs), chief financial officers (CFOs), entrepreneurs, and other business managers. Indeed, with the advent and subsequent explosion in business method patents, there are now few, if any, business functions that need not concern themselves with intellectual property. In addition, the courts are increasingly recognizing the duty of care owed by corporate officers and directors in the management (i.e., the protection, effective utilization, and proper valuation) of a firm's intellectual property.

In the Introduction to this book, intellectual property is defined and its uses described. The reader is then introduced in Chapters 1 and 2 to the various types of IP and how they can be protected.

The book next addresses the management of intellectual property. Two chapters are devoted to documenting inventions and IP portfolio management (Chapter 3) and gathering and using competitive intelligence (Chapter 4). Chapter 5 identifies various approaches to the valuation of intellectual property, and Chapter 6 discusses ways in which this value may be realized.

Chapter 7 addresses the responsibilities of the business manager with respect to IP and presents guidelines as to how these responsibilities can be satisfied. In Chapter 8, the key issues involved in IP enforcement are presented and analyzed, namely, development of an enforcement strategy, law firm selection and management, costs, risks, and litigation risk analysis. Chapter 9 addresses the IP problems created by the Internet and e-commerce, and Chapter 10 deals with the effects that patent portfolios may have on stock price.

The final two chapters are devoted to two different ways in which patent law changes and evolves: Chapter 11 describes how the courts have changed patent law in a number of landmark cases, and Chapter 12 discusses some of the key reforms Congress has proposed to the patent system and what impact those changes would have on inventors and business owners if a Patent Reform Act should pass.

Author's Note

I t is the purpose of this book to introduce the business executive to the principles underlying the identification, protection, and use of intellectual property in the business environment. To this end, key concepts and facts have been described and the authors have attempted to illustrate how these concepts and facts influence (actually, *should* influence) decision making, from the formulation of routine procedures to strategic planning. Of necessity, these descriptions are generalized.

Exceptions abound to every rule stated in the following chapters (your lawyer will, no doubt, be more than happy to enumerate these exceptions for you). Moreover, the law is a living, constantly evolving creature. The rules of the game are constantly changing—often in midplay and sometimes retroactively. A little knowledge is a dangerous thing. Before proceeding, review matters with a qualified professional. Reading this book, however carefully, is no substitute for professional guidance.

Acknowledgments

The authors wish to express their gratitude to Samson Vermont, who has graciously provided many of the patent statistics cited in this book.

Our editors, Susan McDermott, Michael Lisk, and others at John Wiley & Sons, deserve much thanks for seeing this work through.

Without the tireless efforts and unfailing good cheer of Nava Cooper, this work would not have been completed.

While the credit goes to many who have assisted us, the errors are all ours.

About the Authors

Alexander I. Poltorak is the founder, chairman, and chief executive officer of General Patent Corporation (GPC), an intellectual property (IP) management boutique focusing on patent licensing and enforcement as well as IP strategy and valuation. He is also a managing director of IP Holdings LLC, an IP-centric merchant banking organization offering IP-related financial, brokerage, and advisory services. He is the founder and president of a nonprofit industry group, American Innovators for Patent Reform. Alex Poltorak is a Certified Licensing Professional (CLP).

Dr. Poltorak has served as an assistant professor of biomathematics at the Neurology Department of Cornell University Medical College, as an assistant professor of physics at Touro College, and as adjunct professor of law at The Globe Institute for Technology, and has been a guest lecturer on intellectual property law and economics at the Columbia University School of Business and School of Engineering. He has a graduate degree in theoretical and mathematical physics from the State University of Kuban (Russia). He had been awarded a doctorate degree for his research in general relativity, which was rescinded for his anti-communist dissident activities.

Besides *Essentials of Intellectual Property*, Dr. Poltorak also co-authored *Essentials of Licensing Intellectual Property* (John Wiley & Sons, 2004) and contributed a chapter to *Making Innovation Pay—Turning IP into Shareholder Value* (John Wiley & Sons, 2006). He has also authored and co-authored numerous articles on intellectual property, which have appeared in such publications as the *Washington Times*, the *Christian Science Monitor*, *Patent Strategy & Management*, *American Venture*, *Inventors Digest*, and many more. He served on the advisory board of *Patent Strategy & Management*. He was a U.S. co-chairman for the Subcommittee on Information Exchange of the U.S.-U.S.S.R. Trade and Economic Counsel.

Paul J. Lerner is the senior vice president and general counsel of General Patent Corporation (GPC). Before joining GPC, Mr. Lerner was a partner in the Hartford, Connecticut, business law firm of Pepe & Hazard LLP. He has led IP law departments at Olin Corp., Black & Decker Corp., and multinational electrical construction giant Asea Brown Boveri, Inc.

Prior to embarking on a law career, Mr. Lerner was a project manager at the Illinois Institute of Technology Research Institute in Chicago, where he managed a technology transfer and technology forecasting team. Mr. Lerner's education includes a BS in Aeronautical Engineering from Purdue University, an MBA from Loyola University, a JD from DePaul University, and postgraduate legal studies at John Marshall College of Law.

In addition to *Essentials of Intellectual Property*, Paul Lerner co-authored with Alexander Poltorak *Essentials of Licensing Intellectual Property* (John Wiley & Sons, 2004) as well as numerous articles.

Mr. Lerner is a registered patent attorney and an adjunct professor of intellectual property at the University of New Haven.

General Patent Corporation is headquartered in Suffern, New York.

Introduction:
Setting the Stage

Intellectual Capital, Intellectual Assets, and Intellectual Property

Intellectual property has become a cliché du jour of the business world. That intellectual property is important is also evidenced by the fact that, of late, everyone is trying to get into the act. Formerly, only patent attorneys used the word *intellectual*, as in *intellectual property*. Now, however, we have management consultants speaking of *intellectual capital*, while accountants and economists write about *intellectual assets*. Nevertheless, the concepts underlying these terms have significance, and it would be well to understand them.

Intellectual Capital: What They Thought Up

Intellectual capital, in its simplest sense, comprises the sum total of all knowledge in an enterprise. It is what everyone in a firm knows, and what therefore gives the firm its competitive advantage. Intellectual capital includes the knowledge and skills of employees; the processes, ideas, designs, inventions, and technologies utilized by the firm; and the relationships it has developed with both customers and suppliers. It includes software, business methods, manuals, reports, publications, and databases. It includes not only knowledge and information but also the

TIPS AND TECHNIQUES

Intellectual capital is the sum total of all knowledge in an enterprise, as it resides in the minds of its employees, which can be leveraged to create wealth.

intangible infrastructure that facilitates its use, exchange, and retention. Needless to say, intellectual capital includes patents, trademarks, copyrights, trade dress rights, Internet domain names, and the like.

In the broadest sense, intellectual capital is what is left of an enterprise after it has been stripped of all its tangible assets, such as land, buildings, machinery, inventory, and cash.

Intellectual capital = Enterprise value − Value of all hard assets

Intellectual capital cannot exist outside the context of a particular enterprise or independent of its strategy. Intellectual capital that may be at the heart of one business may be utterly useless to another business. Moreover, it is only a clearly defined strategy that can separate useful knowledge from informational noise and disparate facts. It is the structure imposed by a strategy that brings order and meaning to what is otherwise informational chaos. Like a magnet attracts iron filings, strategy and purpose create the discernable informational patterns that we call *knowledge*.

Purpose → Strategy → Information → Knowledge

Intellectual Assets: What They Wrote Down

While intellectual capital is the cornerstone of the modern business enterprise, much of it is tacit knowledge that resides in the minds of its employees. When an employee leaves the organization, so does the intellectual capital that resides in the employee—the employee's knowledge, experience, skills, creativity, and relations with others (customers, suppliers, and other employees). Stated succinctly, intellectual capital is what walks out the door at the end of the day.

> **TIPS AND TECHNIQUES**
>
> Intellectual assets are intellectual capital that is identified, documented, and available to be shared and replicated within the organization.

Obviously, there is a risk that it won't walk back in tomorrow. Moreover, even while an employee is working for an organization, his knowledge cannot be most effectively utilized unless it is identified, documented, and shared with others. Thus, the principal objectives of intellectual capital management are to identify, capture, and document it and to make it accessible to others in the organization. Intellectual capital that has been so captured, preserved, catalogued, and made available for sharing is known as *intellectual assets*.

An organization does not own its employees—they can leave or may be fired. But the organization does own the intellectual assets they create while a part of the organization. Clearly, it is in the best interest of the business enterprise to encourage its employees to disclose and record this intellectual capital (programs to achieve this goal are discussed and described in Chapter 3).

The intellectual capital management process flow looks like this:

Search out → Identify → Capture → Document
→ Index → Store → Augment → Replicate

Intellectual Property: What You Protected

Intellectual assets legally protected under applicable laws are called *intellectual property*. A typical example of intellectual property is a patent that is protected by the patent law (Title 35 of the United States Code).

Intellectual capital, intellectual assets, and intellectual property overlap (see Exhibit I.1). Intellectual assets form a more valuable subset of intellectual capital, and intellectual property forms an even more valuable subset of intellectual assets. The push for growth in value

EXHIBIT I.1

Overlapping Intellectual Property

Intellectual Capital

Intellectual Assets

Intellectual Property

dictates the flow of the management process: to distill intellectual assets from intellectual capital and to further distill intellectual property from intellectual assets. Thus, it is the goal of management to produce intellectual property.

The broad spectrum of intellectual property may be divided into two segments: the (supposedly) well-defined classical or statutory assets and the less-definite contractual or common-law assets (although these, too, may be governed by statute—generally, but not exclusively, state statutes). The former segment comprises the well-known but often-misunderstood trinity of patents, trademarks, and copyrights and, in recent years, has expanded to include mask works and registered designs. The latter segment comprises trade secrets and know-how, as well as noncompetition agreements and confidential disclosure agreements.

 TIPS AND TECHNIQUES

Intellectual property is intellectual assets that are protected under applicable laws.

CHAPTER 1

The Big Three: Patents, Trademarks, and Copyrights

After reading this chapter you will be able to:

- Understand the various kinds of patents and the nature of the protection offered by each.

- Understand what constitutes patent infringement.

- Understand the major considerations and factors to be borne in mind when securing patents.

- Know the factors involved in choosing a good patent attorney.

- Understand the nature of trademarks and service marks and the requirements for registration of these marks, as well as the proper mode of use of a trademark or service mark.

- Know how to choose a mark and determine whether it is available for adoption.

- Understand the nature of copyrights along with the uses of copyrights in nontraditional applications, such as protection of computer software.

- Recognize work-for-hire situations that may call for a written copyright assignment.

- Understand the doctrine of fair use.

IN THE REAL WORLD

"The Congress shall have the power to . . . promote the Progress of Science and useful Arts, by Securing for limited Times to Authors and Inventors the exclusive Right to their respective Writings and Discoveries."

—U.S. Constitution, Article I, Section 8

Patents

A patent conveys to its owner the right to prevent others from making, using, selling, offering for sale, or importing the patented invention. Patents are national in nature, having effect only within the territory of the issuing country.

The patent law of the United States provides for three kinds of patents: plant patents, design patents, and utility patents. Plant patents cover asexually reproduced plants and are primarily of interest only to plant breeders. Design patents cover the ornamental design of an article (i.e., its appearance) to the extent that that design or appearance is dictated by aesthetic, rather than functional, considerations. The majority of patents are of the third kind—utility patents—and it is with these that we shall be mostly, but not exclusively, concerned.

TIPS AND TECHNIQUES

To be patentable, an invention must be:

- Novel
- Nonobvious
- Useful

A utility patent, generally speaking, may cover a device or an article, a composition of matter, a method or process of doing or making something, or, less commonly, a new application for an existing device or material, or a product (otherwise known and, therefore, not patentable) made by a particular new process.

In order to qualify for a patent, an invention must be novel, non-obvious, and useful. The utility requirement is largely self-explanatory and rarely comprises a significant obstacle to patentability. If the invention works, it has utility. A new chemical compound may not be patentable in and of itself, unless there is a useful application for it. The requirement of novelty is satisfied if no single prior art reference discloses all of the features of the invention (i.e., the same invention was not made earlier by someone else). The most challenging, and conceptually most complex, requirement for patentability is nonobviousness. To satisfy this last requirement, the invention must not be merely a combination of elements of prior works, such as would be apparent to a person of "ordinary skill in the art" who was seeking to solve the problem to which the invention is directed (see Chapter 11 for more on this very interesting topic).

Formerly, a United States utility patent had a term of 17 years, commencing on the patent's issue date. Under the current law, however, utility patents have a term of 20 years, commencing on the date of filing of the application on which it is based. The new law applies to patents issuing on applications filed on or after June 8, 1995. Patents issued on earlier filed applications now have a term of either 17 years from the date of issue or 20 years from the date of filing, whichever is longer. Although, in theory, the term of a patent may be extended if its prosecution is unduly delayed by the Patent Office, as a practical matter, a patent term is nonextendable. The primary exception is for those patents directed to pharmaceutical products, in which case the term may be extended to compensate for time lost in securing the applicable regulatory (Food and Drug Administration) approval. Design patents have a term of 14 years from date of issue.

As a result of statutory requirements and rules promulgated by the United States Patent and Trademark Office (USPTO), the format and content of utility patents is relatively standardized. Preceding the textual portions of the patent are one or more pages of drawings of the preferred embodiment of the invention (for all intents and purposes, *preferred embodiment* is synonymous with *best mode*—see the section "What You Don't Tell" later in this chapter for more on this fascinating topic). The patent text begins with a brief statement identifying the subject of the invention. Next comes a background section outlining the problem that is solved by the invention. This statement of the problem may include a description of prior solutions or attempted solutions and the reasons why they were not wholly satisfactory. Following the background section is a section summarizing the invention, including its key features and advantages. Next is a section providing a brief description of the patent drawings, specifying what is being illustrated in each figure. Following this is a rather lengthy section setting forth a detailed description of the invention with reference to the preferred embodiment illustrated in the drawings. These textual portions of the patent are known as the *specification*. The patent concludes with the patent claims, which are the consecutively numbered sentences at the end of the patent document. Preceding the patent text is a cover sheet, which includes a brief abstract and a wealth of other useful information that will be described in a later chapter.

What to Be Concerned About

Few members of the general public have much knowledge about patents. Moreover, much of what is commonly believed about patents is incorrect. Perhaps the most common misconception is that a patent gives its owner the right to practice the patented invention. As noted earlier, a patent conveys the right to prevent others from practicing the patented invention—an exclusionary or negative right. It does *not* convey an affirmative or positive right to the patent owner to practice the patented invention. The difference between the two types of rights—exclusionary or negative and affirmative or positive—is best (and most often) seen in the context of an *improvement patent* that covers an improvement to an existing article or process that is, itself, covered by an unexpired patent. If, as is frequently the case, practice of the improvement necessitates making the underlying basic or unimproved article or performing the basic process, the holder of the patent on the unimproved article or process can prevent such practice. In these circumstances, the owner of the improvement patent cannot practice his own patented invention. This concept can best be understood with reference to the following hypothetical situation, which will be used for illustrative purposes throughout this book.

Example

Suppose there is no such thing as a fire engine. (This *is* a hypothetical situation and we wish to avoid adding technological complexity to the matter.) Jack lives in a rural area of largely wooden houses that lacks a municipal water system. Lack of a ready supply of water makes combating a fire in one of these houses difficult. Perceiving this problem, Jack proceeds to invent and patent (a utility patent) a fire engine, which comprises a vehicle bearing a tank of water, a pump, and a hose and nozzle (for the moment, we need not concern ourselves with a more specific definition of "fire engine").

One fine day Jill happens upon a fire engine, on its way to a fire, caught in traffic. Jill perceives that delays caused by traffic are a problem in that they interfere with prompt firefighting efforts. Jill concludes that this problem would be solved, or at least ameliorated, if other motorists could be made aware of the nature of the fire engine and its mission, namely that it is an emergency vehicle on an emergency mission. Jill determines that such awareness could best be achieved by painting the fire engine a distinctive color (red) and providing it with both visual and auditory warning devices (a flashing red light and a bell). Jill proceeds to patent (again, a utility patent) this improved fire engine, which comprises a fire engine painted red and bearing a flashing red light and a bell.

Under the circumstances of our hypothetical situation, would Jill have the right to make, use, sell, or offer for sale improved fire engines as set forth in Jack's patent (red fire engines with flashing red lights and bells)? The answer to this question is no. In order to make an improved fire engine, Jill must also make a fire engine; Jack, by reason of his patent, has the right to prevent Jill from doing so. Conversely, Jack cannot make, use, sell, or offer for sale an improved version of his fire engine (red paint, flashing light, and bell) because Jill, by reason of her patent, has the right to prevent this. (Cross-licensing often breaks such impasses.)

Another point of misunderstanding with respect to patents is what they cover. Inventors are often a veritable font of misinformation in this regard, speaking broadly (and grandiloquently) about "my invention" or "my basic invention" or—even worse—"my concept," while belittling any "minor changes" or "minor variations" made by an accused infringer. *Do not listen to such people.* What a patent covers is determined by its claims. While the claims are to be construed (i.e., interpreted) in light of the patent specification, it is the claims that determine what the patent covers (more on this subject shortly).

Similarly, technical people, when asked to review a patent (especially after the reviewer's employer has been charged with infringing that patent), will often read the abstract and the summary of the invention, look at the drawings, and opine that the patent is invalid because "it's all old" or "we've been doing that for years." *Do not listen to such people.* Most inventions are improvements on some earlier technology, and most inventions are described in the context of the environment in which they are intended to function. As a result, much of what appears in the patent drawings and is described in the patent specification is old.

However, the scope of a patent is determined by its claims. (We are repeating this point because it merits repetition. It is often overlooked, occasionally even by judges.) A patent examiner, before allowing (approving) the patent, found some limitation in the claims of the patent that, in his (mostly) expert opinion, constituted a legal basis of patentability. This basis can generally be discerned by an examination of the *file wrapper* of the patent, which is a publicly available copy of all of the documents relating to the issuance of the patent. Never accept any opinion as to patent validity or scope that is not based upon a thorough review of the patent file wrapper by a patent attorney (the courts won't, when it comes to a question of willful infringement).

What You Don't Know

It is often said, "What you don't know won't hurt you." This does not apply in business, nor does it apply with respect to patents. Patent infringement is not a specific-intent tort—in layman's terms, this means that one may infringe a patent without intending to do so. While it may be done innocently, it is patent infringement nonetheless. The fact that you were unaware of the allegedly infringed patent is not a defense to a charge of patent infringement (although, as we will see, it may mitigate the damages). It is, therefore, highly advisable to perform a product clearance patent search before marketing a new product or utilizing a new production process. Preferably, such a search should precede any substantial new product or process investment or development effort.

TIPS AND TECHNIQUES

Unintentional infringement is infringement nonetheless.

What You Don't Tell

In addition to questions of patent infringement, there are several basic, but not commonly known, requirements for a patent that, if ignored, may result in the invalidation of any patent thereafter obtained.

A patent must be *enabling* and it must include a disclosure of the best mode of practicing the claimed invention. In essence, this means that, based upon the patent document, a hypothetical person of "ordinary skill in the art" (a phrase that appears frequently in patent matters) must be able to practice the patented invention with only a *reasonable* amount of experimentation; and that where there is more than one way to practice the patented invention, the patentee has disclosed what he considers, at the time of filing of the patent application, to be the best way to practice it, known as the *best mode*. Thus, it is vitally important when disclosing an invention to a patent attorney who will draft a patent application that nothing be withheld or concealed. A choice must be made between maintaining a trade secret and obtaining a patent with respect to an invention. Such choices may be difficult. However, if you try to have both, you may wind up with neither. *Do not try to beat the system.* A patent examiner, when examining a patent application, will not challenge, but will accept, the disclosed embodiment of the invention as being the best mode and may not notice a missing detail that defeats enablement. Opposing counsel, in litigation, will challenge *everything* and will likely have almost unlimited resources, including discovery procedures, available. Expect that opposing counsel will miss nothing. Any victory gained by concealing information is likely to be only temporary.

Another frequently (or conveniently) overlooked aspect of patent law pertains to what are described as *statutory bars*. Simply stated, the law requires that an inventor make a reasonably prompt decision as to whether to seek patent protection for an invention. The need to make this decision is triggered by public disclosure of the invention, or by the first sale, or first offer for sale, of articles made in accord with the invention—even if no sale is actually effected.

Once such an event has occurred, a patent application must be filed and received by the USPTO within one year or the law bars patent protection for the invention. The courts strictly enforce this requirement. The one-year period, known as a grace period, is virtually unique to the United States. Other countries essentially require that a patent application be filed before disclosure or sale of the invention (the so-called "strict novelty" requirement). Therefore, if foreign patent protection is desired, a U.S. patent application should be filed before marketing efforts begin or other public disclosure is made.

What You Don't Disclose

Among the burdens placed on a patent applicant and the applicant's patent attorney (if any—see the later section of this chapter on this topic) is the duty of candor, also known as the duty of disclosure.

Patent examiners have limited time and limited resources with which to search for relevant prior art. In order to aid the examiner in identifying such art and, thereby, preventing the grant of invalid patents, each individual associated with the filing and prosecution of a patent application is impressed with the duty to disclose to the Patent Office all material "known to that individual to be material to patentability." If such an individual fails to satisfy this obligation and withholds known prior art from the Patent Office, such failure, known as *inequitable conduct* (formerly known as fraud on the Patent Office), may result in a patent being found invalid or unenforceable.

 TIPS AND TECHNIQUES

Do not conceal prior art—it will come back to haunt you!

There are those who would point out that, if the patent applicant does not disclose a prior art reference, it is quite possible that it will not be discovered by the patent examiner. Further, even if the examiner *does* discover the reference, no harm will be suffered. The examiner will not inquire as to possible failure to disclose but will merely proceed with examination of the application. The implied advice, therefore, is to forget any information that might imperil the grant of a patent. *Do not listen to such people.* Apart from the ethical considerations, there always exists the possibility that the patent will become the subject of litigation. While the patent examiner was handicapped in searching for prior art, opposing counsel will enjoy substantial, if not virtually limitless, resources. Moreover, opposing counsel has recourse to discovery procedures once litigation commences. Files and records can be examined, and witnesses can be deposed. Thus, the "forgotten" reference may well be discovered. Mere discovery is bad enough. If it is also established that the patent applicant was aware of the reference but failed to disclose it to the Patent Office, *real* trouble may ensue. For example, seeking to enforce a patent known to be invalid may constitute a violation of the antitrust laws. Therefore, do not conceal references from your patent attorney, and do not ask your patent attorney to conceal references from the Patent Office. (Although sometimes tedious, patent attorneys are, as a group, highly ethical.)

Design Patents: Where Less Is More

It is commonly believed (even by some patent attorneys, who should know better) that design patents are very limited in scope and, hence, are of little value, except to prevent exact copying of specific product designs. *Do not listen to such people.* Design patents occupy a significant— if not stellar—position in the intellectual property universe.

Because applications for design patents are, both in principle and in execution, quite simple, attorneys often give them short shrift; indeed, they are most often prepared by paralegals (whereby they yield a significant profit margin to the law firm). Drawings or photographs of the subject product, provided by the client, are simply attached to a largely boilerplate application and filed in the Patent Office. Patents issuing on such applications will, in fact, protect the depicted product design and little, if anything, else. If the scope of such patents is found wanting, however, the fault lies not in the inherent nature of design patents but in the lack of effort on the part of those who prepared the applications.

Drawings utilized in design patent applications should be cleaned up—unnecessary design details should be deleted. The more basic the design is, the more difficult it is to circumvent.

More importantly (and less widely known), a patented design need not encompass an entire "article of manufacture." In a landmark decision (*In re Zahn*, 617 F.2d 261, 204 USPQ 988 [CCPA 1980])—a case brilliantly briefed and argued by one of the authors of this book—the Court of Customs and Patent Appeals (the predecessor to the Court of Appeals for the Federal Circuit, also known as the Patent Court) held that a patented design must pertain to a complete article but that the design need not encompass the entire article. Thus, it is possible to patent a design of a *portion* of a product, whereby the appearance of the remaining portion, which does not bear the patented design, is irrelevant to the question of patent infringement. Such a design patent may be quite broad in scope. No manufacturer should ignore design patents.

Provisional Patent Applications: When You Care Enough to Send the Second-Best

Provisional patent applications are, essentially, utility or conventional patent applications from which the claims have been omitted. They may be viewed as merely an optional, preliminary step in the process of securing a utility patent. The filing of a provisional patent application must be followed, within one year, by the filing of a utility patent application. Failure to do so results in the irreversible abandonment of the provisional application.

When first introduced in 1995, the provisional patent application was touted as a low-cost means of establishing a patent application priority date while simultaneously offering the inventor a period of time (one year) to further develop and refine the invention and to decide whether to undertake the costly filing and prosecution of a regular patent application. A further benefit, ostensibly, is derived from the fact that the term of pendency of a provisional patent application is not included in the 20-year term of a patent. Thus, the provisional patent application, in effect, offered a means of extending the life of a patent by up to a year.

These acclaimed advantages have proven largely illusory, for the simple reason that a provisional patent application is, after all, a patent application and is subject to the same disclosure requirements as a utility patent application—it must be enabling and it must teach each and every limitation that will appear in the claims of the corresponding future utility patent application (i.e., it must provide support for the claims). Indeed, if done properly, a provisional patent application is virtually identical to the specification of the corresponding utility patent application. Thus, while the filing fee for a provisional patent application is considerably less than the filing fee for the corresponding utility patent application, the cost of *drafting* the provisional application is a considerable fraction of the cost of drafting a utility application. Therefore, the total cost savings is nowhere near as significant as some people believe. Moreover, if the further development and refinement of the invention results in technological changes or details not described in the provisional application (how could they be described there if they were created after the filing?), such new developments do not receive the benefit of the filing date of the provisional application.

Finally, there is a serious question as to the value of any patent term extension achieved by the use of provisional patent applications. With the present rapid technological advances, most patented inventions are obsolete long before the patent expires. (Electronics inventions are, on average, obsolete within three to five years of the issuance of the patent.) Thus, it may be much more advantageous to speed the issue of a patent than to delay its expiration. The real advantage of provisional patent applications (if any) may lie in combating the pernicious effects of the *Festo* decision (see Chapter 8).

Some inventors (and, embarrassingly, some patent attorneys) will advocate filing all sorts of technical papers, research reports, and interim project specifications as provisional patent applications. *Do not listen to such people.* Such documents, without revision, invariably lack the level of detail and completeness necessary to support a future utility patent application.

There are, of course, the rare exceptions to this rule. When one is a day short of expiration of the one-year grace period (which has been triggered by publication of a research paper or sale of the product), one may have no choice but to quickly file the provisional application to avoid crossing the novelty bar. Finally, in certain instances it may be beneficial to delay commencement of the patent term by a year (the protection will commence and expire a year later). Even though one will not gain an extra year of patent life, as often thought, one will push the patent term one year forward. In no event should one consider drafting a provisional patent application *pro se*—by oneself. Only in cases of extreme emergency should such practice be allowed. If a development has potential value, and the inventor wishes to file a provisional patent application while considering the matter further, the application should be prepared by a competent professional.

Choosing a Patent Attorney

Accused criminals have the legal right to represent themselves in court. It is widely acknowledged, however, that one who does so has a fool for a client. Similarly, inventors have the legal right to represent themselves in the Patent Office and, similarly, one who does so has a fool for a client.

Patents are not all equal in the eyes of the law. Some afford broad protection and, hence, are of great value. Others are very narrow in scope and are easily circumvented; these are, obviously, of little value. The quality (and value) of a patent is highly dependent upon the skill and knowledge of the person who drafts and prosecutes the patent application. Expertise in both the relevant technology and patent law and procedure are required. Such expertise is not inexpensive. However, as the old saying goes, "If something is worth doing, it's worth doing well." In business terms, the incremental costs of properly drafting and prosecuting a patent application are more than adequately compensated by the incremental value of the patent thus obtained.

It must be borne in mind that the starting point in the preparation of a patent application is a blank sheet of paper (or a blank word processor screen). Drafting a patent application is not a matter of filling in blank spaces in a form. Each patent application is an individually crafted work of art (as noted earlier, depending upon the draftsperson—some are more artful than others). Just as no two inventions are alike, so, too, are no two patent applications alike. For this reason, patent practitioners almost always bill for prosecution services by the hour. The chief exception to this general rule occurs when a client has a substantial number of patent applications to be prepared. In such cases, a law firm may quote a fixed price per application, relying on the law of averages—some applications will be relatively complex (and time consuming), while others will be comparatively simple (and quickly completed).

 TIPS AND TECHNIQUES

Trying to save money on a patent attorney is akin to shopping for the cheapest brain surgeon.

Many inventors, or business managers, search long and hard to find the patent practitioner with the lowest billing rate. *Do not do this.* More often than not, an unusually low billing rate connotes a lack of experience or skill, or both. Moreover, the final cost of an application is the hourly billing rate of the draftsperson, multiplied by the number of hours billed. An inexperienced or inefficient practitioner with a comparatively low billing rate often requires more time to complete an application than a more experienced colleague with a higher hourly rate. Because of the variability in the amount of time billed, there is often little correlation between the hourly billing rate and the cost of the completed patent application. Indeed, the more experienced practitioner may actually prove less costly. If price comparison is absolutely necessary, ask the various candidate practitioners to estimate the cost to draft an application with respect to a specimen invention disclosure.

A factor frequently overlooked when selecting a patent practitioner is the individual's technical background. Patent attorneys and patent agents are, of necessity, quick studies and are generally able to work with inventions in a broad spectrum of technologies. Nevertheless, all other things being equal, it is preferable, in terms of both cost and quality, to secure the services of a practitioner with prior experience in the field of technology to which the invention pertains. Moreover, there are some types of inventions (e.g., pharmaceutical and bioengineering inventions) that should only be handled by practitioners with the corresponding technical education. Inquire as to a prospect's technical background—both education and experience—when making your choice.

A Good Attorney or Another Engineer

Having noted that a patent attorney should have appropriate technical expertise, it must also be borne in mind that a patent is a legal document, the proper drafting of which requires *legal* expertise. Over the past several years, a trend has developed toward ever-increasing levels of technical education among those patent attorneys engaging primarily, if not exclusively, in patent prosecution. This trend is even more pronounced among patent agents. Thus, more and more often one finds patent practitioners with master's degrees or doctorate degrees in technical fields. Some even boast of postdoctoral studies (apparently, they entered the patent field only when spouses—or mothers—insisted they finally get a job).

To an extent, this trend may be driven by the increasing complexity of some of the technologies now being patented and, as such, the trend may be beneficial. To a much greater extent, however, the trend results from one of the most common of management flaws:

the undue attention and preference accorded the familiar and the avoidance of the unfamiliar. Most often, patent practitioners report to a senior member of the client's engineering staff. Such staff members, themselves technologically oriented and having little or no legal knowledge, often prefer patent practitioners who focus on (and talk about) technological rather than legal issues. When retaining patent counsel, make certain to retain a legal adviser, not to hire an addition to the engineering department.

The alert reader will have noticed the use of the term *patent agent*. A patent agent is a person who has passed the Patent Office bar examination. Such a person is entitled to practice in the Patent Office, preparing so-called *patentability opinions* (more on this exciting document follows shortly) and filing and prosecuting patent applications. A patent attorney, by contrast, not only has passed the patent bar but is also an attorney admitted to the bar of one of the 50 states or the District of Columbia. Those activities deemed to constitute the practice of law—rendering patent validity or infringement opinions, engaging in litigation, or drafting license documents—may only be performed by a lawyer, not by a patent agent.

The Process of Obtaining a Patent

Before the drafting of a patent application has commenced, one may request, or the practitioner may recommend, that a *patent search* be performed. Also known as a novelty search, patentability search, or prior art search, this involves searching through the relevant prior art—principally, but not always exclusively, the collection of prior patents and published articles and brochures maintained by the Patent Office—to identify that art which is pertinent to the patentability (novelty and nonobviousness) of the subject invention. While the law does not require such a search, it is almost always a wise measure. Occasionally, such a search will reveal that the invention in question is not patentable—it lacks novelty (it's been done before) or it is obvious in view of the prior art. Such a revelation, while discouraging, at least results in a savings of the cost of the patent application that would otherwise have been drafted and filed.

Much more frequently, however, the search results enable the patent practitioner to better identify patentable aspects or features of the invention and to focus the patent application on these features. After a patent application has been filed, no new matter may be added to the drawings or the specification—they are essentially frozen when the patent application is filed. While the claims may be (and most often are) amended during the prosecution of the application, they cannot cover anything that is not shown in the drawings and described in the specification. Thus, there is great value to foreknowledge ("forewarned is forearmed") such as may be gained through a patent search.

Indeed, a patentability search is becoming almost mandatory in view of the *Festo* decision (more on this later). In essence, the *Festo* decision affixes a steep price to any claim amendment that changes the scope of a claim in order to avoid reading on the prior art. This price is complete loss of the range of equivalents, which would otherwise be available to the patentee under the doctrine of equivalents (a topic discussed more fully in Chapter 8). Thus it is highly advisable to do a patentability search in order to enable drafting of the patent claims in such a manner that they need not be amended later.

Anywhere from 7 to 33 months after an application is filed, depending upon the field of technology to which it pertains and the backlog in that particular section (*art group*) of the Patent Office, a written report known as an *official office action* is issued. In this office action, the patent examiner identifies the prior art believed to be the most pertinent and, generally, rejects some or all of the patent claims as being unpatentable. (If none of the claims are rejected, this may be an indication that you did not claim all to which you were entitled.) A written response to this office action, called either a *response* or an *amendment*, addressing all of the issues raised by the patent examiner, must be prepared and filed—a task for which the practitioner bills by the hour. Additionally, the practitioner may interview the examiner, either by telephone or in person.

In response to all of this, the examiner will, in several months, generally issue a second office action. At this point, the practitioner can usually advise whether (1) it is highly unlikely that any worthwhile patent protection will be obtained; (2) a patent will likely issue in due course; or (3) the examiner seemingly doesn't understand, is unreasonable, or is being stubborn, necessitating an appeal or other lengthy and expensive procedures. Possibilities 1 and 2 make for an easy decision. Dealing with possibility 3 is one of those situations where decision makers earn their pay.

Once a patent is issued, the Patent Office file, known as the *file wrapper*, is laid open to the public. Patent attorneys avidly study file wrappers as an aid to understanding the meaning of various terms and the scope of the patent claims (not surprisingly, such study is time-consuming and, hence, costly).

Patent Marking: Little Things Mean a Lot

Before damages may be collected from a patent infringer, the patentee must establish that the infringer was warned or notified of the infringement. Once notified, damages accrue from the date of the notice. Notice may be either actual or constructive. Traditionally, *actual notice* is what it sounds like—a letter from the patentee, identifying both the patent and the infringing products and including a clear statement that the patent covered the products or, equivalently, that the products infringed the patent. *Constructive notice*, with respect to a commercialized patent, comprises marking the patented product (or, if impractical, its packaging) with the patent number(s). For patents that are not commercialized, or where the commercialization does not yield a markable product, the marking requirement is excused.

TIPS AND TECHNIQUES

Marking products with patent numbers is essential for collecting infringement damages and is also good PR for your company. Marking a product with the number of an expired patent, or one that doesn't cover the product, may expose the patentee to liability for false marking.

Clearly, if the patentee is selling (either directly or through a licensee) patented products, it is advantageous that such products be marked with the patent number(s). Patent marking starts the damages clock ticking without the need for a notice letter to an infringer— a letter that may give the recipient standing to bring a declaratory judgment action (see Chapter 8).

Understanding Patent Claims: Rules of the Road

As previously noted, it is the claims of a patent that determine its scope. An understanding of the basic tenets of claim construction is, therefore, exceedingly important.

TIPS AND TECHNIQUES

Claim limitations are the elements of the claim that determine the scope of the claim.

Patent claims are composed of *limitations*—phrases that identify and describe, or limit, the various components (or steps, in the case of a method or process claim) of the claimed invention. The various words and phrases that appear in the patent claims are to be interpreted or construed according to their normal or accustomed meaning. If no such accepted definition exists—that is, the patent draftsman has created or coined new words or phrases, or has used words or phrases in an unconventional manner (the patent draftsperson is his own lexicographer)—the patent specification is used as a guide to claim interpretation. If no clear definition is provided in the patent specification, the file wrapper is examined. As a last resort (and only then), testimony of expert witnesses may be introduced. If this still fails to resolve any ambiguity, printed materials are considered.

Every word in a patent claim is deemed to have meaning and significance. None may be ignored. Substantive patent law prohibits two patent claims from covering exactly the same invention. Thus, if (as often happens) two patent claims are largely identical, the nonidentical portions *must* be so construed as to have different meanings (this is known as the *doctrine of claim differentiation*).

Claim terms may not be construed in a manner inconsistent with arguments or statements made by the applicant during prosecution of the patent application nor contrary to reasons that may have been enunciated by the patent examiner as the basis for claim allowance (the *doctrine of file wrapper estoppel*). (This may seem comprehensible, but wait, there's more! See Chapter 8 for remarks concerning the *Festo* case.)

Claims—actually constituent claim limitations—must be construed so as to preserve patentability. In the event that a pertinent *new* (not considered during the prosecution of the patent application) prior art reference is discovered, the patent claims must be interpreted, if at all possible, so as to distinguish over the reference and, hence, to maintain the validity of the claims. Also, if at all possible, claims should be construed so as to cover the embodiment(s) of the invention described in the patent specification.

If these rules seem complex and confusing, they are! As evidenced by the number of reversals handed down by the Court of Appeals for the Federal Circuit (CAFC)—the patent appeals court—many trial judges of the federal district courts get it wrong themselves.

Independent Claims, Dependent Claims: A Way
to Simplify the Task of Claim Construction

Patent claims are of two kinds: independent claims and dependent claims. *Independent claims* are those that do not refer to another, preceding claim. Hence, the first claim of a patent (claim 1) is always independent (there *are* no preceding claims). *Dependent claims* incorporate by reference each and every limitation of each of the claims from which they depend (i.e., to which they refer). Many patents include long chains or series of dependent claims, each referring to—and incorporating the limitations of—a preceding claim. Each dependent claim is narrower (i.e., more limited in scope) than the claim from which it depends (see Chapter 8 for a more detailed explanation of this effect). Thus, if an independent claim is not infringed, no claim that depends from it (and, therefore, is of more limited scope) can be infringed. For this reason, attention is inevitably focused on the independent claims, which are generally much fewer in number. In most instances, the dependent claims may be safely ignored.

Provisional Patent Rights: Life before Birth

Among the many popular misconceptions concerning patents, one of the most enduring is that patents have effect as of the date of filing. A surprising number of people believe that a patent springs to life, fully formed, upon filing. Such people occasionally wander into attorneys' offices clutching a copy of a newly filed patent application—more often than not, an application they filed themselves—to seek enforcement of their patent against one or more alleged infringers. Such enforcement is impossible, however, because patents have effect only from the date of issue. Moreover, until recently, patents had no retroactive effect. No liability for patent infringement could arise from any activities occurring prior to the date of patent issue. However, to an extent—and *only* to an extent—this nonretroactivity of patent protection has been altered by changes in the patent law that have created provisional patent rights. These same changes also reversed the prior rule that pending patent applications be maintained in secret, by the Patent Office, until the patent issued.

Under the changed law, patent applications filed on or after November 29, 2000, are published 18 months after their filing date (actually, 18 months after the earliest claimed priority date—discuss this with a patent practitioner). When an application is published, the entire file wrapper is open to inspection and copying by the public. Moreover, members of the public may, within two months of publication, submit prior art documents to the Patent Office to be considered by the patent examiner during examination of the application.

Once a patent application has been published and an accused infringer has been given actual notice thereof, certain provisional rights apply. If the published patent application ultimately matures into an issued patent, having claims substantially similar (although as yet undecided by the courts, the term *substantially similar* probably means "virtually identical") to those previously published, the patentee—upon issue of the patent and proof that the infringer had actual knowledge of the published patent application—may recover, in addition to other damages, a reasonable royalty in respect of infringement of those claims that occurred during the period between the publication of the application and the issue of the patent. Thus, a certain measure of retroactivity has been introduced into the patent system.

Trademarks

A trademark is a word, symbol, or combination thereof that is used to identify the source, albeit a possibly anonymous source, of goods. Examples of trademarks include Nike, Rolls-Royce, and Kleenex. A service mark performs the same function as a trademark with respect to the provision of services. Examples of service marks include FedEx and Roto-Rooter. A trademark or service mark has a potentially perpetual life. Although registration confers several advantages on the owner of the mark, it is not legally required. Registration may be at either the federal or state level. Marks that are unregistered are known as *common-law marks*.

Choosing a Mark

When choosing a mark, it is important to remember the function it is intended to perform, namely source identification. It is not the function of a trademark or service mark to describe the goods or services. Marketing and sales personnel frequently seek to adopt marks that describe the product or tell the customer all about it. Such efforts should be strenuously resisted. Product description should be achieved through advertising copy. Trademarks and service marks should be chosen for their distinctiveness.

Marks are categorized according to their inherent distinctiveness. The most distinctive and, hence, the most desirable marks are coined or arbitrary marks. These are either made-up words, such as Kodak or Xerox, or words that have no relation to the goods or services with which they are used, such as Camel as a trademark for cigarettes.

TIPS AND TECHNIQUES

The *trade dress* of a product encompasses the distinctive appearance of the product and/or its packaging and may include the size, shape, color, and texture.

Next, in decreasing order of distinctiveness, are suggestive marks. These are marks that bear some relation to the goods or services with which they are used. The relation is sufficiently tenuous, however, that the goods or services are not described, nor can they be identified from knowledge of the mark alone (for example, Polar as a trademark for ice cream).

The next lower rung on the distinctiveness ladder (a significant step downward, as we shall soon see) is occupied by descriptive marks. These literally describe some feature or attribute of the goods or services, or are laudatory thereof (for example, Speedy as a service mark for a delivery service).

The bottom rung of the ladder is occupied by what are, technically, not marks at all—generic terms. A generic term is the word or phrase by which a product or service is popularly known (for example, *bicycle* is the generic term for a two-wheeled, pedal-powered vehicle). Generic terms are not protectable.

Trademark Clearance

Trademark clearance is the process of determining or seeking to determine whether a particular mark is available for adoption and use as proposed. Just as many inventors will assure you that no patentability search is necessary because they "know the field of technology and there has never been anything like this," so too will many marketing and sales personnel assure you that no trademark clearance is necessary because they "know the market and no one is using this mark." *Do not listen to such people.* Trademark clearance (if the mark is to be used only in this country) is a relatively quick and inexpensive procedure, especially when compared with the disruptions and costs associated with unwittingly infringing the rights of another—litigation costs, damages, and the costs and chaos of suddenly changing to a new mark. If the mark is to be used abroad, it should be searched in each country where it will appear. Such searches can become costly and time-consuming and, therefore, plans should be made accordingly.

Registering a Mark

While requirements and procedures vary somewhat from state to state, obtaining a state registration of a mark is most often a matter of literally filling in the blank spaces in an application form and paying a small fee. Preparing an application for federal registration is only slightly more complex. As a result, most (if not all) trademark attorneys prepare and file registration applications on a fixed-fee basis. Formerly, use of a mark in interstate commerce was a prerequisite to filing for federal registration. Now, however, the trademark law has changed, and an application for federal registration may be filed based on an intent to use the mark in interstate commerce. Nevertheless, such use must actually commence before the registration is allowed to issue.

TIPS AND TECHNIQUES

A *trade name*, which is the name by which a business is known, cannot be registered as a trademark, but is governed by state and common law.

In order to perform its function—identifying the source of goods— a trademark must be distinctive. A mark that is confusingly similar to other marks cannot serve to distinguish the goods on which it is used from those of others. Some marks—coined, arbitrary, or merely suggestive marks—are deemed to be inherently distinctive. These marks are registerable *ab initio*—immediately upon adaptation and use (the reader is advised that the occasional use of Latin phrases will often impress others).

TIPS AND TECHNIQUES

A trademark may be a slogan, such as Citibank's "Citi never sleeps"; or a package shape, such as the wasp-waisted Coca-Cola bottle; or a color, such as Owens Corning's pink fiberglass insulation.

Marks that lack inherent distinctiveness—descriptive marks—are only registerable upon a showing that they have achieved secondary meaning; that is, that they have become so associated with the goods in the mind of the public that they do, in fact, distinguish those goods. Such a showing may be made through the use of consumer surveys (very expensive) or by establishing that the applicant has used the mark continuously, and substantially exclusively, for at least five years (a so-called Section 2[f] application). This latter approach, quite obviously, requires the trademark owner to endure a lengthy (five-year) period of uncertainty before (hopefully) achieving registration of the mark. The moral of the story: Avoid descriptive marks.

(*Note*: The foregoing paragraph pertains primarily to the issues involved in federal registration. Some states, apparently, will register anything.)

Like the Patent Office, the Trademark Office issues written reports in respect of applications, to which written response must be made. Here the similarity ends. In most cases, prosecution of a trademark application is much less complex and much less costly than prosecution of a patent application.

Once an application has been approved by the examining attorney, it is published for opposition—the mark, the goods or services, and the identity of the applicant are published in the weekly *Official Patent and Trademark Gazette*—and interested parties are afforded 30 days (extensions of time are freely granted) in which to file an opposition setting forth reasons why registration should be denied. If no opposition is filed,

IN THE REAL WORLD

According to a 2010 study by Kantar Retail and BrandZ, the five most valuable trademarks in the world are Google, IBM, Apple, Microsoft, and Coca-Cola.

a registration is issued. If an opposition is filed, there is an *inter partes proceeding* (litigation) before the Trademark Trial and Appeal Board, which decides the matter (subject, of course, to appeal).

Proper Trademark Usage: Use It Right or Lose It

If a trademark ceases to serve primarily as an identification of the source of goods and instead comes to identify the goods themselves (i.e., if it becomes the generic term for such goods), the rights to exclusive use of the mark are lost. Notable examples of such lost marks are escalator, thermos, and aspirin. Proper trademark usage is directed to the prevention of such loss. Prior to release, all publications should be reviewed for proper trademark use. (Although the rules of proper trademark usage are beyond the scope of this book, remember: A trademark is not an adjective and should be followed by the appropriate generic term.)

It is also prudent to monitor the *Official Gazette*, so as to be able to oppose registration of marks that may cause confusion with respect to your own or may dilute or reduce the distinctiveness of your marks.

Once a mark is federally registered, it is identified by the symbol®. The letters TM or, occasionally, SM (for service marks) are used to identify unregistered or common-law marks, or marks that have only state registrations. Thus, the presence of the designation TM or SM after a mark merely means that someone is claiming proprietary rights thereto, not that the claimant actually *has* such rights. This is not meant, however, to suggest that rights claimed under common law may be safely ignored. Many unregistered marks are extremely strong. Check before proceeding.

Having now touched upon the problem of genericness, we should backtrack to an issue relating to the selection of a mark. A trademark, or service mark, is an adjective and should be used in conjunction with the appropriate generic term. If a product or service is truly the first of its kind, no accepted generic term will exist. In such case, or if the existing generic term is awkward and unwieldy—"acetylsalicylic acid" (aspirin) does not fall trippingly from the tongue—a mark may be adopted by the public as the generic term, resulting in loss of the owner's proprietary rights. To avoid such a loss, create a generic term, in addition to the trademark, and foster its adoption and use by the public; for example, "ASPIRIN^{TM} pain reliever."

Copyrights

A copyright is an exclusionary right. It conveys to its owner the right to prevent others from copying, selling, performing, displaying, or making derivative versions of a work of authorship. The duration of a copyright depends upon several factors but in no event is shorter than 70 years. (If your planning horizon exceeds 70 years, consult a copyright specialist.) Although registration confers several advantages on the owner of the copyright and is a prerequisite to a suit for copyright infringement, it is not legally required. Prompt registration provides remedies that make lawsuits affordable. Statutory damages of $150,000 (or more, plus attorney fees) for willful infringement can be obtained if published works are registered within three months of publication or if unpublished works are registered before they are infringed.

Copyrights differ from patents in that they only protect against actual copying. A work created by another, without copying, is not an infringement, no matter how similar it may be to a copyrighted work. Moreover, copyright protects only the expression of an idea, not the idea being expressed. Thus, information or data included in a copyrighted work is not protected against appropriation and use by others, although copying of the presentation and arrangement is barred.

 TIPS AND TECHNIQUES

A copyright protects the expression of an idea, not the idea itself.

Copyrights are generally associated in the common mind with nov-els, movie scripts, music, and song lyrics. For this reason, and because of their limited scope of protection, they are often overlooked or ignored by businesspeople. Copyrights do, however, have application in the pro-tection of product manuals and instruction booklets, training materials, and marketing and sales publications. More importantly, copyright has been utilized to protect computer software, although in recent years, computer software has often become the subject of patent applications.

Copyright Registration

Copyright arises automatically when the original work of authorship is fixed in a tangible medium; for example, music is written as notes on a sheet of paper or its performance is recorded on a tape or CD. Registra-tion of a copyright, which may be done at any time during its life, is merely a matter of filling in the blank spaces on a simple two-page form (instructions are printed on the form), attaching (depositing) one or two copies of the subject work of authorship (see instructions) including a small (currently $35.00) filing fee, and sending it to the Library of Con-gress. Copyright law has no equivalent of the enablement requirement found in patent law. It is perfectly acceptable (and commonly done) to register a copyright on a computer program with significant portions of the program omitted from the copy or copies deposited. This allows registration of the copyright in the program without providing a com-plete and working copy to a prospective infringer.

Copyright Notice

A copyright notice consists of the symbol ©, or the word *copyright*, followed by the year of first publication and the name of the copy-right owner. Formerly, publication of a work without a copyright notice caused loss of copyright. For this reason, some people believe that they are free to copy any work that does not bear a copyright notice. *Do not listen to such people.* This aspect of the copyright law was changed more than two decades ago. While a copyright notice remains a requirement if damages are to be recovered from an infringer, the owner of a work published without a notice may obtain an injunction barring further infringement. Thus, the mere absence of a copyright notice does not indicate that a work may be freely copied. Similarly, a copyright notice should be placed on all of one's own works before they are published.

To clarify a point, copyright registration is not a prerequisite to the use of a copyright notice. Thus, one may include a copyright notice in a publication before registering the copyright with the Copyright Office.

Work for Hire: Sounds Simple, But It Isn't

A *work for hire* is, generally speaking, a work created by an employee within the scope of her employment or, if the parties expressly agree in writing, a work specially commissioned for use as a contribution to a collective work.

The copyright in a work initially vests in the author or authors who created the work. However, in the case of a work for hire, the *employer* is legally considered to be the author. Thus, the copyright of such a work vests in the employer. But what about a work created by a consultant? A consultant is not an employee (if you don't believe this, just ask the IRS); as a result, the copyright in a work (other than a contribution to a collective work) created by a consultant will vest in the consultant, not in the client. Thus, for example, in the absence of a written copyright assignment, a computer program written by a consultant may be used by the client but not duplicated or upgraded by the client (the upgraded program would be a *derivative work*). It is therefore extremely important to ascertain the correct employment status of all of those individuals called upon to create computer programs, advertising and promotional materials, and so forth. If they are not employees, working within the scope of their employment, get a written copyright assignment.

Fair Use or Foul

Not all unauthorized uses of copyrighted material constitute an infringement. Some use of others' works is permitted, even without the approval of the copyright owner. Such use, known as *fair use*, is one of the most important, and least well-defined, limits to copyright protection.

The statutory basis for this doctrine, 17 United States Code §107, sets forth the factors that are to be considered in determining whether a particular use is fair use. In general, uses that advance public interests, such as criticism, comment, news reporting, teaching (including multiple copies for classroom use), scholarship, or research, are favored, while commercial uses are disfavored.

Not all commercial uses are forbidden. Most magazines and newspapers are operated for profit, yet they are not automatically precluded from availing themselves of the benefit of the doctrine. One of the most critical considerations is the extent of the "amount and substantiality of the portion used in relation to the copyrighted work as a whole." If the use is of such an extent and nature as to significantly impinge upon the value of the work or the copyright owner's income derived therefrom, it is not likely to be considered a fair use.

IN THE REAL WORLD

Unlike accidents, which mostly occur in the home, copyright infringement most commonly occurs in the workplace. Otherwise honest and law-abiding citizens routinely make copies of magazine and technical journal articles and duplicate computer software, both for themselves and for their colleagues, without seeking permission from the copyright holders. If you are a part of this mob of scofflaws, beware! There are organizations hunting you.

The Copyright Clearance Center, Inc., enforces the copyrights in a vast array of periodical publications. The Clearance Center offers licenses for the copying of their clients' works and takes action against those who copy without such licenses. Similarly, the Business Software Alliance (BSA) takes action against those who make unauthorized copies of their clients' proprietary computer software. For example, in January 2001, a Chicago firm called ThoughtWorks, Inc., agreed to pay $480,000 to the BSA to settle claims of illegal use of Microsoft and IBM office productivity software by ThoughtWorks' employees.

If you are making photocopies and just can't break the habit or have lots of unlicensed copies of software in use, it's probably best to find these folks before they find you.

Summary

A patent is the legal right to prevent others from practicing the patented invention. A patent does *not* guarantee the right of the patentee himself to practice the patented invention.

There are three types of patents: utility patents, design patents, and plant patents. A utility patent may cover a device or an article, a composition of matter, a method or a process of doing or making something, a new application for an existing device or material, or a product (not otherwise patentable) made by a particular new process. Design patents cover the ornamental design of an article. Plant patents cover asexually produced plants.

In order to be patentable, an invention must be novel, nonobvious, and useful. The requirement of nonobviousness is typically the most significant hurdle to be surmounted. If an invention would be obvious to one of ordinary skill in the art seeking to solve the problem addressed by the inventor, that invention is not patentable. In this regard, it is important to note that inventors and their attorneys are under an obligation to disclose to the Patent Office any prior art of which they are aware that would be relevant to the questions of novelty and nonobviousness of their invention.

Utility patents include a specification and patent claims. The specification comprises drawings and a written description of the preferred embodiment of the invention. The claims determine the scope of the patent monopoly. The specification must provide sufficient information to enable one of ordinary skill in the art to practice the patented invention (the enablement requirement).

Choice of a patent attorney is a complex question involving a trade-off between technical and legal skills. Effective cooperation with a patent attorney may minimize the cost of patent prosecution.

A trademark serves to identify the source of the goods on which it appears. A service mark serves the same function with respect to services. Marks may be registered at either the state or federal level, or they may be used without registration; such unregistered marks are known as common-law marks. Based upon their level of distinctiveness, marks may be categorized as arbitrary or coined, suggestive, or descriptive.

Before adopting a mark, a search should be performed to ascertain whether it is indeed available. Once adopted, a mark should be used properly to avoid loss of exclusive rights therein.

A copyright is the right to prevent others from unauthorized reproduction, dissemination, or modification of a work of authorship. Unlike patents, copyrights do not protect against independent re-creation. Although traditionally considered with respect to music, literature, and works of art, copyright now finds broad application with respect to the protection of computer software.

The exclusive rights afforded by a copyright are limited by the doctrine of fair use, which allows the unauthorized copying of limited portions of another's work under certain specified circumstances.

CHAPTER 2

The Supporting Players: Other Types of IP

Trade Secrets and Know-How, Mask Works, and Noncompetition and Nondisclosure Agreements

After reading this chapter you will be able to:

- Understand the nature of trade secrets and know-how.
- Understand the interplay between trade secrets and know-how and other forms of intellectual property.
- Devise programs to protect trade secrets and know-how.
- Understand the nature of mask works and their relationship to utility patents.
- Register mask works.
- Understand and prepare noncompetition agreements and nondisclosure agreements.

Trade Secrets and Know-How

A trade secret is information that is not generally available and that confers a competitive advantage upon its possessor. It may, for example, comprise a chemical formula, a manufacturing process, a machine design, or a business method. Note that the secret need not be absolute; it is only necessary that the information in question is not widely known. However, general knowledge cannot be converted into a trade secret simply by labeling it as such.

IN THE REAL WORLD

It's Serious

Under the Economic Espionage Act of 1996, the theft of trade secrets is a federal crime, which is punishable by jail terms of up to 10 years and substantial fines.

Know-how is similar to trade secrets. Essentially, it comprises a body of information, the components of which may be individually known but the compilation of which has competitive value. Supplier lists, parts specifications, and quality assurance and testing procedures generally fall into this category.

Unlike patents, trade secrets involve no fees or costs, and no attorneys need be retained. There are no statutory requirements and there is no uncertainty as to what, if any, protection will be secured. All that is necessary is that the subject information be treated as a secret.

This is, nevertheless, a requirement that is often overlooked. Simply stated, if information is to be accorded trade secret status, it must be treated as a secret by its possessor. At a minimum, it must be marked *confidential*, and reasonable (that word again) steps should be taken to assure its security. Storage in locked cabinets, to which access is limited to those with a need to know, is generally considered a requirement, as are written confidentiality and nondisclosure agreements, executed by all those having access to the information, expressly barring any unauthorized disclosure. At the other extreme, it has been held by courts that observation of the arrangement of a partially completed chemical processing plant from an airplane circling overhead was improper and that reasonable steps to maintain the secret details of the plant did not necessitate erecting a roof over the whole facility.

Trade secrets are potentially immortal. Their life extends as long as the secret can be maintained. Of course, this also means that they may be extinguished at any moment if the information is disclosed or otherwise becomes available. Disclosure may result from inadvertence ("loose lips sink ships") or improper conduct (ranging from breaches of confidentiality obligations through industrial espionage). Moreover, the information may be independently discovered or created—actually rediscovered or re-created—by another, either by pure happenstance or through analysis or reverse engineering of the products of the trade secret owner.

Herein lies an important difference between patents and trade secrets: An infringer who has independently discovered the patented invention is an infringer nonetheless but not so with trade secrets. So long as the secret was rediscovered lawfully through independent research or reverse engineering, once the secret is known, it is no longer a secret and, therefore, the trade secret protection is lost. Wait, it gets worse. A competitor who has independently discovered the trade secret may patent the invention (if it is patentable) and, if successful in obtaining a patent, may actually be able to prevent the original owner from using his own trade secret.

Because trade secrets involve neither formalities nor costs, some people promote them as a panacea—the preferred method of protecting virtually all intellectual property. *Do not listen to such people.* While trade secrets have their place in the panoply of intellectual property tools, they also have their limitations. They are, in fact, particularly ill suited to certain applications. Any information that can be ascertained through product examination will remain a trade secret only for so long as it takes a competitor to purchase a sample and inspect it or carry it to an analytical laboratory. As a practical matter, trade secrets are best employed as protection for manufacturing or other processing techniques that are performed in the privacy of one's own facility and that cannot be readily—if at all—discerned from an examination of the product produced thereby. A second suitable application involves information as to which only temporary protection is required. Most commonly, this involves a new product or process for which protection is sought only until market introduction—to obtain the first-mover advantage. Most business methods, if not patented, should be treated as trade secrets.

Another shortcoming of trade secret protection is that, as compared to patent or copyright protection, enforcement opportunities are much more limited, and the likelihood of recovering significant damages for a violation of rights is significantly lower. Violation of trade secret rights arises only from improperly securing access to the secret information. Thus, if disclosure occurs through error—for example, if researchers talk too much at a scientific symposium (or at the bar)—no damages may be recovered from those who innocently acquire and utilize the information. Moreover, when improper activity does occur (the industrial espionage previously mentioned), damages may only be sought from the malefactor. Often, this leads only to a hollow victory.

Let us assume, for example, that a low-down, underhanded competitor bribes a technician to reveal a secret process for heat-treating of machine parts to extend the useful life of certain machine tools. Assume further that this misbegotten slug then utilizes this information to produce hundreds of tools, selling them at bargain prices to the original business's loyalty-impaired customers. The trade secret owner promptly sues this blight on the face of the tool-producing industry, only to find, to his chagrin, that in addition to being dishonest, the odious wretch is also a poor businessperson who declares bankruptcy, leaving a hard-won (costly) judgment unsatisfied. The former customers, meanwhile, having purchased the tools without knowledge of the dastardly bribe, are free to use the same without any obligation to the trade secret's original owner. If, however, the heat-treatment process had been patented (specifically, the patent would include "product by process claims" directed to tools made by this process), an entirely different result would be obtained. In this event, the patentee could sue the purchasers of the tools for *using* the tools and recover damages (hopefully in the form of "lost profits"—see Chapter 8).

Notwithstanding the limitations of trade secrets just described, they represent highly valuable corporate assets and are not to be treated lightly. They may afford a long-lasting monopoly and, at the very least, secure the first-mover advantage. One of the most blatant misuses of trade secrets results from thoughtless mass patenting directed primarily to outnumbering the competitors in patent filings, which is practiced by some of the largest corporations. One needs to keep in mind that in obtaining a patent, one surrenders the underlying trade secret. In many instances, the exchange of a trade secret for a patent is a fair bargain. However, when patents are allowed to collect dust in corporate patent portfolios and are neither licensed nor enforced, the forfeiture of the trade secrets—the price paid for these patents—is nothing short of a total waste.

Mask Works

Semiconductor chips, the heart and soul of the electronics age, are produced by a chemical etching process that utilizes a stencil known as a *mask work*. These chips, which may be very costly to develop, are surprisingly inexpensive to fabricate. The situation positively cries out for copying (known as *piracy* to chip developers and *free enterprise* to chip copiers).

Being useful products, semiconductor chips are not protectable by copyright (although the design drawings of the chips could be so protected—see Chapter 1). Being functional, mask works cannot be protected by design patents, either. Although often complex, the chips frequently lack the nonobviousness required of a utility patent. Moreover, the current pace of technological advancement is such that chips are often obsolete within two years—less than the average period of time to process a patent application in the Patent Office.

To provide intellectual property protection under these trying conditions, Congress passed, in 1984, the Semiconductor Chip Protection Act, creating a new form of intellectual property (actually one closely related to a copyright, with a few patent-like aspects). The act prohibits copying of original mask works that have some degree of originality— they cannot be mere commonplace variations of previous designs (this is one of the aspects borrowed from patent law).

Registration is very similar to copyright registration and is, in fact, administered by the Copyright Office. Protection is effective upon registration or commercial exploitation (first sale, offer for sale, or other distribution to the public), whichever occurs first. However, such protection terminates two years after exploitation has begun, unless an application for protection has been filed. If registered, protection runs for 10 years from the time it began.

Although it is not required, the owner of a mask work may affix a notice (comprising the words "mask work," the symbol **M**, or the letter "M" in a circle, and the name or designation of the owner) on packaging for products employing the mask work, thereby giving constructive notice of its protected status.

Noncompetition Agreements and Confidential Disclosure Agreements

Employees (broadly defined) compose a firm's human capital, a constituent ingredient of intellectual capital. Departing employees deplete a firm's stock of intellectual capital. Worse, they may convey a firm's intellectual capital to a competitor. Indeed, who would value a firm's intellectual capital more highly than its competitors? How, then, is a firm to prevent its intellectual capital from falling into the hands of its competitors? The obvious solution to this problem was barred by the ratification of the Thirteenth Amendment to the Constitution, prohibiting involuntary servitude. The next best solution is the noncompetition agreement.

A noncompetition agreement is a contractual undertaking (lawyer-speak for *agreement*) between an employee and his employer. The agreement limits the right of the employee, upon departure, to accept employment with a competitor of his former employer. Noncompetition agreements create a conflict between two public policy considerations: the need of an employer to protect its intellectual capital and the need of a departing employee to secure suitable new employment. Resolution of this conflict is achieved by requiring that the scope of the agreement be limited to that which is clearly necessary to protect the employer, and no more. The limitations are of three kinds: temporal, geographic, and scope.

Temporal limitations refer to the duration of the agreement, that is, the time that must elapse before a departing employee may accept

IN THE REAL WORLD

Limiting an Employee's Invention Assignments

Some states, including California and Illinois, have enacted statutes that restrict the scope of Employee Invention Assignment agreements. Generally, under such statutes, employees are only obligated to assign those inventions made during the course of employment and at the employer's direction.

employment with a competitor. The employer's goal is to allow sufficient time for the knowledge held by the departing employee to become obsolete or stale. Obviously, from the employer's perspective, the longer the time period is, the better. However, it is wise to remember that the reasonableness of any temporal limitation is a question of fact, to be decided by a jury, and that employees are likely to outnumber employers on any jury. As a practical matter, any period beyond three years is likely to be considered highly suspect.

Geographic limitations refer to the geographic area in which the departing employee may not accept employment with a competitor during the agreed-upon time period. Such limitations are based upon the premise that the employer's business is limited to a specific geographic market and that the departing employee's activities outside this market area cannot harm the former employer. Geographical limitations work well for purely local businesses such as beauticians and barbers, dry cleaners, carpenters, and the like; however, given the national, if not global, nature of most business today, there is a serious question as to the continued validity or relevance of this premise. If, however, the employer's business is truly regional, such a limitation may provide a workable means of resolving the conflict.

Finally, breadth (also known as scope) limitations refer to the definition of *competitor*. For example, if one is in the plumbing supply business, is the competition limited to other plumbing supply companies or does it include all hardware firms? Today, many firms comprise more than one business. This is especially true in the case of vertically integrated businesses and conglomerates. The competitors of such firms are legion. (Consider, for example, how many firms compete in one way or another with some component of General Electric Corporation.) It is necessary, therefore, to define the scope of the prohibition as narrowly as possible. Remember, the goal is merely to prevent the departing employee from utilizing confidential knowledge to the former employer's detriment.

Confidential disclosure agreements, known as nondisclosure agreements (NDAs), are conceptually related to noncompetition agreements. Each is, in essence, an agreement that the recipient of specified information will use that information only for a specified purpose and will maintain it in confidence. Although nondisclosure agreements do not fall under the umbrella of public policy issues applicable to noncompetition agreements, they are subject to certain practical considerations. Because they are so widely used, it is worthwhile to carefully explore and understand these limitations.

Before accepting information in confidence, the prospective recipient should assure herself that the obligations of confidentiality and limited use, at a minimum, will not restrict her from using information already in her possession or information that may subsequently come into her possession from another source, free of any burdens. Obviously, such assurance is difficult if not impossible to obtain, in part because the recipient often cannot ascertain in advance exactly what information will be disclosed, and also because the recipient often cannot ascertain exactly what information her firm already possesses. Moreover, lacking prescience, the intended recipient has no ability to foresee what information may come into her possession in the future or may be independently developed by her staff.

Excepting certain information from the obligations imposed by the confidential disclosure agreement most commonly solves this problem. Although the precise language utilized may vary somewhat, these exceptions apply to information that:

- Is in the public domain.
- Is already in the possession of the recipient.
- Subsequently comes into the possession of the recipient, from a source not known by the recipient to be under any obligation of confidentiality.

- Is disclosed, by the owner of the information, to a third party without any obligation of confidentiality.
- Is subsequently independently created by the recipient without recourse to the disclosed materials. (This last exception is often the subject of some disagreement, as it requires a high degree of trust.)

Notwithstanding the presence of these standard exceptions, the intended recipient should seek as clear—and narrow—as possible a description of the information to be disclosed. Finally, there should be a time limit on the obligation. Ideally, it should expire when the information to be conveyed has become stale. Commonly, confidential disclosure agreements have terms not exceeding three years. See Appendix C for a sample Nondisclosure Agreement.

Summary

Trade secrets are information not generally known that confers a competitive advantage upon its possessor. Similarly, know-how is a body of information, the components of which may be individually known but the compilation of which has competitive value. Reasonable steps must be taken to preserve the confidentiality of trade secrets and know-how.

Trade secrets and know-how may be lost through inadvertence, improper activity (industrial espionage), or independent re-creation, including re-creation resulting from reverse engineering. When improper activity does occur, only the actual wrongdoer is liable for damages.

Trade secrets are forfeited when disclosed in a patent application. The surrender of the trade secret is the price one pays for obtaining a patent.

Mask works, which are the stencils used in the fabrication of semiconductor chips, may be legally protected by registration in the Copyright Office. Such registrations provide quick and inexpensive, albeit limited, intellectual property protection.

EXHIBIT 2.1

Comparative Table of Intellectual Properties

	Utility Patent	Design Patent	Trademark/ Service Mark	Copyright	Trade Secret	Mask Work
Protects	Products, devices, processes, business methods	Industrial design	Words, phrases, or symbols that identify the source of goods or services	Expressions of creative works, such as pictures, novels, music performance, advertising copy, etc.	Confidential information that is maintained as secret	Mask works— stencils used for semiconductor chip manufacturing
Term (in years)	20	14	Perpetual, so long as used	70 minimum	Perpetual, as long as secret is maintained	10
Registration required	Yes	Yes	No	No	No	Yes
Examined	Yes	Yes	Yes	No	N/A	No
Cost to obtain and maintain	High	Medium	Low	Low	Low	Low

EXHIBIT 2.2

Intellectual Property Protection Table

	Utility Patent	Design Patent	Trademark/Service Mark	Copyright	Trade Secret	Mask Work
Article of manufacture	Yes	Yes			Possibly	
Manufacturing process	Yes				Possibly	
Computer software	Yes			Yes	Possibly	
Business method	Yes				Possibly	
Brand name			Yes			
Product manual				Yes		
Training manual				Yes	Yes	
Semiconductor chip						Yes
Corporate logo			Yes			
Chemical compound	Yes				Possibly	
Fabric print pattern		Yes		Yes		
Photograph				Yes		
Novel				Yes		
Movie script				Yes		
Musical performance				Yes		
Series of movements in sports	Yes					
Web page		Yes		Yes		
Internet domain			Possibly			

Noncompetition agreements limit the right of a departing employee to accept employment with a competitor of his former employer. These agreements are designed to protect the intellectual capital of the employer, and public policy dictates that such agreements include such temporal, geographic, and breadth limitations as to not unduly bar the former employee from securing new employment.

Confidential disclosure agreements, also known as NDAs, are intended to allow a controlled, or limited, disclosure of confidential information. Under such an agreement, the recipient of proprietary information agrees to maintain it in confidence and to use it only for specified purposes.

Exhibits 2.1 and 2.2 provide a quick reference on the various types of IP, their terms, and a sampling of the types of intellectual assets that they may be used to protect. These tables are for illustration purposes only. Many exceptions exist, and in every instance, a professional should be consulted. The applicability of any IP tool is dependent on the particular facts of the situation.

Protecting the Fruits of Your Research and Development

After reading this chapter you will be able to:

- Recognize the importance of proper disclosure in protecting an invention.
- Successfully motivate inventors.
- Understand the parts of the invention disclosure form.
- Ensure that anything invented by your employees for your company actually *belongs* to your company.

Getting It Down on Paper

Developing new technology is only half the battle. The technology, or any other intellectual asset, must be protected if its potential value is to be fully realized.

Intellectual capital is a creation of the mind. Before it can be protected, or even used, it must be disclosed by its creator(s). More specifically, it must be disclosed to those who will be responsible for its use and those who will undertake to secure and protect it.

TIPS AND TECHNIQUES

Laboratory notebooks are necessary for every R&D project. Each step of the inventive process should be carefully documented in a lab notebook on a daily basis, and every page must be dated and witnessed by two people other than the inventor(s).

Proper disclosure is particularly important with respect to inventions that may be protectable by patenting or as trade secrets. Obviously, no steps can be taken to protect an invention until its existence and nature are known. Unless suitably encouraged and directed, many inventors will not disclose their inventions in such a manner as to bring them to the prompt attention of those charged with securing and protecting them. Some inventors are too busy with other tasks, or simply too lazy, to prepare a proper disclosure of their work. Some inventors are excessively humble, refusing to recognize the significance (and value) of their work. Some do not understand intellectual property and the rules pertaining to its protection. Such lack of understanding can be overcome by periodic brief talks or presentations.

Organizations are well advised to prepare standardized invention disclosure forms and to include invention disclosure and a performance review into R&D staff job descriptions, as well as those of middle management (remember, business methods and processes can now also be patented).

The other hindrances to disclosure are best overcome by resorting to that most powerful of human motivators: self-interest (there's no interest like self-interest).

Many organizations, especially larger organizations with long—and depersonalizing—channels of communications, institute what are known as inventor award or inventor incentive programs. Although these programs vary in detail, they generally provide a cash reward to the inventor or co-inventors when a patent application is filed. A second, generally larger, reward is paid to the inventor(s) upon the issue of a patent. The purpose of this second reward is to induce the inventor(s) to cooperate in the prosecution of the patent application. In many instances, these rewards are inadequate and fail to sufficiently motivate personnel.

It should be noted that these rewards are not in the nature of compensation for the invention. Rather, they are a token—a form of acknowledgment or recognition of the contribution the inventor has made to the firm. Attempts to compensate inventors with a portion of the profits earned from their inventions have proven counterproductive. Although not common in this country, such programs are mandated by law in several European countries. To the extent that they were intended to encourage innovation, such programs have failed. The major results seem to be suspicion, on the part of inventors, that they are being cheated (management, after all, does the bookkeeping); anger on the part of those not named as co-inventors; corporate politicking to have one's invention commercialized; jealousy; and, in general, a balkanization of the workforce. Moreover, the ability to license or assign IP rights is compromised by the demands of the inventors who, in effect, become parties to any negotiations. It may prove more productive to reward the inventors with a one-time monetary award of appreciable value.

In virtually all organizations, the creation of inventions is subject to the Pareto 80/20 rule—that is, 80 percent of the inventions are created by 20 percent of the technical staff (note that the term *engineers* was not used—many of the most prolific inventors are product designers). Identify these people and keep them happy.

The Invention Disclosure Form

Invention disclosure forms are adapted to elicit from the inventor(s) the information that is required for the preparation of a patent application. A sample disclosure form may be found in Appendix G. As seen in the illustration, such forms typically request a brief description of the problem being solved by the invention and a description of the prior solutions, or attempted solutions, and the reasons why they were not wholly satisfactory. Identification of known prior art is requested. A description of the invention is also requested, preferably to include drawings or sketches. Next, the inventor is generally requested to highlight those aspects of the invention believed to be novel and to consider what modifications or alterations could be made to the invention. These questions are intended to elicit information of use in the preparation of the patent claims. Finally, questions are often presented as to possible applications of the invention, date of first sale, offer for sale, or disclosure of the invention in a written publication, its estimated value or significance, and where it is likely to be of use. These last questions are intended to elicit information of use in establishing priorities as to the filing of patent applications and in identifying those foreign countries where patent protection should be sought (more on this issue later).

TIPS AND TECHNIQUES

To establish the conception date of an invention, one may utilize Internet-based digital notary services such as www.digistamp.com, www.genuinedoc.com, or others that can be found via a search for "digital notary service."

It is also worthwhile to ask the inventor(s) to identify possible uses of the invention in industries other than those in which the organization competes. This will facilitate the future licensing of the invention to others.

It will be recalled that patent practitioners most commonly bill by the hour for time spent in drafting patent applications. It should be appreciated, therefore, that a well-prepared invention disclosure form

TIPS AND TECHNIQUES

The invention disclosure form may be submitted to the U.S. Patent Office under the Invention Disclosure Program, where it will be kept for two years and may be referenced in a subsequent patent application filed within this time.

will not only improve the quality of a patent application based thereon but will also reduce the cost of such an application by reducing the amount of time the patent practitioner must devote to its preparation. In an ideal situation, the patent practitioner would merely be required to draft the patent claims—in fact, such a method of preparing patent applications is widely utilized in Japan. The quality of patent disclosure becomes even more important in those situations in which a patent practitioner has little or no contact with the inventor and thus has only the invention disclosure to work with.

Make Sure You Own It

Probably few things are as frustrating, embarrassing, or potentially career-threatening as creating, or having created for you, a valuable piece of intellectual property, only to find that you have lost it or, perhaps worse, don't own it—it is owned by someone else.

It is well settled in the law that inventions made in the course of their employment by individuals whose duties encompass such inventive efforts belong to the employer. Notwithstanding, it has been common practice (which one should follow) to have those employees involved in tasks likely to result in the creation of inventions—that is, engineers, product designers, and, more recently, software designers execute written agreements, known as *invention assignment agreements*, acknowledging that any invention that they may make during the course of their employment belongs to their employer and obligating them to disclose such inventions and to cooperate in securing patents or other protection for them. A sample invention assignment agreement may be found in Appendix D.

Today, however, the advent of business method patents has opened the patent office doors to a host of professionals, such as accountants, salespeople, and marketing specialists, who were not formerly considered potential inventors and, therefore, were not generally required to execute invention assignment agreements. These days, *all* employees should be required to execute invention assignment agreements. (*Caution*: This matter should be reviewed with a labor lawyer. Ask about the need for additional consideration.)

Not all inventions are patentable. Some inventions that are patentable should (for reasons discussed later) be left unpatented. Many such inventions, however, can still be protected as trade secrets—if they are maintained in confidence. Thus, after disclosure (our old friend, the invention disclosure form), they must be maintained in confidence. For this reason and others, it is important that all personnel with access to confidential information (which includes practically everyone) take a vow of silence. Such vows, when made in a business setting, are generally known as *confidentiality agreements*. A sample confidentiality agreement may be found in Appendix C.

Plan Ahead for Protection

Many business corporations, as well as individual inventors, consider patents only when an invention is completed and ready to bring to market. Indeed, many prospective patentees wait until literally the last day possible before filing a patent application (occasionally, they wait until the day *after* the last day, creating ulcers for patent attorneys' malpractice insurance carriers). This approach, known as *retrospective patenting*, is primarily defensive in nature—it is intended to defend the market for the new product. Moreover, such corporations typically limit, or narrowly focus, their inventive efforts to what are considered core business areas and, as a result, develop correspondingly limited or narrow patent portfolios. They view patents as valuable only with regard to technology that falls within the scope of their current business.

Increasingly, however, inventions are being patented before the invention has been demonstrated physically. Instead of awaiting the building, testing, and refining of prototypes before seeking patent protection, many inventors are now filing patent applications in respect of the results of thought experiments. This approach is known as *prospective patenting*. There seems to be a strong probability that retrospective patents will be defensive or core patents, while prospective patents are rather likely to be offensive or noncore patents.

In addition to the traditional function of protecting the market for a newly developed product, prospective patents are also being used as bargaining chips for cross-licensing negotiations with other organizations, allowing a patentee to trade away patent protection for an invention it chooses not to commercialize, in exchange for the right to proceed with respect to a product otherwise blocked by a competitor's patent(s). Prospective patents, comprising bases for potential counterclaims, may also serve to discourage competitors from crossing litigation swords with the patentee. They may add revenue through licensing or sale and, in today's economy, they may facilitate (or even enable) the patentee to raise capital.

Summary

An invention can only be protected after it has been disclosed to those responsible for its protection. The invention disclosure form is a vehicle for securing such disclosure. Various inventor award or incentive programs may be organized to encourage disclosure of inventions and cooperation in securing protection for those inventions.

An organization should ensure that it will own the inventions and other intellectual assets created by its employees. This may be accomplished through the use of invention assignment agreements.

CHAPTER 4

Know What You Have (IP Audit) and What the Other Guy Has (Competitive Intelligence)

After reading this chapter you will be able to:

- Know the goals of an intellectual property (IP) audit.
- Understand the advantages conferred by having an outside organization (rather than in-house personnel) perform the IP audit.
- Identify core, noncore, and useless patents in your portfolio.
- Gain useful information about your competitors' business and product plans through monitoring their patents and patent applications.
- Understand patent mapping's advantages and limitations.

The Intellectual Property Audit

Often a firm does not know, or may not fully appreciate, the scope and applicability of its intellectual property. To paraphrase one business executive, "Had we known then what we know now, we would be twice the size." The means to correct this lack of knowledge is an intellectual property audit.

An IP audit has several goals:

- To identify all of the intellectual property a firm may possess.
- To ensure that all identified property is properly assigned and protected.
- To identify those intellectual assets that are worth protecting, thereby converting them into intellectual property.
- To identify any gaps in the systematic extraction of knowledge and conversion of intellectual capital into intellectual assets.
- To identify any gaps, problems, or failures in the procedures followed by a firm in identifying and safeguarding such assets.

The audit can, theoretically, either be performed by an outside organization, such as an intellectual property law firm or intellectual property management firm, or be done in-house. While the in-house approach offers a clear advantage (it's free), it is almost always the worse choice. Essentially, doing an effective audit in-house requires that the personnel involved either (1) admit to their own shortcomings and mistakes (not likely) or (2) point out the shortcomings and mistakes of their colleagues (everyone knows where that leads). Let the professionals handle it—it's worth the cost.

Typically, at the commencement of the audit, the auditors will submit a detailed list of questions to be answered by the firm being audited (hereafter the *auditee*). Submission of this questionnaire is often followed by a meeting with liaison personnel and key executives of the auditee, where the questions are discussed and answered.

The questionnaire is largely designed to elicit information as to what intellectual property has been created or acquired, and what steps (if any) have been taken to protect this property. A thorough audit will also delve into the procedures followed by the auditee in documenting and protecting its intellectual property. A sample intellectual property audit questionnaire may be found in Appendix E.

Based on the answers to the questionnaire and the results of follow-up investigations, an inventory of intellectual property is produced. This inventory generally includes both an identification of the individual items and a description of their legal status. Recommendations are provided as to any further steps to be taken to protect or secure these specific items. Often, an audit will indicate that intellectual assets *may* have been created in the course of a given project or program, or that there exists a substantial probability that assets may, in the future, be so created. In the former event, further analysis may be required before a definite response can be provided. In the latter event, a heightened awareness and careful monitoring of the project or program is generally prescribed.

In this regard, it should be considered that intellectual property is, potentially, being created whenever and wherever efforts are being directed to the solution of a problem or the satisfaction of a need. This concept is generally accepted with respect to technological research and product development. It also applies, however, to market research, preparation of sales and promotional materials, and development of accounting and control systems and new methods of doing business. Tools are available that, under the appropriate circumstances, may provide for the protection of the results of all of these efforts. Examine everything. Overlook or ignore nothing.

In addition to recommendations with respect to individual property items and specific projects or programs, an intellectual property audit should include policy or procedural recommendations directed to the identification and protection of intellectual property that may be created in the future. Once such policies and procedures have been adopted and implemented—and with the experience gained through participation in the audit process—subsequent, periodic audits may be adequately performed in-house. Nevertheless, independent (a diplomatic way to say *outside*) personnel should perform audits upon the occurrence of critical or unusual events, such as the acquisition or divestiture of a business unit, or when the business to be audited is a joint venture with another party.

Without proper invention assignment agreements, the firm may not own all of the IP discovered by the IP audit. Therefore, the audit should include a review of all consulting agreements and verification that all employees have executed invention assignment agreements and non-disclosure agreements (NDAs).

In the event of a recent merger or acquisition, the IP audit should assure that the surviving entity not only owns intellectual assets contractually but that the transfer of ownership had been properly recorded (e.g., patent assignments were recorded in the U.S. Patent and Trademark Office).

IN THE REAL WORLD

Don't Assume—Verify

Even large, supposedly sophisticated organizations screw up occasionally—like when the Volkswagen Group purchased all of the assets of the Rolls Royce Motor Car Company. Volkswagen acquired the plant, equipment, parts, and tooling. To their surprise and chagrin, however, Volkswagen did *not* get the famous Rolls Royce trademark. Subsequent investigation revealed that the Rolls Royce Motor Car Company did not own the trademark; rather, the Rolls Royce airplane engine company, a completely separate entity, owned it. Moreover, under its terms, the license terminated upon a change in ownership by the car company.

The Patent Review Committee

One of the questions that must be answered with respect to each (hopefully) patentable invention is where (in which countries) patent protection is to be sought. A subsequent question, which should be raised and answered after a patent is issued, is whether maintenance of the patent (i.e., payment of the periodic government patent maintenance fees) is economically justified. This question is best answered by a patent committee.

A patent committee generally includes, at a minimum, representatives from the legal, marketing, and engineering departments of the business. In some cases, the engineering contingent may include specialists in manufacturing, product development, and basic research. Collectively, the committee members should be aware of the current state of their employer's product plans (emphasis on *current*) and the available intelligence as to the products, processes, and plans of competitors. In addition, they should possess the breadth of technical expertise and foresight to assess the present and future applicability or utility of an invention. If available, an in-house patent practitioner and a licensing executive should also be included.

It is the function of the committee to periodically review the entire patent portfolio, including invention disclosures, pending patent applications, and issued patents, to decide:

- Which invention disclosures should be made the subjects of patent applications.
- Whether continued prosecution of pending patent applications is warranted.
- Whether foreign patent protection is to be sought and, if so, in which countries.
- Whether issued patents should be maintained or allowed to lapse.

The appropriate frequency of meetings is proportional to the size of the portfolio to be reviewed and, to a somewhat lesser extent, to the rate of change of plans and technologies in the industry. The committee should hold meetings at least quarterly. Most large organizations hold monthly meetings.

The importance of the committee in protecting the organization's intellectual property, while still controlling costs, should be emphasized. Because committee deliberations occupy time that would otherwise be devoted to meeting departmental goals, departmental heads may be inclined to delegate their least productive personnel for committee membership (this kind of selection process should be familiar to those with military experience). A committee composed of such people may well be worse than no committee at all. Every effort should be made to assure all concerned that the committee is composed of the most—not the least—capable personnel.

In the event the IP audit is conducted internally (which is not recommended), the place to start may be to create simple schedules of all patents, trademarks, service marks, copyrighted materials, trade secrets, and so forth.

After the schedules have been compiled, remove expired or lapsed patents and trademarks and verify the status of every intellectual asset identified (if some of the rights have recently lapsed, such as for failure to pay patent maintenance fees, they may be reinstated if acted upon immediately).

Create a schedule of critical dates (on which patent maintenance fees must be paid or licenses renewed, etc.) and create a mechanism to act in time to prevent future loss of rights.

Portfolio Audit—Triage for Patents

An IP audit is directed to the identification and protection of intellectual property. A portfolio audit, which may be considered the next step in the IP utilization process, sorts through the patents in a portfolio in order to separate the wheat from the chaff.

Over the years, large companies tend to accumulate significant numbers of patents in their portfolios. Some of these patents are acquired as the result of corporate mergers and acquisitions. Many such patents are orphans—unknown and unloved by anyone at the acquiring or surviving company. Another cause of portfolio growth (or bloat) is the natural reluctance of anyone to take responsibility for abandoning a patent or a pending patent application. New patents are constantly added to the portfolio but none, or few, are deleted (rather like the Roach Motel^{TM}—"they check in, but they don't check out").

The maintenance of a patent portfolio involves both direct (explicit) costs and indirect (implicit) costs. The direct costs are, of course, the prosecution costs and maintenance fees incurred in prosecuting and subsequently maintaining the patents in the portfolio. Less obviously but more importantly, the indirect cost is the loss of value of the trade secrets disclosed in the patent application. The indirect costs are also the so-called opportunity costs—the revenues foregone by failure to license patents that are of interest to others and the losses suffered as the result of failure to enforce those patents that are being infringed. To the extent that funds are being expended in prosecuting patent applications and maintaining issued patents that do not further business objectives, such expenditures are wasted.

Similarly (although less noticeably), the failure to extract value from the patent portfolio also constitutes a waste of the business's assets. Effective management (and retention of cushy jobs) requires that such waste be avoided or eliminated. (For more on the exciting topic of who's responsible, see Chapter 7.)

The patents and patent applications that make up the patent portfolio may be divided into three categories: core, noncore, and useless.

Core patents are those that cover key technologies. They provide exclusivity with regard to production processes, products, or services of the enterprise. Core patents are to be vigorously enforced so as to maintain the exclusive franchise they were intended to secure. Failure to enforce core patents results in the two great ills attendant upon competition: loss of market share and price erosion. (See Chapter 7 for a discussion about liability regarding the licensing of core patents.)

Noncore patents are those that cover technologies that are useful, or potentially useful, but not critical to a firm's competitive position. They may, for example, pertain to products or services that the firm has decided not to market or to processes it has chosen not to utilize. These very products, processes, or services may, however, be of interest to others (*interest* in this sense means willingness to pay). Thus, revenues may be realized by the assignment (lawyerspeak for *sale*) or licensing of noncore patents. Such businesses, however, will rarely beat a path to your door. Licensing of noncore patents is a complex and time-consuming (although often extremely lucrative) task (see Chapter 6). Setting up a patent licensing or IP management group dedicated to extracting value from the existing IP portfolio may prove to be a very worthwhile undertaking.

Useless patents are exactly what they would seem to be. Generally, they pertain to obsolete technologies or to technologies that seemed promising but failed to develop as anticipated—technological dead ends. In other cases, they may represent sound technological developments that were sidestepped by the standard-setting bodies, rendering them mostly useless. They confer no competitive advantage and offer no reasonable likelihood of generating any revenues. A business should cut its losses and abandon such patents.

Who is to perform this patent triage? The answer is, primarily, the patent review committee. Indeed, if the committee has been properly fulfilling its role, there should be no such accumulation of useless patents—such patents would be promptly identified and abandoned. Similarly, in making its group decision that an invention merited the filing of a patent application, the committee had determined that it was either critical to the firm's competitive position (a core patent) or held the promise of financial gain (a noncore patent). This preliminary decision was revisited each time the committee considered further expenditures with respect to the patent application—prosecution costs, issue fees, foreign filing costs, and maintenance fees.

Thus, due to changes in a firm's plans, an invention once thought to be critical may be downgraded to noncore status. (Changes in the state of the art or developmental failures generally result in an invention being considered useless.) It is a function of the committee to react to such changes. The committee should have, in effect if not in fact, a list of noncore patents ripe and ready for licensing. The committee members should also be able to offer much useful advice as to potential uses and licensees of such technologies.

Competitive Intelligence

Competitive intelligence is the art of knowing what your competitor has and using that to your own advantage. Patent monitoring and patent mapping yield information that is valuable in many ways—from indicating the nature and direction of your competitor's research and development efforts to helping you determine if a competitor is infringing *your* patents.

Patent Judo—Turning Your Competitors' Strengths against Them

In business, there are two kinds of patents: one's own and one's competitors'. The former protect the fruits of an organization's skill, labor, creativity, and capital investment. They prevent unimaginative, unprincipled, and ruthless competitors, both present and potential, from misappropriating the organization's work—reaping where they did not sow, stealing the organization's inventions.

The competitors' patents are monopolistic tools—obstacles to market entry that stifle competition. One cannot be too objective about this: One's own patents are assets; one's competitors' patents are a problem. It all depends on one's vantage point.

Obviously, significant benefits flow from the first kind of patents and, for this reason, such patents are or should be a matter of serious attention. Less obviously, value can also be derived from the second kind of patents—those owned by competitors—as they contain much valuable information about such competitors' developments, products, and plans; for this reason, they too should be accorded a measure of attention.

Each of a competitors' patents describes a product, or a process, or an improvement in a product or process, which that competitor believes to be of sufficient value to warrant the cost of the patent (practitioner's fees for drafting and prosecution, filing fees, issue fees, and maintenance fees, not to mention the loss of the value of the underlying trade secret forfeited in the patent application). Clearly, one should not ascribe too much significance to a single patent or published patent application. Plans and markets may change, and apparently promising developments may prove to be limited or flawed. Nevertheless, a competitor's patent, at a minimum, identifies a technology or product of interest to the patentee. Moreover, the existence of multiple patents on closely related technologies or products might be considered a reliable predictor of future activity. Simply stated, the competitor is paying a lot of money to tell the world what he plans to do, and it would be ungracious and downright foolish not to take appropriate notice.

There are several ways in which this valuable information may be obtained. The least costly method is simply to examine the *Official Gazette* of the U.S. Patent and Trademark Office (USPTO). This publication contains the abstract and a representative drawing from each patent issued in the previous week, together with the name(s) of the inventor(s) and (if the patent has been assigned) the name of the assignee. The patents are arranged in the *Gazette* according to their Patent Office classification. Thus, all patents pertaining to a given field of technology are grouped together and may be readily scanned to identify those of interest.

In addition, the *Gazette* includes both inventor and assignee indexes, permitting the ready identification of patents assigned to particular competitors or those with particular inventors. Once patents of interest have been identified, copies may be ordered from the Patent Office or obtained online from any of a variety of providers. Alternatively, a standing order may be placed with the USPTO for copies of all patents issuing in designated technological areas. A patent practitioner may perform the same continual monitoring of newly issued patents—not surprisingly, this is known as a *patent watch*. (Practitioners are generally eager to offer such services, as they provide an opportunity to bill at substantial rates for work done by paralegals or clerks or, sometimes, computers.) Such patent watches may be limited to U.S. patents and published patent applications or may extend to European (EPO) and Japanese patent applications, which are *laid open* or published prior to issue.

Formerly, U.S. patent applications were maintained in confidence, and one would need to monitor the Patent Cooperation Treaty (PCT) filings, which are published after 18 months, in order to gain a glimpse of the content of the corresponding U.S. patent applications. However, as noted in Chapter 1, all patent applications filed in the United States after November 29, 2000, will also be published after 18 months. (Some inventors may choose to forgo the option of filing corresponding foreign patent applications and request that their applications be kept secret in the USPTO.)

TIPS AND TECHNIQUES

Most patent searches can be done now on the Internet and can easily be automated. Information providers such as Nerac, Inc. (www.nerac.com) can monitor all newly issued patents, identifying those that are assigned to a particular company, pertain to a particular technology or classification code, or contain keywords of interest.

To search for U.S. patents, one may also visit the web site of the USPTO (www.uspto.gov) or the Delphion Intellectual Property Network (www.delphion.com). One of the most useful databases is Thomson Reuters (http://science.thomsonreuters.com/). One can similarly monitor scientific and technical literature for any articles either published by competitors' staff, pertaining to a particular field of technology, or containing certain keywords. Such services are provided, for example, by Nerac.

Further information on a competitor's activities may be gleaned by closely examining the front pages of the competitor's patents. Patent title pages contain a wealth of information, including lists of the prior art cited during the prosecution of the patent. Prior art citations in a patent are of three kinds: (1) patents, (2) foreign patents, and (3) research publications (scientific papers and conference proceedings) and other nonpatented prior art. Calculating the median age of the cited patents, a parameter called technology cycle time (TCT) may help in deducing how close the competitor's R&D activities are to cutting-edge research. Citation of more recent patents may indicate that the R&D program is in step with or at least close to the state of the art, while a predominance of old patent citations may indicate that the development activities are merely directed toward improvements of old technology.

Similarly, the mean number of references to scientific publications among the patents issued to a company, called the *science linkage index*, may reveal whether this company's R&D program is directed more toward basic research or toward product development. A predominant focus on basic research indicates long-term planning that may secure such a firm a future competitive advantage (more on this in Chapter 10). Similar watch programs may (and should) be implemented with respect to a firm's trademarks and copyrighted materials.

Signs of Opportunity

The question is often asked (or should be), "How can I find out who, if anyone, is infringing my patent?" One answer to this question is, "Look at other people's patents."

Conveniently printed on the top sheet of each patent is a list of the prior art references cited during the course of its prosecution. In a broad sense, these prior art references identify the technology on which the patented invention rests. Stated in another way, the patented invention is, to a greater or lesser degree, an improvement on the cited prior art. Remember the red fire engine? If a patent is cited as prior art in a patent owned by another inventor, then it is quite possible that practice of the other's invention will constitute an infringement of the patent cited as prior art.

Monitor newly issued patents—especially those assigned to competitors—to identify those wherein your patent is cited as prior art. If such a patent is found, determine whether the assignee of the new patent is practicing the previously patented invention. If the patented invention *is* being practiced, carefully examine the newly patented product or service to determine whether infringement has occurred. There may well be a patent enforcement opportunity (patent infringement is an enforcement opportunity in the same way that a cruise on the *Titanic* was a swimming opportunity). If the newly identified patentee is not practicing its own patented invention, this may be due to a variety of factors, including concern over infringement of the cited prior art patent. Thus, this may be a licensing opportunity (see Chapter 6).

Patent Mapping

One of the popular topics in current writings on intellectual property is *patent mapping*. Patent mapping sounds terribly complex but in actuality it is quite simple. Patent mapping, simply stated, is the visual—actually, graphical or tabular—presentation of patent data.

The data being presented may relate to one's own patents or to patents of competitors (i.e., competitive intelligence data).

Among the more common applications of patent mapping are the following:

- *Benchmarking.* This is a presentation of the number of patents held by various competitors, especially those that are considered to be the best of breed. The numbers may be simply presented in gross (the total number of patents owned by an organization) or they may be divided into classes based upon subject matter. Benchmarking is intended to facilitate the comparison of a firm's intellectual property portfolio with the corresponding portfolios of its competitors. The weakness of this analysis, however, is that it fails to account for patent quality. Rather, it rests on the implicit assumption that all patents are of equal scope, equal validity and enforceability, and, hence, of equal value, which, of course, is not so.

- *Competitive predictions.* As previously noted, an analysis of a competitor's patent portfolio can help predict new products and the overall direction the competitor is likely to take. This analysis can be refined if one focuses on the *changes* in a portfolio (i.e., what is the competitor patenting *now?*). Such current efforts can be masked if one merely examines a complete portfolio, which has been developed and accumulated over many years.

- *Patent clusters.* Patents may be categorized by the field of technology to which they appertain. For categorization purposes, the Patent Office classification scheme may be utilized (the Patent Office has kindly done this work for us) or any other convenient system may be employed. When plotting a number of patents in a portfolio, related categories are grouped together. It is thus theoretically possible to both identify broad areas of concentration, which would have been otherwise masked, and also determine the regions of concentration within the broader area.

- *Profiling.* Related to cluster analysis is portfolio profiling (don't worry, it raises no civil rights issues). Once a patent portfolio has been analyzed and plotted in terms of numbers of patents in various technological categories, it will be seen that the resultant plot describes the portfolio—and, by inference, the portfolio owner—in the same manner that a plot of a DNA sample describes the sample donor. By comparing such plots or *profiles*, one may, theoretically, identify likely licensees, acquisition targets, or merger partners. The critical question here, of course, is "What are we searching for—strength or weakness, similarity or dissimilarity?" The answer depends upon the reason that the inquiry is being made.

- *Miscellaneous portfolio information.* It has been suggested in the literature that patent mapping may be used to highlight various features of a patent portfolio. Thus, for example, the number of patents issued in the name of various inventors may be graphed. The idea here is that the high points on the graph identify the most prolific inventors (well, duh!). It has even been suggested that this analysis be refined to identify the number of patents whose inventors are no longer employed by the patentee organization (inventor employment analysis). It is implied that having many inventors leave an organization is not a good thing (again—well, duh!). Similarly, one may graph numbers of patents against patent age. This is intended to provide an indication of portfolio aging and warn of impending expiration or technological obsolescence.

While useful, the concept of patent mapping has been somewhat oversold. It is most applicable to analysis of sizable portfolios where it can disclose trends. It can be misleading when applied to small portfolios. Moreover, it has a significant lag time—patent applications are not published until 18 months after the earliest claimed priority date.

Summary

An IP audit provides the means for taking inventory of a firm's intellectual property and assuring that all such property is properly assigned and protected. It also provides for the identification and documentation of valuable intellectual assets and corrects any shortcomings in the procedures followed by the firm in handling such assets.

A patent review committee periodically reviews the firm's patent portfolio to decide questions pertaining to the continued prosecution of patent applications, maintenance of issued patents, and the advisability of filing foreign counterpart applications.

Much information about a competitor's developments, plans, and products may be gleaned from an examination of its patents. This information may be gathered by simply reviewing the USPTO's *Official Gazette* or obtained from any number of service providers. Examination of competitors' patents may also give warning that one's own patents are being infringed. Patent mapping is the visual presentation of patent data.

CHAPTER 5

What Is It Worth?
Putting a Value on Intellectual Property

After reading this chapter, you will be able to:

- Understand the various IP valuation models.
- Understand how factors such as infringement, corporate culture, national culture, and the patentee's ability to enforce patent rights can affect patent value.

Having devoted such effort to creating, identifying, and protecting intellectual property, the reader is probably wondering what it is worth. (If not, the reader should be.) Certainly, venture capitalists, bankers, shareholders, and other investors—actual or potential—are asking this question.

Valuation Models

Intellectual property (IP), like any property that is bought and sold, is worth what it will bring in the market. In the absence of an efficient market (a market with many buyers, many sellers, and freely available information as to prices) for trading technologies, it may be quite difficult to ascertain what the market value of a particular technology may be. Nevertheless, there are several valuation models that may be employed in valuing intellectual property. Among the most widely used models are historical R&D cost, replacement cost, discounted revenue stream (also known as the income approach), market value (also known as the comparables approach), and incremental value.

Replacement Cost

The historical R&D cost approach values a technology at the historical cost of the R&D that led to its development. It is, simply, the sum of the actual expenses incurred (research, development, and legal costs) in creating the property. As practiced, this method rests on the implicit assumption that the result of each dollar invested in research is equal to the result of every other dollar so spent. The fallacy of this assumption should be readily apparent to all. By this thinking, an expensive failure is worth more than an inexpensive success. However, because replacement cost is based solely upon precise, verifiable, historical data, it is dearly beloved by accountants and others of their ilk. *Do not listen to such people.* Its only (very limited) value is its use as a surrogate for the replacement cost.

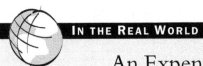

IN THE REAL WORLD

An Expensive Failure

An attempt to develop a nuclear-powered aircraft was, perhaps, the most expensive R&D failure of modern times. According to the replacement cost valuation method, the end result of this failure would be worth billions of dollars (for which no one would pay a dime).

Replacement cost is, theoretically, what it would cost to replace or reinvent the property. Although the theory is sound, the practice is weak. In practice, replacement cost is considered to be the same as development cost, although there is a theoretical difference (development cost is a historical value—what it actually cost to develop the technology at the time it was developed—while replacement cost is an estimate of what it would cost to achieve the same result now, which may be considerably different).

This does not mean, however, that the replacement cost approach has no place under the sun. It does have some applicability to the valuation of trade secrets and patents. Recall that trade secrets may be legally discovered by reverse engineering or independent research. Based on this, the price of a trade secret should never exceed the cost of rediscovering it in one's own lab. Hence, the replacement cost (cost of independent development or reverse engineering) effectively places an upper limit on the value of a trade secret.

The upper value of the trade secret, in turn, is the minimum value of a patent based on the invention covered by the trade secret. Since, as previously noted (see Chapter 1), the filing of a patent application generally results in a loss of the underlying trade secret pertaining to the invention, a patent applicant must be convinced that the ensuing patent will be more valuable than the surrendered trade secret or the patent application would not have been filed. This implicit assumption establishes the minimum value for the patent as the cost of replacement of the underlying trade secret. Needless to say, the value of the patent could be considerably higher.

Discounted Revenue Stream
or Income Approach

The *discounted revenue stream* or income approach (also known as the *capitalized revenue stream* approach) to intellectual property valuation is based on the assumption that the property will produce a stream of revenues. Obviously, if the property is licensed there will be revenues in the form of royalties. A forecast of such royalties is prepared—as to both amount and timing—and the present value of the forecasted stream is calculated. Clearly, the calculated value is highly dependent upon the discount rate applied. However, the rate may be chosen to reflect the perceived risk and may, in this way, constitute a valuable adjustment mechanism.

The capitalized revenue stream approach is best suited to situations where the property owner neither uses the underlying technology nor seeks to deny its use to competitors (see Exhibit 5.1). In such circumstances, the property has no value to its owner other than the revenue stream it may produce. If, however, the property owner competes in the market to which the technology appertains (a word beloved by attorneys for its archaic sound), the valuation question becomes much more complex.

Market Value

Like many people (probably including the reader), we regularly scan the notices of home sales in our respective communities. When we find

---

EXHIBIT 5.1

Value of Unused IP: Capitalized Revenue Stream

$$V = \sum_{i-1}^{n} \frac{R_i}{(1 + I_i)^i}$$

Where: $V =$ is the value of the subject intellectual property

$R =$ is the revenue derived from the property (i.e., royalties) in year n

$I =$ is the applicable discount rate chosen to reflect the risk factors

$n =$ is the number of years in which revenue is received

that a house similar to ours has been sold, we can assume that the value of our house is approximately equal to the sale price of the similar house. This is an example of the *market valuation* or comparables method.

While this approach to valuation works reasonably well for valuing homes, it is difficult to apply to the valuation of patents. Since, by definition, all patented inventions are unique (actually referred to as *novel*, but that's the same thing), it is virtually impossible to find other patents sufficiently similar to the one to be valued (in real estate, this is called *lack of comparables*). Moreover, there is no efficient market for patents—even if we could find comparables, there is no information available as to recent sales prices of such patents. In short, it works for houses but not for patents.

IN THE REAL WORLD

How Wall Street Valued a Patent

From time to time, bankruptcy auctions and stock market reactions to a patent loss place a market value on an intellectual property. On August 9, 2000, Eli Lilly lost 31 percent of its market value, which erased $35 billion from its market value, due to the loss of the latter to expire of its two Prozac patents. This event clearly indicated that the lost patent, invalidated for double patenting, was worth $35 billion in the eyes of the investors.

Incremental Value

The *incremental value* of intellectual property is the value it adds to its owner. It is the difference between the value of an enterprise with the property and the value of the same enterprise without the property—brilliant in its theoretical simplicity, complex in its practical application.

Consider a proprietary process owned by a manufacturing firm that utilizes the process in the production of a product it sells. Assume further, for the moment, that the firm does not license this technology. Under the capitalized revenue stream method, therefore, this property has no value. If one were to apply a measure of common sense—it does seem old-fashioned, but sometimes nothing else works as well—one might measure, for example, the cost savings effected by the use of the technology and consider this a revenue stream. Discounted to the present, such future cost savings (viewed for our purposes as periodic cash flows) represent the incremental value of the patent.

If use of the technology resulted in a superior product that commanded a premium price, this price increment could also be treated as a revenue stream. Indeed, adding a dash of sophistication to common sense, one might impute a reasonable royalty (the rate the firm would have willingly paid for an exclusive license of the process if the intellectual property protecting the process was owned by another) as a revenue stream. Such an approach is, however, still a mere theoretical approximation. It fails to distinguish between the value of the technology and the value of the intellectual property.

If the firm did not have proprietary (exclusive) rights to the technology (if, for example, the technology was not patented or protected as a trade secret), the firm would still be free to use it but so, too, would its competitors. The existence of such competition would certainly affect (for those readers who failed Economics 101, it would reduce) the market share and sale price enjoyed by the firm. For example, pharmaceutical companies typically lose half of their market share when the patent protection of a brand-name drug is lost or expires, and generic drug manufacturers begin producing a no-name version. If the reader were to forecast the annual profit of the firm under monopoly conditions and subtract the corresponding profit of the firm employing the same technology under competitive (nonmonopoly) conditions, the difference is the value created by the intellectual property. The present value of these profit differentials, over the life of the intellectual property, is its true value (see Exhibit 5.2).

EXHIBIT 5.2

Value of a Patent Portfolio Being Used by Its Owner

$$PV(PP) = \sum_{i=1}^{n} \frac{\Delta_i}{(1 + I_i)^i}$$

Where: $PV(PP) =$ is the present value of the patent portfolio

$\Delta_i =$ is the incremental annual profit due to the patent monopoly in year i:

$$\Delta_i = \langle PR_i \rangle - PR_i$$

where $\langle PR_i \rangle$ is the profit derived from the patented product or process, under patent monopoly conditions, in year I

$PR_i =$ is the profit derived from the same product or process, under hypothetical freely competitive conditions, in the same year I

$n =$ is the number of years remaining of the patent's life

Assume now that the firm licenses the intellectual property. This may have occurred for any of a variety of reasons. Perhaps the firm granted a license in exchange for a license of technology owned by the licensee (a cross-license arrangement). Perhaps the firm was unable to satisfy the entire market demand for the product produced by the subject technology and concluded that it would maximize its return by licensing one or more competitors. Does this sharing of the intellectual property destroy its value? No. It creates a shared monopoly or, more precisely, a franchise. The same valuation models may still be employed, although, unfortunately, they become still more complex.

The Formula

A variation on the incremental value model just described is known as the *formula* or the *excess earnings* or *residual value* model. It differs from the other models in that it purports to determine the value of a firm's intellectual property as a whole, rather than the separate value of any piece or component thereof. Moreover, it is only applicable to a profitable business. For these reasons, its applicability is somewhat limited. It does, however, enjoy the acceptance of the Internal Revenue Service (IRS Revenue Ruling 68-609) and, for that reason if for no other, it merits a brief explanation.

In essence, the formula involves first determining the portion of a firm's profits that were attributable to its intellectual property and then capitalizing those profits at a suitable rate—one that reflects the risk associated with the firm's business (see Exhibit 5.3). The profits attributable to the IP are calculated by subtracting from the firm's total profits those that are attributable to the firm's tangible assets. This, in turn, is calculated by applying an industry average return rate to the actual amount of the firm's tangible assets.

Obviously, this model has its conceptual flaws, the most significant being that it takes no notice of the demise of any of the IP (patent expiration or obsolescence, trade secret loss through disclosure or independent reinvention). Rather, it implicitly assumes that the pool of intellectual property will be constantly replenished at the same rate it is lost, such that a constant level is maintained. Moreover, it should be apparent to the alert reader that any factor causing a reduction in the firm's overall earnings—including factors unrelated to IP—will have the effect of reducing the calculated value of the IP portfolio.

EXHIBIT 5.3

Example of the Formula Valuation Method	
Value of the firm's tangible assets	$1,000,000
Average rate of return in the industry	10%
Earnings attributable to tangible assets	$ 100,000
Total earnings of the firm	$ 700,000
Less: earnings attributable to tangible assets	(100,000)
Earnings attributable to IP	$ 600,000
Discount rate reflecting the cost of capital and business risk	15%
Value of IP	$4,000,000

Mathematically Correct Patent Valuation Models

The authors will now proceed to present their own (obviously superior) valuation models. For those readers who are mathematically inclined (or simply masochistic), equations for the theoretically correct valuation of a single patent or a portfolio of related patents are derived and appear in Appendix F. These formulas describe values in both a perfect world (i.e., where patents are respected, not infringed) and the real world (where patents are routinely infringed). Models are also derived for the valuation of the individual constituents of a portfolio of related patents.

Patent Value: A Model for a Perfect World

In nonmathematical, more generally comprehensible terms, a value is first derived for the entire portfolio of related patents—patents all directed to different aspects of a single product, product line, or service. This value, as noted earlier, is defined as the difference between the cash flows enjoyed by the portfolio owner under exclusive conditions afforded by the patent(s) (this is a perfect world model) and the corresponding cash flows that would result under purely competitive conditions (as if there were no patent[s]). Summing these differences over the expected life of the patent(s) produces a total value. Thus, for each period (usually, but not necessarily, these are annual periods), sales volume, the sale price, and variable costs must be estimated (forecasted, guessed) under both the monopolistic (with patents) and competitive (without patents) market assumptions. The difference between the cash flows with and without the patents is the annual value of the market monopoly.

This is, of course, the weakness of the model: The calculated value is no better than the estimates on which it is based, and the estimation process itself is lengthy and tedious (it is especially suited to performance by summer interns, graduate students, and similar sources of intelligent but cheap labor). The present value of the patent portfolio is found by discounting the cash flow differences in succeeding years; that is to say, taking the present value of the previously calculated stream of annual cash flow enhancements due to the patent monopoly.

Having calculated the value of a portfolio of related patents, one can approximate the value of a single, constituent patent. First, divide the value of the entire portfolio by the number of constituent patents to calculate an average value per patent. This average value is then adjusted with regard to two factors: patent term and relative merit.

The *patent term* adjustment factor is essentially a fraction whose denominator is the number of periods (again, usually, but not necessarily, years) or the term over which the portfolio valuation was calculated. The numerator is the number of periods, during the valuation term, during which the subject constituent patent was active (issued and subsisting). For example, if the portfolio was valued over a five-year term, and the subject patent was issued at the beginning of the third year of that term and remained subsisting (did not expire and was found neither invalid nor unenforceable by a court), the term adjustment factor would be three-fifths or 0.6.

The *relative merit* adjustment is, unfortunately, more subjective. As should be apparent to the reader by this point, the relative value of the various patents in a patent portfolio is affected by the scope or breadth of the patent claims (if this is not apparent, please see Chapter 1).

Patent Value: A Model for the Real World

The foregoing valuation model assumed that patents are universally respected—that they are not infringed (actually, it simply ignored the possibility of infringement). Unfortunately, in the real world, infringement does sometimes (frequently) occur (it is hoped that the reader is outraged by this revelation). The question to be asked is what effect infringement has on the value of a patent or a patent portfolio.

The answer to this question depends upon the likelihood that the patent owner will successfully enforce the patent rights. The likelihood of successful enforcement depends on two factors: (1) the probability that the patent owner will undertake enforcement action and (2) the probability that enforcement action, undertaken by the owner, will be successful. The probability that the patent owner will seek to enforce the patent is, in turn, composed of two elements: (1) the owner's willingness to undertake enforcement and (2) the ability to do so.

Many companies that are aware of acts of infringement of their patents are unwilling to enforce those patents for a variety of reasons. Some firms have a litigation-averse or risk-averse corporate culture. In some instances, internal corporate politics (e.g., whose department budget is going to pay for litigation?), management complacency, fear of upsetting an existing supplier or customer relationship, or fear of being accused of monopolistic behavior produce inaction, if not to say passivity.

National culture plays a role in this, too. Europeans are much less likely than Americans to become engaged in patent litigation, while in Japan, patent litigation is quite rare (and Japan is one of the largest patent filers in the world!). Needless to say, a patent portfolio owned by a company that is unlikely to enforce it is worth considerably less (if anything at all!) than a similar portfolio owned by a company that vigorously enforces its patents, all other things being equal.

The ability to enforce the patents is often a matter of finance. With the median cost of patent infringement litigation at $5.5 million (in 2009) and rising, one needs to have the necessary capital before embarking on this expensive journey. Thus, a patent portfolio owned by a garage inventor or struggling start-up is probably worth less than a similar portfolio owned by a company with plenty of cash.

The probability of prevailing at trial is also composed of several factors, which include (1) the probability that at least one of the patents in the portfolio will be found to be infringed; (2) the probability that at least one of the infringed patents will be found valid; and (3) the probability that at least one of the infringed and valid patents will be found enforceable.

The most authoritative research studies on patent litigation statistics performed in the 1990s showed that the statistical probability of these values during the 1980s and 1990s was as follows: The probability that a given patent would be found infringed was 66 percent. The probability that a given patent would be found valid was 67 percent. The probability that a given patent would be found enforceable was 88 percent. One cannot assume that these values are independent, as judges rule in favor of the same party on all issues in 74 percent of cases and juries in 86 percent of cases. *In toto*, patent owners prevailed 58 percent of the time at trial (68 percent in jury trials).

These numbers are no longer valid and are now significantly lower. The most recent PricewaterhouseCoopers study has the overall probability for a patentee to prevail in litigation at a mere 29 percent.

As stated earlier, the value of a patent portfolio is not proportional to the number of constituent patents. It was also noted that this is true only in an ideal world. In the real world, where one must deal with the realities of infringement and patent enforcement, the value of a patent portfolio increases with its size: The more patents, the better.

Summary

Various models may be employed in an effort to determine the value of a patent or a patent portfolio. The most basic, and least accurate, valuation model is *replacement cost*. The *capitalized revenue stream* is best suited to valuation of patents used exclusively as licensing vehicles.

The *market value* method is rarely useful for valuing intellectual property, unless it is offered for sale, due to lack of efficient markets and the difficulty in comparing intellectual properties. The *incremental value* model values a patent, or patents, as the difference between the value of an enterprise with the property and the value of the same enterprise without the property. The *formula* model, also known as the *excess earnings* or *residual value* model, values all of a firm's intangibles as a whole. Although it is limited in its applicability, the IRS accepts it for tax purposes.

CHAPTER 6

Make More Money by Sharing (Licensing)

After reading this chapter you will be able to:

- Understand why selling a patent is often a complex and difficult matter, making licensing an attractive alternative.
- Properly manage a license once it's signed.
- Make sure you get what the licensee has agreed to pay.
- Recognize the difference between a joint venture and a strategic alliance.
- Understand the choice between *paid up* and *running royalty* licenses.
- Understand how to increase the value of a patent or a patent license.

Introduction

The question is often (but not often enough) asked: How can we (or I, or, in one instance, at a cocktail party, a friend) make money from our intellectual property? Briefly stated, there are three ways to make money from any property: sell it, rent it, or use it. The choice depends upon which approach or combination of approaches yields the greatest return.

To Sell or Not to Sell—That Is the Question

Conceptually, the simplest way for a company to make money from intellectual property that it is not using is to sell it. The company or patent holder approaches the transaction with intellectual property and the responsibility for its maintenance and protection, and departs with money, or its equivalent (is there anything truly equivalent to money?) and no responsibilities. What could be better? Complexity, however, arises from the need to set a price. There will be only one chance to get it right.

The sale price is generally set at some fraction, typically one-quarter to one-half of the expected benefit to the buyer. Obviously, a problem will arise if the buyer and seller have significantly different views as to the amount of this benefit. Almost always, the benefit to be realized is proportional to the future sales of a given product or product line. These sales may be influenced by a host of factors, many of which are difficult or impossible to predict.

Perchance to License

One way to avoid or minimize disagreements as to future benefits is to license, rather than sell, the intellectual property. If the license provides for a royalty based upon actual sales of the licensed product(s)—a *running royalty*—the need to forecast future sales volumes and prices is obviated. It is what it is, and the patent owner gets an agreed percentage of it, generally payable quarterly. Of course, this still begs the question of how to set the royalty rate. In theory, the factors that are used to determine the royalty rate of a patent license are the same factors used in setting a sale price—in essence, the royalty effects a sharing of the benefits enjoyed by the licensee by reason of the license. Thus, ideally, the royalty rate is set at one-quarter to one-half of the expected benefit. In practice, the rates tend to be at the lower end of the range.

TIPS AND TECHNIQUES

If you haven't a clue what royalty rate to request, start with a demand for 5 percent, and you won't be far wrong.

As usual, however, real life is not as simple as theory. Either or both of the parties may seek to improve their position by reference to the royalty rates of other existing licenses, the implicit assumption being that the rates in these other licenses are somehow relevant to the question of the appropriate rate for the license at issue. Thus, for example, licensors will generally point to the royalty rates in licenses they had previously granted under the same patents. This, in fact, has some relevancy. Either party may argue about "typical" or "standard in the industry" rates (the terms in quotations are often euphemisms for "unverifiable"). This, in fact, is largely irrelevant. Licensees may occasionally point to the royalty rates in other licenses they have taken or licenses they have granted. This, in fact, is completely irrelevant, if not totally inane.

It Ain't Over Till It's Over

Many patentees believe that the battle is over when a license is finally executed. Wrong! After a license is executed, it must be policed. First and foremost, is the licensee making all royalty payments required under the license agreement in a timely manner? Note that the foregoing is a compound question (lawyerspeak for unfair or tricky); let's parse it:

- *Timely*—was payment received in the allotted time?
- *All*—were all sales covered by the license reported?
- *Made*—were all required payments actually received?

A surprising number of licensors file away (and forget) their executed licenses without docketing scheduled payments. *Do not do this.* Some licensees, for example, forget to make their quarterly royalty payments. It is up to the licensor to provide a *written* reminder when a payment is overdue. This, of course, requires that the licensor knows when a payment is overdue.

Not all licensees report all licensed sales (surprise!). Keep track of all licensees' payments. Does the current payment seem unusual as compared to past payments or the payments of other licensees? If a licensee claims business is poor, check the licensee's web site. Is the licensee boasting to the world about how business is expanding? Check sales reported by licensees with purchases of their known customers. Are there any inconsistencies? If the licensee is a public company, peruse their 10-Q filings. What are they telling their shareholders?

Licenses should include a provision allowing the licensor to audit the books of a licensee to the extent of verifying the accuracy of the licensee's reports of sales of licensed goods. Such audit provisions should provide that the licensee will bear the cost of an audit if a material discrepancy—usually 5 percent or more of the amount properly due—is discovered. Audits can be rather costly and, therefore, are not to be undertaken lightheartedly. Often, however, the mere threat of an audit will produce the desired result—the licensee discovers an unfortunate error and tenders a check (sometimes with apologies, sometimes without).

Monitor the licensee's product literature (most often, this is available on the licensee's web site). Are there any new products or new models of old products that are subject to the terms of the license but are not being reported (and for which no royalties are being paid)? In this regard, it may be advantageous to include an arbitration provision in a license, whereby any dispute as to whether a new product is subject to the license may be (reasonably) promptly and inexpensively resolved.

Finally, demand periodic verification that the licensee is complying with the patent marking and any similar provisions of the license. (If this doesn't seem familiar, for shame!—see Chapter 1.)

Nothing Ventured, Nothing Gained

The situation may arise that the owner of intellectual property wishes to capitalize on this property yet lacks an essential element to do so. For example, the property owner may have insufficient manufacturing capacity or may lack an effective distribution system. The property owner may believe that marketing muscle, in the form of a well-recognized trademark or service mark, would be necessary to get the new product (or service) off the ground. If another firm can supply the missing element, a *joint venture* may be an effective vehicle for commercializing the property.

Basically, a joint venture is an entity, such as a partnership or corporation, created for a specific limited purpose and owned by two or more parties. The contributions or investments of each of the joint venturers (owners) are usually in kind, not in cash. In this instance, the intellectual property owner would contribute the intellectual property, either by assignment or license, while the other venturer(s) would, perhaps, contribute appropriate manufacturing or distribution services and a trademark or service mark (again, either by assignment or license). Hopefully, the whole is greater than the sum of its parts.

Because a joint venture is a separate entity, it allows its owners to continue their own existence with minimal interference. The joint venture is most often dissolved when its purpose is accomplished. For this reason, it is especially important that the parties agree, during its formation, upon a plan of termination, including the question of ownership of any intellectual property created by the joint venture itself.

A *strategic alliance* primarily differs from a joint venture in that it is not a separate entity. Rather, it is simply an agreement between its various members (the allies) to cooperate in some specified manner. Generally, the allies offer each other preferential or exclusive terms with respect to the sale of goods or the provision of services. The goods or services subject to the agreement most commonly are those in which the supplier enjoys some competitive advantage. The alliances are constituted so that each member receives, under most favorable terms, those goods or services it needs to enable it to most effectively capitalize upon its own area of strength or comparative advantage. Because it is not an entity, a strategic alliance cannot develop or hold intellectual property. For this reason, dissolution or expiration of a strategic alliance presents few of the problems inherent in the termination of a joint venture.

Risk and Price—Package Deals in IP Licensing

Businesspeople, as a rule, prefer to avoid or minimize risk. Given a choice, they gravitate toward those investments or projects that involve the least uncertainty. Obviously, the prospect of a large reward may tempt people to accept risk; but, as between different investments offering similar potential rewards, the one perceived as presenting the least risk will be the most popular and, hence, will command the highest price. This principle lies at the heart of the franchising industry.

Franchise purchasers pay a substantial premium over the costs they would otherwise incur in starting a similar business *ab initio* (the Latin is so much more impressive than the corresponding "from scratch"). What does the franchise purchaser receive in exchange for this premium? Greater certainty—as much as anything can be certain in business. The franchisee receives detailed specifications, formulas, and process directions for the products or services that the new business will offer. Lists of suppliers are also provided, as is training for employees. All necessary equipment and tools arrive in a package. Frequently, the franchisor includes assistance with such things as site selection, application for necessary permits and approvals, and establishing accounting and other control systems. Moreover, and most importantly, the franchise includes a license under the franchisor's trademarks.

The same principle applies to intellectual property licensing. It is, most certainly, possible to assign or license a patent, for example, without offering anything more. Such transactions, however, are generally in the nature of patent enforcement actions. In these instances, a matter of patent infringement is (more or less) amicably resolved when the infringer acquires the infringed patent or a license thereunder (so-called *stick licensing*). Such a license engenders little technological risk—the infringing product is already on the market. Indeed, by taking a license, the former infringer actually reduces its risk by eliminating the risk of being sued for patent infringement.

Quite a different situation results, however, when a party is not already using the patented technology. In such a case, the party is under no compulsion to acquire the patent or take a license. Adoption of a new—and therefore untested and unproven—technology presents substantial risks. The technology may prove to be flawed. It may require further (expensive) development before it is ready for the market. Even if there are no technological problems or if such problems are successfully solved, the technology may still fail in the market for any of a variety of reasons. The greater the perceived risk associated with a new technology, the greater the reluctance to invest substantial resources to acquire and commercialize it and, as a result, the lower the price the technology can command. Once this relation between price and risk is recognized, the solution becomes obvious: Reduce the risk associated with a technology, and the price it commands will increase.

Risk reduction is, in essence, a matter of providing solutions to those problems that would otherwise constitute risks. Just as a franchisee willingly pays a premium for a turnkey business operation, so too will a prospective assignee or licensee pay a premium for a market-ready or market-proven technology. In other words, a tested and proven new product or service, covered by a patent, will fetch a much higher price than the patent alone. Therefore, whenever possible, sell a product, not a patent. Package the patent with applicable trademarks, design specifications, blueprints, test results, process know-how, quality assurance procedures, lists of qualified suppliers, market research data, and anything else that will facilitate commercialization of the patented technology. Such information is of value to a prospective buyer in two respects: It reduces the additional investment required to achieve commercialization, and it reduces the risk of failure. It is comparatively easy to sell a successful product or service. The closer an invention is to market—the fewer the remaining problems—the more it will bring. Moreover, a package license, including trademarks and know-how, may continue generating royalties after the patents in the package have expired.

Since (some) patents have value, they may, under appropriate circumstances, be used as collateral for loans. While most banks still refuse to make loans collateralized solely by patents, there are now certain specialized (and more enlightened) financial institutions that will do so.

IN THE REAL WORLD

The Odds against an Inventor

Only about 1 patent in 20 is licensed, and only about 1 in 100 patents generates any royalties.

The Carrot and the Stick

Two terms commonly used (actually, overused) in the licensing biz are *carrot license* and *stick license*. For this reason and no other, the authors feel compelled to explain them.

In plain English, a carrot license is a voluntary license, while a stick license is taken under duress. Generally, an infringer or an accused infringer takes the stick license in settlement of a lawsuit or under threat of one. Thus, a stick license should be viewed as a patent enforcement tool. (A stick license is an offer you can't refuse; a carrot license is one you can.)

Although the meaning of the term *carrot license* is clear, the underlying concept is barren. Virtually no one comes knocking on a patentee's door, hat and checkbook in hand, politely inquiring about the availability and cost of a license. As a practical matter, convincing a noninfringer to take a patent license is a tough job, consisting, as it does, of two parts: (1) convincing the party that they *want* to use the patented technology and then (2) convincing them that they have to *pay* for it. The first part essentially consists of the tasks of finding a party that actually could benefit from the use of the technology and then overcoming the natural reluctance of that party to adopt technology from outside (the infamous "not invented here" syndrome). Upon successfully completing the first task, the prospective licensor must then convince the party that unlicensed use will be vigorously opposed (i.e., via lawsuit). Thus, even a carrot license has elements of the stick.

Summary

There are three ways to make money from a patent: use it, rent (license) it, or sell (assign) it. The sale price of a patent is typically one-quarter to one-half of the expected benefit to the buyer. Ideally, a royalty in a license effects a similar sharing of the benefit derived from the use of the patented technology. Royalties may be paid in a lump sum (a *paid-up* license) or may be based upon sales of the licensed products (a *running royalty*). Once a license has been executed, it should be policed to assure that all payments are made in a timely manner and in the proper amount.

The price that a patent or a patent license may command is often increased if the patent is packaged with corresponding know-how and other information that facilitates commercialization of the patented technology by the assignee or licensee.

CHAPTER 7

Corporate Officers and Directors Beware: You Can Be Liable for Mismanaging Intellectual Property

After reading this chapter you will be able to:

- Understand the responsibilities of corporate officers and directors with respect to the management of intellectual property and the extent to which such responsibilities may be delegated.

- Understand the liabilities that may attach to corporate officers and directors who fail to satisfy their duty of care with respect to the management of intellectual property or are responsible for acts of infringement.

- Develop a program to satisfy officers' and directors' intellectual property management responsibilities.

Recent changes in the value and role of intellectual property present the business corporation with newfound opportunities; however, they also expose its officers and directors to newfound risks and potential liabilities. In times past, directors and senior officers could—and almost universally did—ignore intellectual property, leaving it to clerical staff who filed and forgot it. It was a rare company indeed where the intellectual property portfolio was accorded a fraction of the attention directed to tangible assets. Now, however, the increased importance of the intellectual property portfolio mandates a commensurate increase in the care with which it is managed. It must, in fact, be managed with the same degree of care and attention as is devoted to the company's tangible assets. Failure to meet this new standard may well have serious legal implications for the firm's officers and directors.

Nature of Injuries Arising from Mismanagement of Intellectual Property

Every officer and director of a corporation, as a fiduciary, has an affirmative duty of care, which is, broadly stated, a responsibility to diligently manage the affairs and assets of the corporation, and to consider the possible ramifications of its actions (or inaction).

The business laws of the state in which the business is incorporated govern the duty of care and any liability arising thereunder. Aside from any liability arising under state statutes related to the duty of care, the officers and directors of publicly traded companies may also incur liability under federal securities laws.

Injuries arising from the mismanagement or nonmanagement of intellectual property fall, most commonly, into two general categories: waste and misvaluation.

Waste occurs when an asset is not utilized, or not utilized fully, or is sold for much less than its true value. Avoidance of waste of intellectual property requires, among other things, identification of all of its possible uses and the estimated extent of such uses, determination of the existence and merits of competing technologies, and, where a patent is involved, assessment of the strength of the patent and the scope of its claims.

Patents protecting unused technology are a prime example of unutilized assets. Failure to license such unused intellectual property and produce an income stream may be a waste of corporate assets, which may expose officers and directors to liability.

Novel technology is an asset. The failure to aggressively patent the results of corporate research and development (R&D), like the failure to insure valuable plant and equipment, may be deemed mismanagement. Most U.S. companies face a dilemma of whether to obtain foreign patents or trademarks in addition to their U.S. rights and in which countries to seek such protection.

Failure to enforce intellectual property rights is another example of mismanagement of corporate assets. Many technology-related corporations are rushing to file as many patents as possible, which may or may not be a prudent strategy. However, patents afford only exclusionary rights. Failure to enforce these rights by bringing a patent infringement action creates a double waste: loss of a valuable monopoly on the use of the patented technology as well as a waste of the capital spent on obtaining and maintaining the unenforced patents. Furthermore, any delay in enforcing the infringed patents may result in laches and estoppel (see Chapter 8), which may ultimately reduce the damage awards when an action is brought at a later date or render the patents unenforceable. Therefore, there may well be an affirmative duty for corporate officers and directors to vigorously enforce corporate intellectual property rights in a timely manner.

Although it causes different injuries, misvaluation is closely related to waste. Where waste can be described as a *realized* loss, misvaluation is a *book* loss. Both spring from the same errors and omissions. Misvalued intellectual property can adversely affect the total valuation of the transaction in a merger, acquisition, divestiture, or equity financing.

Oops!

It has been estimated that nearly 40 percent of the market valuation of the average company is missing from its balance sheet.

Failure to communicate the value of the intellectual property of a publicly traded company to the financial community may result in undervalued stock, thus causing loss of value to shareholders. Such matters, for example, as a patent, newly issued to a competitor, which may be infringed by the company's product, need to be disclosed to shareholders, regardless of whether actual infringement notice has been given. Reasonable apprehension of a possible patent infringement lawsuit should be disclosed, as should the expiration dates of important patents, which may adversely affect the company's market share. Such disclosures may need to be made in press releases, in annual and quarterly financial statements, and in the "Management Discussion and Analysis" section of registered financial statements filed with the Securities and Exchange Commission (SEC). Failure to accurately and in a timely way report information relevant to corporate intellectual property to the shareholders, in the initial prospectus as well as in quarterly and annual reports, may result in their ill-advised decision making and subsequent losses, prompting them to seek relief in a class-action suit against the officers and directors.

Standard of Responsibility for Portfolio Management

Waste that occurs by not exploiting (or by underexploiting) corporate intellectual property assets need not involve any wrongdoing or evil intent, such as would incur criminal liability. It may be merely negligence, a proverbial sin of omission. Negligent waste may be established by showing that no person of ordinary sound business judgment would say that a fair benefit had been derived from the challenged transaction. In this regard, it must be borne in mind that intellectual property is almost always a wasting asset—patents expire, technology becomes obsolete. Thus, waste may result from any or all of the following:

- Inadequacy of return for the license or sale of intellectual property.
- Failure to utilize intellectual property.
- Undue narrowness of its utilization.
- Undue utilization delay.

While there is no relevant case law specifically dealing with mismanagement of corporate intellectual property assets, there is no reason to believe that the standards the courts will apply for directors' and officers' responsibility for management of intellectual property assets will differ from the well-established criteria and standards for duty of care in managing other corporate assets. With the recent market downturn (or collapse), however, it seems only a matter of time until some disgruntled shareholders of a publicly traded technology company, having seen their stock price plummet or the company dissolved in bankruptcy, will attempt to recoup their losses in a derivative class-action suit against officers and directors for mismanaging corporate intellectual property assets. Directors and officers of publicly traded companies are well advised to take prudent steps today to protect themselves from future liability.

One of the factors considered in determining whether a firm's officers and directors have met their duty of care with respect to management of the firm's intellectual property is the nature of the company's business. Thus, it has been held that a director's duty may be greater where the company engages in a business affecting the general public, especially where there is an established regulatory scheme for such business. Chief among such businesses is banking, including investment banking. Bank officers and directors are typically held to a higher standard than are the officers and directors of other businesses. While IP portfolio valuation is always a prudent step in the management of corporate assets, obtaining an opinion as to the value of an IP portfolio involved in an initial public offering (IPO), merger and acquisition (M&A), divestiture, or corporate reorganization may be considered virtually obligatory. (Although the legal standard applied by courts to the publicly traded companies may be the same as for privately held nonbanking concerns, the SEC itself is a powerful potential plaintiff whose mere presence can have a marked, chilling effect.) As expected, in determining what would be prudent under similar circumstances, the courts look to the practices and procedures of similar businesses; a failure to adopt such practices and follow such procedures as are accepted as necessary by the officers and directors of similar businesses is almost invariably held to establish negligence.

Therefore, should the directors and officers of other high-tech companies expect to be held to the standards of IBM, which generates over $1 billion a year in licensing revenues? Probably not. They are certainly well advised, however, to look into adopting some of the IP management strategies employed by IBM, Texas Instruments, Dow Chemical, and a number of other standard-setting companies.

Typically (when all other avenues of escape are blocked), officers and directors seek to defend their acts (or, more often, their omissions) on the basis of the *business judgment rule*. The courts, however, have begun to more clearly invoke the threshold requirement that the challenged decision must have resulted from the exercise of *informed business judgment*, based upon all information *reasonably available*. A reasonable investigation is generally deemed necessary to satisfy this requirement.

Acceptance or rejection of a settlement offer in patent infringement litigation, for example, is a decision—if made on an informed basis—that can be justified under the business judgment rule. If, however, the management and the board fail to analyze the litigation risk and consider other relevant factors, they may be exposed to potentially serious liability in the event the litigation results in an unfavorable judgment and a substantial loss.

Finally, it is to be noted that the acceptance of the office of a director implies a competent knowledge of the duties assumed. A director cannot be excused for imprudence on the grounds of ignorance or inexperience. Serving without compensation or merely as an accommodation does not negate the director's responsibilities.

While the burden of proof to establish officers and directors liable for waste is a heavy one, the question is, nonetheless, one of fact. Thus, in the absence of substantial justification for challenged transactions, one accused of waste may well be forced to face the perils and uncertainty of trial.

Delegation of Responsibility

While responsibility for management of the IP portfolio may be delegated, such delegation must comply with certain requirements if it is to satisfy the duties of the corporate officers and directors. A director's ability to delegate responsibility to nondirectors is essentially limited to activities that are in the ordinary and usual course of business. The director should, despite any delegation, remain informed as to the policies and affairs of the corporation and maintain a general knowledge of the employment of the corporation's resources. He is chargeable with knowledge that he might have possessed had he diligently discharged his functions and, thus, is presumed to know everything concerning corporate affairs that he might have learned by the exercise of reasonable care and diligence. Where the duty of knowing facts exists, ignorance due to neglect of duty may create the same liability as actual knowledge and a failure to act on that knowledge.

Where a board of directors appoints a committee of its members to assume responsibility for a task, a nonmember director is expected to still comply with the standard of care in satisfying himself that the committee, upon which he proposes to rely, reasonably merits his confidence. This would require, as appropriate, that he generally familiarize himself with the investigative or other activities of the committee.

Moreover, neither the designation of such committee, the delegation of authority to the committee, nor the action of the committee pursuant to such authority alone constitutes full compliance by any nonmember director with his duties as a director.

One measure often taken by directors is to seek the advice of experts. Indeed, relevant precedent suggests that failure to seek advice from outside experts may, in some circumstances, itself constitute a breach of the duty to be informed. There are a number of IP management firms providing businesses with such expert advice. Where directors seek expert advice and honestly act under it, they are protected from personal liability, even though the advice ultimately proves erroneous. In order to be entitled to rely on an expert's report, statement, or opinion, the director must have read it or have been present at a meeting in which it was orally presented, or have taken other steps to become generally familiar with its contents.

Liability for Failure to Meet Duty of Care

Where an officer or director fails to meet his duty of care, and a waste of the corporation's intellectual property assets results from that failure, that officer or director may be held personally liable for the loss suffered. One or more of the shareholders or the directors may bring an action, on behalf of the corporation, to recover the damages. Under some statutes, officers and directors may be held liable to corporate creditors for losses suffered as a result of their mismanagement. If the corporation is in reorganization or liquidation, the corporation's trustees or receivers may bring an action against negligent officers or directors. A director of a holding company may be liable to that company for the diminished value of its share resulting from his waste of intellectual property assets of the subsidiary company, even though he might also be liable to the subsidiary corporation for the same act.

Misrepresentation or omission of material information pertaining to the intellectual property of the issuer of securities may be a violation of

Section 10(b) of the Securities Exchange Act of 1934, as is presentation of values for IP assets that are based on invalid data or techniques. Further, decline in the price of stock resulting from the dissemination of false information as to the value of corporate IP assets constitutes a direct, and hence actionable, injury to individual shareholders. Repeatedly, the courts have held that the failure to determine the actual (as opposed to book) value of a corporation engaged in a merger is a breach of the director's duty of care. Intangible IP assets are a major factor contributing to the discrepancy between the actual and the book value of an enterprise. Moreover, where directors did not make reasonable inquiry into the methods used to value a corporation's assets, their decisions were not entitled to the beneficial presumption of the business judgment rule.

What to Do

Intellectual property and its management can no longer be relegated to middle management or even to an in-house patent counsel overburdened with filing and prosecuting patent applications. It must be addressed by corporate directors and officers. Despite the obvious complexities involved, they should devise and establish a reasonable IP management program, and make reasonable inquiries and keep diligently informed as to the implementation of such a program.

An intellectual property portfolio audit (see Chapter 4) is a necessary first step to avoid waste of the enterprise's assets. Prudence would dictate that a specialist manager and/or IP management firm be retained to perform such an audit and to otherwise manage a corporation's IP portfolio. The advisability of this course of action is highlighted by the growing presence and acceptance of such firms. As the employment of such firms becomes more widespread, it may have the effect, as previously noted, of raising the standards to which others are held. Thus, there is a strong impetus to jump on the bandwagon. Given the higher standards to which bankers are traditionally held, this advice should apply with even greater force to investment bankers and underwriters.

In choosing a manager or management firm, certain criteria should apply if reliance upon their advice is to be deemed reasonable. Obviously, the individual(s) involved must have appropriate education and experience, particularly in the field of IP management, IP law, and the technologies of interest to the corporation. There should be a documented history of success in the management of intellectual property. Further, the chosen managers should be required to provide regular and complete reports of their activities, including reasonably detailed descriptions of methodologies employed.

Damned If You Don't, Damned If You Do

Not only may corporate officers and directors be held liable for their mismanagement of the firm's IP—generally acts of negligence or omission—they may also, under certain circumstances, be held personally liable for the company's acts of patent infringement.

Many officers and directors believe (profess to believe, try to believe, wish to believe, or in some cases, pretend to believe) that personal liability will attach only if there is a "piercing of the corporate veil." Piercing of the corporate veil is a legal doctrine that permits the court to disregard the existence of the corporation and proceed against individual officers and directors, if this is necessary to prevent (among other evils) fraud, injustice, or a thwarting of public policy. As a practical matter, the doctrine is applied when the corporation is inadequately capitalized, has failed to comply with organizational formalities, or is being used for fraudulent purposes. Efforts to pierce the veil are rarely successful. Thus, the belief in the invulnerability of officers and directors was, in most cases, well founded. This has now changed.

The Court of Appeals for the Federal Circuit (CAFC) has now held (*Hoover Group Inc. v. Custom Metalcraft, Inc.*, 94-1285 [Fed. Cir. 1996]), that it is not necessary to pierce the corporate veil in order that a person in a control position be held personally liable for the tortious acts of the corporation (patent infringement being a tortious act). Rather, the court is to consider several factors, including the nature of the wrong-doing, the culpability of the act (and the actor), and whether the person sought to be held personally responsible acted in his own interest or the interest of the corporation (in some small, owner-managed businesses, the two are the same). In many cases, this new standard is more encom-passing than the old one. Thus, the corporate charter may no longer be proof against all attacks on those in control positions—one more good reason for officers and directors to exercise reasonable care in patent matters.

Summary

Intellectual property must be managed with the same degree of care and caution as is devoted to a firm's tangible assets. Injuries arising from mismanagement of intellectual property generally fall into two catego-ries: waste and misvaluation.

The standard of care demanded of corporate officers and directors may be more stringent where the company engages in a business, such as banking, that implicates the general public.

In determining whether an action or decision was prudent, the courts generally look to the practices and procedures of similar busi-nesses; failure to adopt such practices and procedures is almost invariably held to be negligence.

A corporate director may delegate his responsibilities with respect to IP management but must still remain informed as to such affairs.

Personal liability may result where an officer or director fails to meet his duty of care and a waste of the corporation's IP assets results. Such liability may be to the corporation itself, the shareholders, and, in some circumstances, to creditors and trustees or receivers. Where there is a failure to disclose material information pertaining to intellectual property, or if such information is misrepresented, criminal liability may attach.

Prudence suggests that directors retain a qualified specialist manager and/or an IP management firm to perform an audit and to manage the firm's IP portfolio.

It is no longer necessary to pierce the corporate veil to find officers and directors personally liable for acts of patent infringement committed by the corporation. Instead, the court will examine the personal culpability of the individuals involved.

CHAPTER 8

Enforcing Your Rights

After reading this chapter you will be able to:

- Understand the types of infringement (literal and under the doctrine of equivalents).

- Know the importance of having the broadest possible claims coverage when drafting a patent application.

- Understand the ramifications of the *Festo* case for patentees.

- Choose the best venue for your litigation.

- Communicate with patent infringers in the most effective (and least self-defeating) way.

- Anticipate an infringer's preemptive strike—the declaratory judgment action.

- Understand the two kinds of damages (lost profits and reasonable royalty) that may be awarded in a patent infringement case and the requirements for each.

- Understand the role of convoyed sales in assessing a reasonable royalty.

- Understand the usual path of patent litigation and some factors that contribute to the individuality of each particular case.

- Understand two common defenses, laches and estoppel, and the differences between them.

- Prepare a quantitative analysis of litigation risk.

- Choose a law firm to represent you in litigation matters.
- Protect yourself against overbilling by your law firm.
- Identify which infringer(s) to sue first and which defendants will be the most aggressive.
- Determine if pendant claims are also involved in a company's infringement of your patent.
- Present a positive image of your company to a jury.
- Understand reexamination and the issues regarding its use.
- Understand the advantages of settlement as opposed to litigation.
- Understand the forms of alternate dispute resolution, along with their benefits and drawbacks.

Patent Infringement

When a patent is infringed, it's never just a simple case of telling the infringer to cease and desist. (Indeed, doing so could give the infringer grounds to sue *you*.) From knowing what constitutes patent infringement at the most basic level, to identifying contributory or induced infringement—that is, when a direct infringer leads other companies and individuals to infringe the patent—there's a lot to consider before embarking on a patent enforcement campaign.

Patent Claims—Where Less Is More

The scope of a patent is determined by its claims. If each and every limitation of a claim is found in an accused device or process, the claim is said to *read on* that device or process and is infringed thereby. If a single limitation is missing from the accused structure, there is no infringement (this requirement is known as the *all elements rule*). However, the presence of additional features in the accused structure does not negate infringement.

It Ain't Kosher

Basically there are two kinds of patent claims: article claims and method or process claims. (For any nitpickers among our readers, article claims include the more esoteric *product by process* and *composition of matter* subclasses.) Article claims are composed of multiple article limitations, and method claims are composed of multiple steps or process limitations. Both types of limitations are fine but, just as those who keep kosher are forbidden to mix milk and meat, so too we are directed—albeit by a different authority—not to mix article limitations and process steps in a single patent claim.

This was demonstrated in *Rembrandt Data Technologies, LP v. AOL LLC et al.* The patent claim in question was directed to a "data transmitting device" comprising (1) first and second buffer means, (2) fractional encoding means, (3) trellis encoding means for trellis encoding frames (whatever that means), and (4) *transmitting the trellis encoded frames*.

The defendant moved for summary judgment of invalidity, asserting that the patent claim was "fatally flawed." The plaintiff, accepting the undeniable, conceded that the claim contained an error and sought to invoke the court's power to correct such an error in a patent. The plaintiff argued that "the error is so plain and known by anyone in the field there can be no question that the claim as written includes an obvious error" and that the claim element "transmitting the trellis encoded frames" should be edited to "a transmitter section for transmitting the trellis encoded frames."

The defendants, as would be expected, argued that the proposed correction "would significantly alter the meaning of one element, changing it from a method step to an apparatus step." They further argued that "there is no evidence to support Rembrandt's assertion that a 'typographical' error occurred." (Typographical—was Rembrandt serious? This sort of argument could give patent trolls a bad name.)

The court sided with the defendants, noting that "Rembrandt has failed to demonstrate that the language at issue is anything other than what it submitted to the Patent and Trademark Office."

TIPS AND TECHNIQUES

The lesson to be learned from *Rembrandt*. There are article claims and there are method claims and never the twain shall meet.

Not infrequently (only lawyers and politicians talk like that—in double negatives), an inventor reviewing a draft of a patent application prior to filing will complain that lots of things were left out of the claims. This is not an error or failure on the part of the patent practitioner. It is, in fact, a measure of the practitioner's skill (assuming the claim is, ultimately, allowed by the patent examiner). The goal of the practitioner is (or at least should be) to secure the broadest possible claims coverage. This is accomplished by drafting patent claims with the fewest possible limitations. Each limitation in a patent claim is a potential avenue to claim circumvention. The greater the number of limitations in a patent claim, the greater the probability that the subject invention can be substantially copied or imitated, while one claim limitation is omitted. If this occurs, the copy does not infringe the patent claim—remember the all elements rule. When reviewing a draft patent application, object to patent claims that appear too detailed, not to those that appear too general.

Infringement may be either literal or under the doctrine of equivalents. *Literal infringement* occurs when the claim language literally reads on the accused device or process. If, however, one or more claim limitations are not literally met by the accused device, all may not be lost.

In order to prevent the perpetration of a fraud on the patent—circumvention of the patent by means of a trivial change or modification—the courts long ago created the *doctrine of equivalents*. Under this doctrine (which, as the reader shall see, is subject to a number of limitations), if a claim limitation is not literally met, but the corresponding structure in the accused device, or the corresponding step in the accused process, "performs substantially the same function, in substantially the same way, to achieve the same result," the claim may still be infringed. Note that the doctrine is applied on a limitation-by-limitation basis, not on the basis of an entire claim.

The chief limitation on the interpretation or construction of words or phrases in a patent claim is *file wrapper estoppel*, a doctrine created by the courts that prevents a patentee from recapturing, through a broad interpretation of words or phrases in a claim, that which was previously surrendered in securing allowance of the claim. Thus, the scope of a patent claim is largely determined by the prosecution history of the patent (i.e., the file wrapper).

The *Festo* Case: You May Not Have What You Thought You Had

Charles Dickens created the ghost of Christmas past, which haunted Ebenezer Scrooge for his past acts of avarice. The courts (including the U.S. Supreme Court) have created *Festo* (*Festo Corp. v. Shoketsu Kinzoku Kogyo Kabushiki Co., Ltd. et al.*), which haunts patentees for their past acts of claim amendment committed during the prosecution of their patent applications.

Patent claims are to be written so as to apprise the reader of the precise limits of that in which the patentee claims an exclusive right—the so-called *notice requirement*. When infringement is literal, this notice requirement is rather easily satisfied. When infringement is founded upon the doctrine of equivalents, however, the clarity of a claim becomes less certain. The range of equivalents to be accorded a claim limitation was traditionally determined—more precisely, limited—by the doctrine of file wrapper estoppel. Thus, traditionally, an analysis of the scope of a patent claim necessitated a review of the file wrapper and a detailed analysis of the estoppels (if any) created by each and every amendment made to the patent claims during prosecution. This was a complex task, even for experienced professionals.

Enter the Court of Appeals for the Federal Circuit (CAFC), eager to reduce complexity and restore clarity to claim construction. Seizing the opportunity presented by the *Festo* case, the court, overturning lengthy and substantial precedent, decided, essentially on policy grounds, that the necessity for identifying and analyzing file wrapper estoppels was inimical to the requirement of claim clarity. The solution it chose was to simply eliminate *all* equivalents of any claim limitation that had been amended during prosecution. No need to analyze the extent of an estoppel—if a limitation had been amended, henceforth, it had no equivalents. The limitation would now be construed to cover that which had been disclosed in the patent specification and no more. Simple but deadly. With the stroke of a pen (or a word processor), the court had narrowed the scope of tens of thousands of subsisting patents—patents that had been prosecuted in reliance upon a body of law now suddenly, and retroactively, reversed. Approximately 1.2 million currently subsisting patents include claims that were amended during prosecution and are, therefore, affected by this decision.

Dickens allowed Ebenezer to escape the haunting by reforming (actually, old Eb overreacted by becoming a spendthrift). The courts offer patentees no such escape. Various prosecution tactics have been proposed in an effort to deal with the effects of the decision. While the efficacy of these tactics is yet to be determined, the universal result (surprise!) has been to vastly increase the costs of patent prosecution.

Partners in Crime: Contributory Infringement and Inducing Infringement

A party who, without authorization, practices the patented invention of another is a direct infringer. There are circumstances, however, that may render it difficult—if not economically impractical—to sue the direct infringer(s) of a patent. Suppose, for example, that you have a patent on a new and improved water-based paint. Suppose further that an odious and unprincipled paint manufacturer mixes all of the ingredients of this new paint, save only the water, and sells the dry mix to consumers who take it home and mix it with water, thereby completing the production of the patented paint. Clearly, each of these consumers is a direct infringer of the patent. However, while there are many of these infringers, each one has produced only a small amount of paint. It would be extremely difficult, if not impossible, to identify them; if they were identified, the amount of damages recoverable from any one of them is far less than the costs of even uncontested litigation. Does this mean that you are without an effective remedy? No! The paint manufacturer is a *contributory infringer* and, under the law (35 USC 271[c]), is liable for all of the direct infringement resulting from his sale of the dry mix.

A contributory infringer is one who sells, offers to sell, or imports into the United States a component that is a material part of a patented invention, knowing that the component is especially made or adapted for use in an infringement of the patent, where the component is not a staple item having a substantial noninfringing use. Note that it is not necessary that the seller actually know of the existence of the patent that is being infringed, merely that he know of the use to which his component will be put.

Assume now that the dry paint mix could be combined with linseed oil, in place of water, to produce an oil-based paint. This would be a substantial noninfringing use. In such case, the paint manufacturer would not be a contributory infringer.

Finally, assume that the owner of the paint store where the dry mix is sold recommends to purchasers of the mix that they combine it with water. The paint store owner is inducing infringement and, under the law (35 USC 271[b]), is liable for all of the direct infringement resulting from his ill-advised recommendation.

The lesson here is this: Whenever there occurs an epidemic of infringement of a patent, look for one who is inducing the infringement or contributing to it. If such a party is found, sue him.

Risks of Patent Litigation

Every grab for the brass ring carries the risk that you will fall off the merry-go-round. This also holds true for patent litigation.

In order to *prevail*, a patentee must establish that the patent-in-suit is infringed and must also successfully defend that patent against any defense (almost certain to be raised) of invalidity and/or unenforceability. To *succeed*, the patentee must also recover damages in an amount appreciably in excess of the costs of litigation.

Invalidity

A patent enjoys a presumption of validity unless found by a court to be invalid. A patent may be found to be invalid for any of several reasons. An accused infringer will inevitably search the prior art in an effort to find pertinent references not considered by the Patent and Trademark Office when the patent was granted. The extent of such a search is limited only by the determination of the accused infringer and, faced with a potential liability for tens of millions of dollars in damages, such a party can be very determined indeed. Newly discovered prior art may establish that the claimed invention lacks novelty or would have been obvious to one of ordinary skill in the art at the time the invention was made.

Although a more difficult defense, the accused may also seek to establish that the inventor has concealed the best mode of practicing the invention or that the patent is not enabling (see Chapter 1). An infringer may establish that the patent application had been filed more than a year after the patented product was introduced in the marketplace. Moreover, if the infringer can prove to the court that the patentee had concealed relevant prior art from the Patent Office (i.e., engaged in inequitable conduct), the patent may be declared unenforceable (i.e., good for nothing).

Noninfringement

It may be found that the accused product does not infringe the patent-in-suit. In this regard, two recent cases have tipped the scales of justice in favor of the defendant.

The Supreme Court, in the famous (or, depending on one's point of view, infamous) *Markman* decision (*Markman vs. Westview Instruments, Inc.,* 52 F.3d 967 [Fed. Cir. 1995] aff'd 116 S.Ct. 1384 [1996]), held that patent claims are to be construed (i.e., interpreted) by the court (the judge) as a matter of law (more on this later). To perform this function, the trial judge holds what has come to be known as a Markman hearing. After both sides have submitted proposed constructions of any disputed patent claim terms, the judge hears arguments, examines the patent and its file wrapper (see how important the file wrapper is?), and issues a decision. Except in very rare cases, expert testimony or other extrinsic evidence is not admitted. Once the court has construed the patent claims, it is often clear to both sides whether the claims, as construed, are literally infringed. The claim constructions adopted by the trial judge tend to be narrower than those that would have been adopted under similar circumstances by a jury.

As noted earlier, the *Festo* case has effectively eliminated the doctrine of equivalents with respect to any claim limitation that was amended during the course of prosecution of the patent. Thus, the effective scope of many patents has been severely reduced.

Avoiding Pyrrhic Victories

For reasons that will soon become apparent, patent infringement litigation is very costly. The costs of litigation, except in rather rare circumstances, are *not* awarded to the prevailing party. Thus, as a general rule, a patentee should not undertake litigation unless the expected or probabilistic recovery, including damages and the value of a permanent injunction barring further infringement, substantially exceeds the anticipated litigation costs (more about this shortly). Attorney's fees may be awarded to a prevailing patentee, in a so-called exceptional case, when it is found that the infringer lacked a good faith belief in its defenses or otherwise raised meritless or frivolous defenses. Similarly, however, the case may be found to be exceptional where the patent-in-suit is found to be invalid or unenforceable for reasons known to the patentee. In such event, litigation costs may be awarded to the defendant. Generally, this occurs when the patentee has:

- Concealed a known prior art reference from the patent examiner (inequitable conduct).

- Concealed the best mode of practicing the patented invention.

- Failed to disclose a prior sale, offer for sale, public use, or description in a written publication (statutory bars).

- Misused the patent in a tying arrangement.

- Sought to enforce the patent beyond its term.

Indeed, seeking to enforce a patent known to be invalid, or otherwise misusing a patent, may itself be an antitrust violation known to us patent professionals as a Walker process violation, opening the offending patentee to counterclaims and possible multiple damages.

Jurisdiction and Venue—Location, Location, Location

In military science, much weight is accorded the advantages conferred by fighting a battle on ground of one's own choosing. In litigation, much weight is accorded the advantages conferred by trying the case in a courtroom of one's own choosing. A plaintiff, however, does not have complete freedom in deciding where to sue. The available choices are limited by the twin requirements of *jurisdiction* and *proper venue*.

Jurisdiction is of two kinds. *Subject matter jurisdiction* is the authority of the court to hear (try) cases of a particular type. *Personal jurisdiction* is the authority of a court to exercise control over a particular defendant. *Proper venue* is, similarly, that court or courts, among all those having jurisdiction, where the case *properly* (an elegant term meaning "according to the rules provided for such matters") may be heard. The federal courts have exclusive jurisdiction over patent and copyright infringement matters, meaning that any such case can only be brought in federal court.

Personal jurisdiction is conferred on a court by residence or, in some circumstances, by the actions of a party. Thus, a court has personal jurisdiction over any party that resides within its district. Moreover, if a nonresident party commits acts having an impact within the district, such party may, as a result, subject itself to the personal jurisdiction of the courts of that district; this is known as *long arm jurisdiction.*

Proper venue is, as you should by now suspect, a matter of statute. For a long time, the applicable law—set forth in the Federal Rules of Civil Procedure (FRCP) (Title 28 of the U.S. Code)—was that actions pertaining to patent infringement could be brought only "in the judicial district where the defendant resides, or where the defendant has committed acts of infringement and has a regular and established place of business" (28 USC 1400[b]). Thus, an infringer could only be sued in those jurisdictions where it had a place of business. Obviously, such a requirement could comprise a serious limitation on a plaintiff's choice of forum.

In 1990, however, following certain changes in the law, it was determined that a defendant corporation could also be sued for patent infringement "in any judicial district in which it is subject to personal jurisdiction at the time the action is commenced" (28 USC 1391[c]). This meant that a corporation could be sued in a jurisdiction where it had no place of business, if it had committed acts sufficient to subject it to long arm jurisdiction. Given that many infringing companies commit their nefarious acts on a nationwide basis, this change in the law is indeed liberating to plaintiffs. (*Note*: This does *not* mean that such an infringer may be sued anywhere the plaintiff may choose; other requirements must still be satisfied. Consult an attorney.)

At this point, the reader is likely asking, why read this arcane (euphemism for "boring") stuff? What difference does it make where suit is brought? The answer is: It makes a lot of difference.

The first difference is one of convenience. Given a choice of venues, a plaintiff may choose the most convenient one (*convenient* is a euphemism for "least costly"). For example, by choosing a court near its principal place of business, a plaintiff may reduce the travel time and expense of its witnesses. Selection of a court near the offices of the plaintiff's trial counsel obviates the need for a local counsel—a significant cost savings. The plaintiff's selection may prove to increase the defendant's costs, but this, of course, is purely coincidental (right!).

A plaintiff may choose a venue where it expects to receive public (jury) sympathy and support, or it may choose to avoid a venue where the defendant enjoys such popularity.

Finally, although there is now a great deal of similarity, indeed homogeneity, between federal courts, some differences still remain. Different precedents may be followed. Also, backlogs and scheduling practices vary among the districts. In some districts, it can be reliably predicted that trial will follow the initiation of an action by three or even four years. In other districts (the so-called "rocket dockets"), trial may commence in less than a year. All of these factors must be identified and weighed before a venue is chosen

A Jury Is a Good Thing

It has long been believed—often correctly—that juries are unable to comprehend the complex technical questions presented by a patent infringement lawsuit. For that reason, most litigants formerly waived their right to a jury trial, opting instead for a bench trial—a trial in which the judge both applies the law *and* determines the facts to which the law is applied (the function performed by the jury when one is present). Bench trials tend to result in approximately equal numbers of verdicts for the plaintiff/patentee and the defendant/(alleged) infringer. (The actual historical number is 51 percent of decisions in favor of the plaintiffs.)

About two decades ago, however, a truly brilliant (but unknown) member of the plaintiffs' bar (the good guys) realized that this lack of understanding could be turned to the plaintiffs' advantage. This is because, by law, an issued patent is presumed to be valid. If, as is virtually always the case, a defendant alleges that the patent-in-suit is invalid, the defendant has the burden of proving the invalidity by "clear and convincing evidence." This burden of proof is considerably more demanding than the ordinary burden in civil (noncriminal) matters, where a mere "preponderance of the evidence" is required. Thus, a jury, which is almost certain to be totally confused by the esoteric technical evidence adduced (lawyerspeak for "introduced") by the learned (lawyerspeak for "expensive") counsel, is unlikely to find that the defense has met this burden. Rather, the jury will find—in effect, by default—that the patent-in-suit is "not invalid." (Just as criminal suspects are not found innocent but rather "not guilty," so, too, patents are not found "valid" but rather "not invalid.")

Lest the jury overlook this factor, plaintiff's counsel reminds them of it during closing arguments. Moreover, juries (more so than judges) are apt to decide *all* of the issues in favor of the same party. If a jury finds in favor of the plaintiff with respect to the validity of the patent-in-suit, so too is it likely to find that the patent is infringed. The ultimate result is that a jury is considerably more likely than a judge to enter a verdict in favor of the plaintiff (historically, the probability is 68 percent). The conclusion to be drawn is that, in most cases (lawyers rarely speak in absolute terms—there are too often exceptions to any rule), *a plaintiff should request a jury trial.*

Juries do, nonetheless, present some special problems, most of which derive from the simple fact that juries are composed of normal people. They become bored. They become irate. Unlike the attorneys and the expert witnesses (and, to a somewhat lesser extent, the judge), they are not receiving substantial compensation for their courtroom duty (as anyone who has served on a jury can attest, jury pay is a pittance).

It is, therefore, extremely important that case presentation in a jury trial be entertaining. Communication skills are paramount (bear this in mind when selecting counsel). Maximum use should be made of visual aids, especially video presentations and computer simulations (if it comes out of a computer, it must be correct!). Do not give the appearance of prolonging the proceeding, and do not appear condescending to the jury. Every opportunity should be seized to present the party in a favorable light—a righteous David locked in mortal combat with a rapacious corporate Goliath.

Declaratory Judgment Action: The Preemptive Strike

In essence, a declaratory judgment action (in lawyer's jargon, a "DJ action") is a jurisprudential implementation of the old adage, "Do unto others as they would do unto you—only do it first!" It is an opportunity to strike first, rather than waiting for a patentee to file a suit alleging patent infringement. A party, having *standing* (to be discussed in a moment), may file an action in the appropriate federal court (proper venue) seeking a judicial declaration that a patent is invalid, unenforceable, and/or not infringed by anything the party is doing. Such an action is, in fact, the mirror image of a conventional (euphemism for "boilerplate") patent infringement action. Indeed, the near-universal (knee-jerk) response to a declaratory judgment action is the filing, by the declaratory judgment defendant (the patentee), of a counterclaim alleging (surprise!) patent infringement.

The reader (especially one who has not been paying close attention) may, at this point, ask, "So what? The end result is pretty much the same." The answer is: The end result is not necessarily the same.

First, by filing a declaratory judgment action, the loathsome infringer is able to choose the battlefield. (If this doesn't seem important, reread the section of this chapter entitled "Jurisdiction and Venue.") Second, the disgusting swine is able to choose the timing of the action. This may be significant for several reasons. A patentee may, for example, have planned, indeed prepared, to take action against another infringer (remember that infringement is often industrywide). These plans and preparations may well be totally upset when the patentee is unexpectedly hauled into a different court to face a different infringer. It is also possible that the patentee is engaged in some activity, such as an IPO, a merger, or an acquisition, which renders litigation especially burdensome at that time.

Finally, many knowledgeable experts (euphemism for "someone who has actually observed a patent infringement trial") maintain that there is a psychological advantage that accrues to the plaintiff. There may well be something to this theory. Certainly, it is difficult for a patentee to convincingly present a courtroom image of righteous indignation when the only reason he is in court is that the (alleged) infringer dragged him there.

Standing, which is a prerequisite to the bringing of a declaratory judgment action, was for a long time essentially a requirement that the plaintiff (the pestilential infringer) have an objectively reasonable apprehension of imminent suit by the (righteous, oppressed) patentee. (Now the requirements for standing have been substantially loosened; see Chapter 11.) An express charge of infringement by the patentee is not required to create such an apprehension. Rather, the courts look to the totality of the circumstances. Briefly and bluntly put, almost any assertion concerning the scope of a patent will confer standing, whether such assertion is made directly to actual or potential infringers or indirectly, through advertising. Indeed, recent case law has significantly expanded the range of acts that will create standing.

The few *possible* exceptions include the offer of a license without an accompanying charge of infringement; sending copies of one's patents to a competitor (again, without a charge of infringement); and (the authors' personal favorite) lighthearted banter falling short of a threat (the "smile when you say that" exception).

The lesson to be learned is this: Take care when communicating with possible infringers or an inconvenient declaratory judgment action may result.

Damages

The court will award to a successful patent infringement plaintiff damages sufficient to place the plaintiff in the position that the plaintiff would have occupied had the infringement not occurred. Just as there are two kinds of infringement (literal infringement and infringement under the doctrine of equivalents), so too are there two kinds of damages—lost profits and a reasonable royalty.

Lost profits are, in fact, exactly what they would seem to be—the profits lost by a patentee when an infringer makes sales that, but for the infringement, would have been made by the patentee. The profits in question are incremental profits (i.e., the excess of sale price over variable cost), not net profit, which is gross profit less overhead and other fixed and apportioned costs.

In order to satisfy the "but for" requirement, the patentee must establish that (1) it had the ability or capacity to make the sales it claims to have lost; and (2) there was no noninfringing alternative, such that the subject sales of the defendant were possible only through infringement. It is this second requirement that now may prove to be the greatest stumbling block to a successful patent infringement plaintiff seeking an award of lost profits. Formerly, an infringer was required to show actual possession of this noninfringing alternative—an unlikely situation.

Clearly, if one actually possessed a substitute for the infringing product or process, there would have been no point in infringing.

IN THE REAL WORLD

Losing Lost Profits

In *Grain Processing Corp. v. American Maize-Products Co.*, 185 F.3d 1341 (CAFC 1999), the CAFC affirmed a lower court ruling that a patent owner could not recover lost profits if non-infringing substitutes would have been available at the time of infringement.

Recently, however, the court has greatly relaxed this requirement (see the "Losing Lost Profits" box). Today, an infringer merely needs to establish that the noninfringing alternative was reasonably available. Indeed, it need not have actually been in existence at the time of the infringement, so long as it could have been made available if desired. The effect of this altered requirement is to greatly reduce the probability that a plaintiff will be awarded damages in the form of lost profits.

The damages awarded by the court shall be "in no event less than a reasonable royalty" (35 USC 284). Clearly, therefore, a reasonable royalty is the minimum amount of damages that may be recovered. Often, it is only a small fraction of the amount that would have been awarded had the lost profits standard been applied. That being said, the question remains, what constitutes a reasonable royalty?

In theory, a reasonable royalty is the royalty that would have been agreed upon by a willing licensor and a willing licensee at the time the infringement began. The factors that theoretically would have been considered by the parties are set forth in the Georgia-Pacific case (*Georgia-Pacific Corp. v. United States Plywood Corp.*, 318 F.Supp. 1116 [S.D.N.Y. 1970]). In practice, of course, a reasonable royalty is whatever

EXHIBIT 8.1			
Royalty Rates by Industry			
Automotive	4.7%	4.0%	79.7%
Chemicals	4.7%	3.6%	25.9%
Computers	5.2%	4.0%	34.4%
Consumer goods	5.5%	5.0%	30.8%
Electronics	4.3%	4.0%	51.3%
Energy and environment	5.0%	5.0%	52.9%
Health care products	5.8%	4.8%	22.4%
Internet	11.7%	7.5%	492.6%
Machines/tools	5.2%	4.5%	35.8%
Pharma and biotech	7.0%	5.1%	17.7%
Semiconductors	4.6%	3.2%	8.5%
Software	10.5%	6.8%	22.6%
Telecom	5.3%	4.7%	35.5%

Source: John Jarosz, Carol Mulhern, and Robert Vigil, "Industry Royalty Rates and Profitability," presented at Licensing Executives Society Annual Meeting, October 31, 2001.

the court decides it to be. The factors that seem to weigh most heavily, however, are the royalty rates in other licenses, if any, granted by the patentee, and that old standby, "the standard rate in the industry" (see Exhibit 8.1).

But Wait, There's More!

Damages are intended as recompense for the ill effects of the infringement. Yet what are these ill effects? It may be that the patentee suffered a loss of sales, in respect of which it will seek to recover its lost profits. But did it not suffer more? Probably it did; just ask an economist or an accountant (and be prepared to pay for the answer).

Initially, a patentee, by reason of its patent, enjoys a monopoly and may price the patented product or service accordingly. When this monopoly is broken by the despicable acts of an infringer, competition may force the patentee to reduce its price for the patented product. The revenues and, hence, profits lost as a result of this price erosion may be recoverable as damages by the patentee. Although sometimes difficult to establish (to the satisfaction of the court), price erosion can constitute a very significant portion of the total damages resulting from an infringement.

In addition to lost sales of the patented product, the patentee may suffer a loss of sales of associated products or services. Such associated products may be supplies or consumables normally purchased and used in conjunction with the patented product (for example, film purchased in conjunction with patented cameras, or razor blades purchased in conjunction with patented razors). Furthermore, along with sales of the patented product, the patentee may have lost sales of spare or replacement parts (which often enjoy a high profit margin) and service or maintenance contracts. The profit lost with the loss of sales of these associated goods, known as *convoyed sales*, is, under appropriate circumstances, recoverable.

A similar rule may apply where a patented improvement is incorporated in a much larger product (as an extreme example, consider an improved carburetor incorporated into an automobile). If the patentee can establish that sales of the automobile are driven (pun intended) by the presence of the improved carburetor, the price of the entire automobile may be used as the basis for the calculation of damages. This is known as the *entire market value rule* (EMV rule).

In those cases where the patentee is in competition with the infringer but the court nevertheless awards only a reasonable royalty as damages (indicating that a noninfringing alternative was available), the patentee may argue for inclusion of the convoyed sales in the base against which the reasonable royalty is applied or, alternatively, may use the existence of such convoyed sales to support an argument for a higher royalty rate (the argument here being that, in view of all the benefits accruing to a licensee, willing parties would have agreed on a higher royalty rate).

Patent Infringement Litigation—An Overview

In a very general sense, all patent litigations follow a predictable path. However, it must be borne in mind that each case is unique. This individuality arises from a number of factors, including peculiarities of the local rules of the court where the action is being tried, tactical decisions made by the opposing party, and the personal preferences of the trial judge. If patent infringement litigation seems contradictory and uncertain, it is!

Patent infringement litigation, like all civil litigation, commences with the filing and service upon the defendant(s) of a summons and complaint. The *summons* is essentially a notice to the defendant that it is being sued, identifying the court and the parties and directing the defendant to file an *appearance* identifying the defendant's attorney. The *complaint* sets forth, in numbered counts and paragraphs, the specific allegations being leveled against the defendant (i.e., charges of direct infringement, contributory infringement, and inducement to infringe) and ends in a *prayer for relief*, listing the various forms of relief being sought. Such relief, at a minimum, comprises unspecified monetary damages (How do you spell relief? M-O-N-E-Y) and an injunction against further infringement, and frequently extends to multiple damages, attorney's fees, costs, interest, and so on. (The list is limited only by the creativity and imagination of the plaintiff's counsel.)

Once served with the summons and complaint, the defendant appears and files an *answer*, which is a lighthearted denial of all of the material allegations of the complaint, together with a list of affirmative defenses ("I didn't do it, but even if I did—which I deny—it doesn't matter because . . ."). Most defendants will also search high and low for any possible counterclaims, which, if found, are appended to the answer. The plaintiff responds to the answer by filing a *reply* (this depends upon local rules and the plaintiff's legal budget), including a jocular denial of the allegations of the affirmative defenses. If counterclaims have been made, the plaintiff (now more properly known as the "plaintiff and counterclaim defendant") will jovially deny the allegations thereof as well. At this point, the pleadings are closed and, in most civil litigation (i.e., civil litigation not involving patent infringement), *discovery*—also known as the discovery process—commences. Patent infringement litigation, however, has been marching to a different drummer since the landmark Supreme Court decision in the *Markman* case.

In *Markman*, for reasons known only to themselves, the Supreme Court justices decided to consider who should *construe* (define, delineate, guess at) the scope of the claims of the patent-in-suit. Being unimpressed by nearly 200 years of consistent American practice, they hearkened back to those thrilling days of yore, in Old England, when juries were composed of ignorant peasants and contracts, when in dispute, were construed by the more learned (as compared to the peasants) judges. Deciding, by analogy, that modern-day American juries were incapable of comprehending the intricacies of patent claim construction (often true), they decided that the task would best be accomplished if guided by a wise and experienced jurist (often untrue). To this end, they decided that, henceforth, the question of claim construction was one of law, not fact, to be decided by the court (i.e., the trial judge). Thus, we have the genesis of the so-called Markman hearing, which continues to plague us even today.

Although the Supreme Court, in effect, mandated a Markman hearing, it did not specify when in the litigation process this was to occur. Most often, it takes place rather early, following a limited period of discovery directed solely at claim construction issues. In some cases, the Markman hearing amounts to a trial before the trial, complete with expert witness testimony and the introduction of excerpts from all manner of printed reference works. Most judges, however, eschew extrinsic evidence, especially the testimony of self-proclaimed experts, and limit the hearing to attorney argument. Indeed, some judges rely solely on written briefs, thus delivering the *Markman* decision without the hearing.

However achieved—either through a full, evidentiary hearing or by divining the entrails—the Court ultimately decides the scope and meaning of the patent claims-in-suit. At this point, patent infringement litigation rejoins the regularly scheduled legal programming. Full discovery now commences, with all its breathtaking billing opportunities for the lawyers (discovery costs sometimes run to seven or even eight figures). At the close of discovery, the impoverished but unbowed parties appear at trial, to finally be accorded their day (frequently a week or two) in court. Total time elapsed from filing of the complaint to entry of a verdict: at least nine months, most often about two to three years. It is not uncommon, however, for a case to drag on for four years or more (for further reading, see the case of *Jarndyce v. Jarndyce* described in the novel *Bleak House* by Charles Dickens).

Popular Misconceptions—The Cloakroom Defenses

A charge of patent infringement often elicits one of two indignant responses: (1) "I'm not infringing your patent because I invented the accused product/service myself," or (2) "I'm not responsible because I purchased the product in question from XYZ Company—talk to them" (invariably, XYZ Company is an offshore entity, well beyond the patent holder's reach). These responses are similar to the little placards posted in restaurant cloakrooms that say "Not responsible for lost or stolen property"—they are only effective if one is gullible enough to believe them.

Unlike copyrights and trade secrets, patents protect against independent re-creation—reinventing the wheel. (This, in part, justifies the greater cost of patents.) Thus, so long as the patent in question is valid and the accused did not make their invention before the patentee did, their subsequent independent invention is not a legal defense. (*Note*: Many are those who claim prior invention; few are those who can prove it. Go ahead and sue them.)

As the reader should remember from Chapter 1, a patent bars the unauthorized practice of the patented invention—making, using, selling, or offering for sale. It matters not that the seller of a product bought it from another. Everyone in the chain of distribution is equally liable for any infringement. As a practical matter, the (supposedly innocent) seller probably has (or certainly should have) an indemnification agreement with his supplier. Indeed, under the Uniform Commercial Code (UCC), the seller implicitly warrants that noncustom goods are free of patent infringement. So again, go ahead and sue them. Let *them* chase the miserable, misbegotten supplier to recover any damages awarded to you.

A slightly less common, but still popular, response (also invariably delivered with great indignation) is "I'm not infringing; I, myself, have a patent on this product." (Usually, however, the grammar isn't this good.) Even if it is true, this will avail the speaker naught. Remember the red fire engine. A patent is a negative right (some things bear repetition); it does not convey the affirmative right to make the patented product. Go ahead and sue.

 IN THE REAL WORLD

How to Lose $388 Million in Five Easy Steps

Whatever else you may want to say about Microsoft Corporation, they certainly know how to overcome an adverse jury verdict in a patent infringement case. Of course, sometimes the plaintiff goes out of its way to help them.

In *Uniloc USA, Inc. and Uniloc Singapore Private Limited v. Microsoft Corporation*, the jury found the patent-in-suit valid and infringed. They found the infringement to be willful. They awarded the plaintiffs damages of $388 million—before any enhancement. Undaunted, Microsoft moved for judgment as a matter of law (JMOL) with respect to all of the issues presented to the jury and (figuratively) walked out of court successful on *all* counts. In a lengthy (66 pages) but surprisingly readable decision, the court catalogued the various sins—some of commission and some of omission—committed by the plaintiffs.

After much thoughtful analysis, and a couple of shots of Jack Daniels (a much favored aid to legal analysis), we are able to present five rules for overturning a jury verdict:

❶ *Confuse and mislead the jury.* Simplification is good; oversimplification is not. Microsoft's overall theme was that the jury failed to grasp the complexity of the case due to Uniloc's "ceaseless rhetoric and innuendo." The court found that Uniloc's approach was "to boil down complex computer software programs to a kind of generic word find puzzle, that ignores how the allegedly infringing system actually works and, most important, the actual disclosure in the '216 patent." As a result, the court concluded that the jury "lacked a grasp of the issues before it and reached a finding without a legally sufficient basis."

❷ *When drafting a patent application, limit disclosure of claimed algorithms.* Although the jury found the patent infringed, the court disagreed, finding that "[t]he skeletal disclosure in the '216 patent with three plus signs and the phrases 'by addition' and 'items to be summed' cannot be so broad as to capture within its scope (to one of ordinary skill in the art) virtually any and all software algorithms that include addition as one mathematical component, no matter how minor."

   The court held that allowing the jury's embrace of Uniloc's "simplistic and clever gloss on the patent's disclosed structure" would impermissibly broaden "the scope of [the] means-plus-function claim language beyond the structure disclosed in the specification and its equivalents."

❸ *Rely on a limited and simplistic expert's report.* This rule may be deemed a corollary to rules 1 and 2. The court found that the Uniloc expert's report "disclosed next to nothing about his opinions . . . or the principles he discussed." This created a "problem with relying upon [the expert's] incomplete, oversimplified and frankly inappropriate explanation to support the verdict." The court solved this problem by largely ignoring the opinion.

❹ *Get greedy, and ignore the court's instructions.* Microsoft objected to Uniloc's introduction of a demonstrative pie chart wherein Uniloc sought to apply the EMV rule to Microsoft's total sales ($19.27 billion) of accused products, to yield a royalty of about $565 million. The court "instructed counsel to stay away from the $19 billion figure. Yet, the figure continued to rear its head through the back door during cross-examination of Microsoft's expert and in closing." The court held that this improperly encouraged "awarding damages far in excess of the contribution of the precise patented invention . . . [s]hould the need for a new trial arise, Microsoft is entitled to a new determination of damages without the taint of this irrelevant evidence. . . ."

❺ *Always argue that infringement was willful—even if you lack any real evidence.* The court held that Uniloc's "evidence" of willfulness "could not, as a matter of law, have left the jurors with a 'clear conviction or firm belief' that Microsoft knew it infringed because it stole some idea of Uniloc's," thus denying any enhanced damages.

More importantly, however, the court also held that Uniloc's abundance of copying "evidence" could not be deemed "harmless insofar as its likelihood to confuse, distract and taint consideration of the other issues." This was the tipping point in the court's decision to grant Microsoft a new trial on liability to "prevent a miscarriage of justice." Thus, an ill-conceived claim proved to be Uniloc's possible undoing—at least with respect to patent validity.

Time Can Mean So Much—Laches and Estoppel

Although not unique to patent litigation cases, two often-encountered defenses are laches and estoppel (some writers mention laches and estoppel as a single defense—this is both incorrect and intellectually sloppy).

Laches is the unexcused failure to take action in a timely manner (in lay terms, sitting on your hands). Having once discovered an infringement, a patentee must take action (file suit) with reasonable promptness. If the patentee fails to so act, and the delay causes material prejudice to the (alleged) infringer, the patentee may be barred from recovery of any damages for past acts of infringement—those occurring prior to the filing of the suit. The patentee may, nonetheless, obtain an injunction barring further infringement of the patent-in-suit.

"Prejudice to the (alleged) infringer" refers to a handicap in presenting a defense. A defendant may allege, for example, that critical documents have been discarded as no longer needed, or that key witnesses are no longer available, or that their memories have dimmed (such dimming often proves to be surprisingly selective). The length of delay is measured from the time the infringement was discovered or reasonably should have been discovered. A patentee cannot, like Admiral Nelson, turn a blind eye to such evidence of infringement as would prompt further investigation by a reasonable patentee (so-called *inquiry notice*). Finally, a delay of six years is presumed to be unreasonable (well, duh!) and creates a "rebuttable presumption" of laches. This has the effect of shifting the burden of proof from the defendant (who otherwise must prove prejudice) to the plaintiff (who must now prove some legally cognizable excuse for the delay).

Estoppel, or more properly *equitable estoppel*, is closely related to laches. Whereas laches involves a mere failure to act, equitable estoppel requires some affirmative act by the patentee that leads an accused infringer to believe that it will remain unmolested (in lay terms, barking, but then failing promptly to bite). The accused infringer must reasonably rely on this act to its detriment. (*Detriment*, in this context, is largely synonymous with *prejudice* in the context of laches.) Although mere silence does not give rise to equitable estoppel, extended inaction after issuing a notice of infringement may well do so. Equitable estoppel not only bars recovery for past acts of infringement, it renders the patent completely unenforceable with respect to that defendant. The lesson to be learned: Don't bluff. Never accuse others of infringement, nor threaten suit, unless you are prepared to take legal action.

Litigation Risk Analysis

Litigation in general, and particularly patent infringement litigation, involves an untold number of decisions: settlement decisions, pretrial discovery decisions, trial strategy decisions, and appeal decisions. Lawyers and business executives are constantly striving to make the right decisions. The process of making these decisions is rendered more difficult by the complexity of the problems being addressed and the uncertainties associated with their various constituent factors. The decision-making process may be facilitated, however, through the use of litigation risk analysis.

Litigation is fraught with uncertainty, which is a condition or a state inherent in situations offering more than one possible outcome. Uncertainty also arises from the inherently probabilistic nature of some of the events affecting the ultimate outcome, as well as from the imperfect information available about certain facts and the concomitant need to make assumptions. Risk is the likelihood that the actual outcome will be unfavorable or undesired. Complexity results from uncertainty piled atop uncertainty. From a business decision-making point of view, litigation management is to a large degree a risk management problem.

Risk is most often difficult to precisely measure or assess. Commonly, it is described with generalities such as "a good chance," "probably," "in all likelihood," or (only slightly better) "more likely than not." Such terms are vague and uncertain, conveying different meaning to different people. More importantly, they cannot be combined to describe the risk presented by a situation involving more than one uncertainty. Such methods of description are obviously unsatisfactory.

Clearly, there is a need to rationalize complex problems—that is, to identify the constituent uncertainties (at least the most significant ones) of the problem and the relations between them; to assess the risks associated with these uncertainties and present them in a precise and mathematically sound manner; and to combine these constituent risks so as to determine the risk presented by the entire problem. Litigation risk analysis, which is both a disciplined approach to the analysis of problems involving uncertainty and a systematic method of dealing with complexity, meets this need. Properly applied, it will lead to the identification of the best decision (which, as we will see, is not always the right decision). In addition, it will provide a basis for clear, precise communications.

Identification of Uncertainties and Drawing the Decision Tree

The first step in litigation risk analysis, indeed in any risk analysis, is to identify and organize all (or at least the significant) uncertainties that make up a given problem. These uncertainties are then schematically arranged in chronological order, starting with the present and progressing into the future, to produce a flowchart encompassing all of the uncertainties and all of the possible outcomes of the problem. The flowchart is then converted or reformatted as a decision tree. (Some practitioners prefer to omit the flowchart and commence organization and representation of a problem as a decision tree.) Each point of uncertainty causes the tree to branch, with one new branch being created for each possible outcome of the uncertain event. Each possible outcome of the problem is found at the tip of at least one branch. The process of preparing a flowchart and/or a decision tree can best be explained and understood with reference to the following example.

Example

The client company (the "Client") is one of a small number of firms in the business of producing a mineral product that is first fused in a kiln and then ground. An executive of the client company (the "Executive") has quit his job and immediately thereafter invented and subsequently patented an improved kiln. The client company claims ownership of this patent but has taken no action with respect thereto.

Utilizing the invention, the Executive started a business that competes with the Client. The Client, wishing to upgrade its technology, retained a consultant (the "Consultant") to design improvements to its own kilns. The Client chose not to disclose the patent to the Consultant, who remained unaware of its existence. Based on the Consultant's design, the Client built new kilns, which bear a marked resemblance to those described and claimed in the patent. The Client also improved its grinding procedures. The Client's various changes have caused a marked improvement in the quality of its product, allowing it to dominate the market.

With his market share and price being steadily eroded, the Executive brought a lawsuit against the Client for patent infringement. The Executive claims that the alleged infringement is willful and seeks lost profits and treble damages.

The Client has responded to the suit by denying infringement and asserting that the patent is invalid. The Client further asserts its ownership of the patent, alleging that the Executive made the invention while in the Client's employ. Obtaining a stay of proceedings in the infringement action, the Client has petitioned for reexamination of the patent on the basis of prior art not considered during examination of the original patent application. This reexamination resulted in a final rejection of all of the claims-in-suit. An appeal of this rejection to the Patent Office Board of Appeals is now pending.

The Client has calculated that, if found guilty of patent infringement, a reasonable royalty for use of the patented kiln would be $500,000, while the Executive's lost profits would amount to $10 million. It is believed that the choice of the appropriate measure of damages will depend upon a finding as to whether the improvement in quality of the Client's product was the result of the change in the Client's kiln design (i.e., whether the output of the accused kilns is unique).

Finally, it is anticipated that in-house staff will handle all proceedings in this matter and, hence, no legal fees will be incurred.

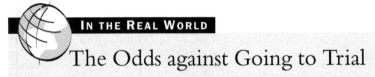

IN THE REAL WORLD

The Odds against Going to Trial

Historically, 76 percent of patent suits settle. Only about 4 percent of patent infringement lawsuits proceed through trial.

The Client has requested a decision as to the settlement value of this case. As a first step in reaching such a decision, a model or flowchart of the litigation, as shown in Exhibit 8.2, would be prepared. The top or first three boxes are included merely to place the problem in its historical context. As past events, they could have been omitted.

Exhibit 8.3 shows the same problem analysis, presented in the form of a decision tree. The decision tree lists all of the identified uncertainties composing the present problem and graphically illustrates the relations between them. All of the possible outcomes are listed in the column to the right of the tree. As yet, however, there has been no consideration of the risks engendered by these uncertainties. We cannot, therefore, determine the likelihood of any of these outcomes actually occurring.

Assessing the Risks

Having identified all of the uncertainties and, therefore, being aware of what *can* happen, we must now assess the risks associated therewith; which is to say we must determine the *likelihood* or probability of each of the possible outcomes actually occurring.

In general, attorneys are loath to assign probabilities to risks. This may be due to a perceived inability to make an accurate assessment or (more likely) a fear that the assessment may prove inaccurate and come back to haunt them. (One attorney claimed that his malpractice insurance carrier would not permit him to offer percentage assessments of risk.) However difficult it may prove to be, there is, unfortunately, no

EXHIBIT 8.2

Flowchart of Litigation

Decision Tree Analysis of Litigation

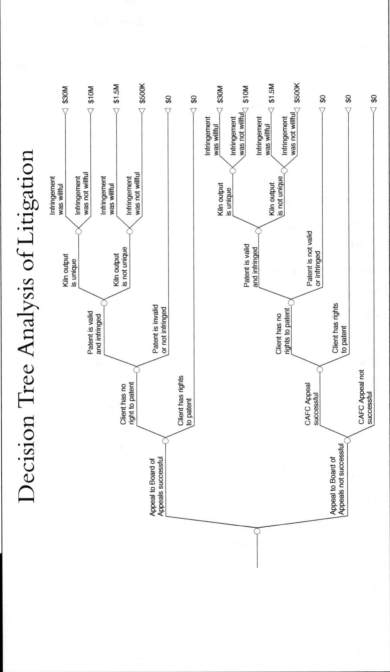

alternative to obtaining risk assessments from the people most intimately involved and knowledgeable about the problem. Soliciting assessments from several individuals and assuring them that only the resulting average will be utilized can sometimes overcome this reluctance. (This approach has been compared to recruiting members for a firing squad by assuring them that one of them will have a blank cartridge in his rifle.)

A better approach (although much more cumbersome and time-consuming) is the so-called Delphi method, which involves soliciting opinions (in this case risk assessments) from a number of individuals, who are most commonly kept separated and anonymous to prevent status, authority, or other intimidating influences from prejudicing their views. After all of the participants have submitted an assessment, those who have submitted the most extreme opinions (in our case, the highest and lowest risk assessments) are informed of the opinions of the others and offered an opportunity to reconsider (euphemism for "change") their own opinions. If they decline this opportunity, they are required to state their reasons for maintaining their extreme position. These reasons are then conveyed to the other participants who are then offered the opportunity to reconsider *their* opinions. If they decline to alter their opinions, they must respond to the reasons provided by the extremists. Any reasons so provided are then conveyed to the extremists, who are once again presented with the choice of revising (another euphemism for "changing") their opinion or defending it. Generally, after two or three such iterations, something approaching consensus is reached.

Continuing with this example, the risks therein were assessed as shown in Exhibit 8.4.

Having obtained these risk assessments, we are now ready to complete our example litigation risk analysis.

Putting It All Together

Once the risks inherent in a problem have been assessed, they are entered on the previously prepared decision tree, as shown in Exhibit 8.5.

EXHIBIT 8.4	
Risk Assessment	
Probability that the Patent Office Board of Appeals will reverse the patent examiner's rejection of the critical reexamined claims	30%
Probability that the CAFC would reverse a decision of the Board of Appeals affirming the claims rejection	30%
Probability that the Client is found, by the court, to have rights to the patent-in-suit	10%
Probability that the reexamined patent is found by the court to be both valid and infringed	80%
Probability that the court determines that the patented kiln caused the increase in quality of the Client's product	80%
Probability that, if defendant is found guilty of infringement, the court will determine the infringement to have been willful and wanton	50%

The probability that a given outcome will actually occur may now be calculated. It is the mathematical combination of each of the risks encountered along the path between that outcome and the start point. (Risks are combined by multiplying them together.) The probability of occurrence of each of the possible outcomes is listed in Exhibit 8.6. The sum of the probabilities of occurrence of each of the possible outcomes is 1.0 (or 100 percent), meaning that (if our model is accurate) one of these outcomes must occur. (If this total is other than 1.0, or 100 percent, an arithmetic error was made somewhere.) The third column in the Exhibit 8.6, entitled "Expected Value," lists the product of each possible outcome multiplied by the likelihood or probability that it will actually occur. The sum of the expected values is the expected value of all possible outcomes and, hence, the probabilistic outcome of the problem. In our example, it is the effective value of the case— $2.46 million—that represents the effective potential liability or *exposure* to the Client.

Once the analysis is complete, it should be subjected to a sanity test. In other words, is the result so outrageous as to suggest that it is likely to be erroneous? (*Hint:* If the result seems unreasonable, but the sum of the possible outcomes is 1.0, the error is likely in the model; either the flowchart is wrong or an error was made in converting it into a decision tree.)

EXHIBIT 8.5

Risk Assessment Decision Tree

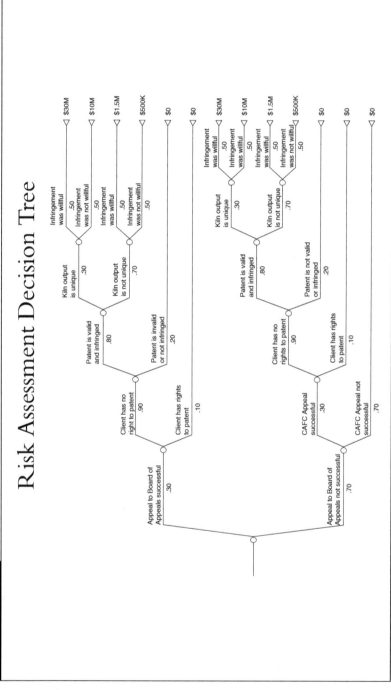

EXHIBIT 8.6		
Probability Table		
Possible Outcome ($ Million)	**Probability**	**Expected Value ($ Million)**
$ 30.0	3.24%	$ .97
$ 10.0	3.24%	$ .32
$ 1.5	7.56%	$ .11
$ 0.5	7.56%	$ .04
$ 0	5.40%	$ 0
$ 0	3.00%	$ 0
$ 30.0	2.27%	$ .68
$ 10.0	2.27%	$ .23
$ 1.5	5.29%	$ .08
$ 0.5	5.29%	$ .03
$ 0	3.78%	$ 0
$ 0	2.10%	$ 0
$ 0	49.0%	$ 0
Totals: $ 84	**100%**	**$2.46**

Once reasonably confident that the risk analysis is sane, it may be enlightening to determine the sensitivity of the model or the criticality of the various uncertainties that compose the problem. This is done by altering the assessment of the risk associated with the uncertainty and observing the impact on the sum of the expected values (a procedure known as *sensitivity analysis*). Such sensitivity analysis may disclose the importance of a seemingly minor issue or, conversely, may reveal that a supposedly key issue is actually of relatively little significance.

Finally, the analysis should be examined to determine whether it contradicts any conventional wisdom or other widely accepted views. For instance, in our example, despite the rather pessimistic views regarding the Executive's chances of securing allowance of the critical patent claims, we learn that, in fact, he has a 51 percent probability of success. This is composed of a 30 percent probability that the Board of Appeals will reverse the patent examiner and a 21 percent probability $(0.70 \times 0.30 = 0.21)$ that an appeal will be taken to the CAFC and decided in favor of the Executive. It is "more likely than not," barring settlement, that the Client will have to face him at trial.

TIPS AND TECHNIQUES

When making decisions based upon a decision tree risk analysis, it must always be borne in mind that, in real life, unlikely outcomes do sometimes occur. Indeed, our analysis calculates the finite probability that such outcomes will occur. If such an outcome would have a serious (or even catastrophic) effect, it cannot be safely ignored.

The likelihood of being unpleasantly surprised by such a probabilistically unexpected outcome can be reduced if the decision tree is updated as each of the included future events becomes an historic event. After the time for an event to occur has passed, its probability of occurrence is either 100 percent (it did occur) or 0 percent (it did not occur), and the previously estimated probability for the event should be replaced with the historically determined one.

IN THE REAL WORLD

The Real Deal

The example used in this chapter was drawn from a real case managed by one of the authors. As the case unfolded:

❶ The Board of Appeals affirmed the patent examiner's rejection of the critical reexamined claims.

❷ The CAFC reversed the Board of Appeals.

❸ The Court found the Client did not have any rights to the patent-in-suit.

❹ The Court found the reexamined patent to be valid and infringed.

❺ The Court found the patented kiln caused the increase in the quality of the Client's product, awarding damages on a "lost profits" basis.

❻ The Court found the infringement to have been willful and wanton, and awarded treble damages.

Dealing with Complexity and Moving into the Modern Age

As mentioned at the beginning of this chapter, patent infringement litigation presents an exceedingly large number of risks, some of which are common to all litigation, while others are peculiar to patent matters. The patent-specific issues relate to the questions of patent validity, patent enforceability, and patent infringement, and to damages calculation. These questions, and some of the subissues that they comprise, are set forth in the following list.

IN THE REAL WORLD

More Patent Litigation Odds

Only 1.1 percent of all patents are ever litigated. About 67 percent of patents litigated through trial remain valid, and only 11 to 12 percent of patents are held unenforceable; 66 percent of patents are found infringed at trial.

How likely is it that the patent will be found to be:

- Invalid due to
  - Prior art (anticipation, obviousness).
  - Lack of enablement.
  - Failure to disclose the best mode.
- Unenforceable due to
  - Inequitable conduct.
  - Laches.
  - Estoppel.
  - Patent misuse.

EXHIBIT 8.7	
Infringement Analysis Questions	
1	What is the probability that a motion seeking a preliminary injunction will be granted?
2	What is the probability that a motion for summary judgment on (1) invalidity, (2) unenforceability, (3) noninfringement, or (4) infringement will be granted?
3	After a decision for the plaintiff, will the damages be assessed based on lost profits or reasonable royalties?
4	Will infringement be found to have been wanton (i.e., will multiple damages be awarded)?
5	Will the case be deemed exceptional (i.e., will attorney's fees be awarded)?

- Not infringed as to
  - Claim 1.
  - Claim 2.
  - Claim X.

Infringement analysis should preferably be performed for each claim of the asserted patents (at the very least, the independent claims). Once this analysis is completed, further questions may be asked (see Exhibit 8.7).

In addition to the foregoing, it is to be considered that the level of complexity of patent infringement litigation has been vastly increased by the requirement of a so-called Markman hearing, which, in effect, adds another layer of litigation—a trial before the trial—to the resolution of a patent infringement case.

By this time, the keen observer will have noted that each uncertainty added to a decision tree results in a substantial increase in the number of tree branches. Indeed, a single uncertainty (with only two possible outcomes) added at the roots of the tree may double the number of branches in the completed tree. It will be appreciated, therefore, that as an analysis of a problem becomes more detailed, the resultant decision tree spreads even further, becoming cumbersome, if not impossible, to handle manually. Combining closely related or intertwined uncertainties may sometimes ameliorate this problem. Thus, in our example, patent validity and infringement were combined. However, combining—as a single uncertainty—the validity of all claims in a patent (based on the notion that all claims stand or fall together), or even so considering the validity of several patents within a portfolio of patents, may be a reasonable simplification. Indeed, if an assessment of the risk of patent validity is impossible (or inconvenient) to obtain, historical data may be substituted. For example, juries have historically held patents not invalid 67 percent of the time, and judges, in bench trials, have held them not invalid 57 percent of the time.

It should also be noted that, despite the considerable effort required, the risk assessments in the example given were developed as a single number. Obviously, a range of probabilities, rather than a single number, is more likely to be correct and less troublesome to obtain. Although mathematical formulas exist allowing for the use of ranges rather than discrete assessments of risk, such approaches are exceedingly complex and unsuitable for use by the ordinary practitioner. Fortunately, this problem is neatly solved by what is known as Monte Carlo simulation.

Simply stated, Monte Carlo simulation utilizes random numbers to determine the actual outcome of the various uncertainties composing a problem. Each complete simulation represents one possible outcome of the problem. The simulation is repeated many times to create a statistical analysis of all possible outcomes of a problem. Thus, unlike the simple analysis of our example (which produced a single number representing the *expected value* of all possible outcomes), Monte Carlo simulation yields a *distribution* of all possible outcomes with their corresponding probability of occurrence. Rather than purporting to tell *what* will happen, Monte Carlo simulation specifies *how likely* any possible outcome actually is. Such a simulation also offers a fine opportunity to perform a sensitivity analysis.

TIPS AND TECHNIQUES

As might be expected, various computer software pack-
ages are available that both assist in the creation of
decision trees and facilitate the simple or Monte Carlo analysis
thereof. For decision tree analysis, the authors highly recommend decision analysis software from TreeAge Software, Inc.,
which was used for this chapter.

Choosing and Managing Your Counsel

One cannot fight a war without an army. Similarly, one cannot litigate a
patent without a squad of lawyers. Selecting a law firm is a critical, but
not unduly complex, task. Only three basic factors need be considered:
quality, flexibility, and price.

A Few Good Men/Women

There is an ancient Chinese proverb that holds, "Gold will not always
buy you good soldiers, but good soldiers will always bring you gold."
Despite this long-standing recognition of the primacy of quality over
price, many prospective plaintiffs focus on price when selecting a law
firm to litigate their patent(s). *Do not do this.* Pay what is necessary to
retain the best people. If one wins, few will worry about the cost. If one
loses, the saving of a few dollars offers little consolation.

Having decided to hire the best counsel, the question remains how
to identify them. Often, people look to recent, newsworthy trials, seeking to hire the firm that represented the prevailing party. While this
approach has some basis in logic, it is good to remember that even a
clock that has stopped is right twice a day. Therefore, inquire also about
those cases that the firm has lost.

For all of its shortcomings, the newspaper technique, along with
recommendations from colleagues, may be the best means of assembling

a list of candidate firms. To select a firm from amongst these candidates, they must be interviewed and critically analyzed.

Interviewing can best be accomplished by first preparing a brief (one-page) synopsis of the case and forwarding it to each of the candidate firms—having first verified that they have no conflicts that would prevent them from accepting the matter and that they are also willing to accept the synopsis and discuss it. Some firms may be unwilling to accept the proffered synopsis, either because of a preexisting conflict or because they hope to be retained by the opposing party. Thus, the identification of such firms may be a useful bit of intelligence. Further, those firms that review the synopsis may be thereby barred from later representing the opposing party. Thus, even an unsuccessful interview is not without its benefit.

Law firms do not litigate cases—lawyers do. When interviewing a law firm, insist on speaking with the lawyers who will actually handle the case. Do not be satisfied with platitudes from the firm's managing partner whose only involvement with the matter, after a retainer agreement has been signed, is to review and increase (more on this later) the billings in the matter. When speaking to the attorney who would be chiefly responsible for the matter, ask what strengths and weaknesses are perceived in the case and what strategy is planned. Obviously, such preliminary opinions and plans are subject to revision as further information is acquired. Nevertheless, the interviewee attorney should be familiar with the information provided, should have identified the key issues presented by the case, and should be able to propose a comprehensive and realistic case strategy.

Occasionally, an interviewee will have researched the matter prior to the interview. Such efforts show initiative or at least a strong desire to secure a new client. If such research was done, consider it carefully. Did it focus on relevant matters? Was it productive (i.e., did it increase the likelihood of success)? Not all research is relevant or productive (although it is all expensive). An attorney who lacks focus at an interview will almost certainly lack focus throughout the case.

No sane, responsible attorney will undertake to litigate a patent infringement case of any significance alone. Most commonly, the lead attorney will be a partner or senior associate of the firm. A colleague, generally a midlevel associate, will assist the lead attorney. Inquire about this assistant and, if possible, include the assistant in the interview. How long have the assistant and lead counsel worked together? Long association indicates that the lead counsel prefers to work with this associate, which, in turn, suggests a measure of respect for the associate's abilities.

Many Are the Soldiers, Few Are the Fighters

Many attorneys hold themselves out as litigators. Do not confuse *litigators* with *trial attorneys*. The bulk of the work in litigation takes place outside of the courtroom—discovery (interrogatories, requests for production, document review, depositions) constitutes the vast majority of any litigation effort, especially in intellectual property litigation. Legal issues must be resolved and briefs must be drafted. Arguing of motions and the trial itself make up a very small, but crucial, fraction of the litigation effort. Many litigators spend virtually their entire careers on such preparatory matters and have little or no experience in presenting a case to a trier of fact—either a jury or a judge.

Effective presentation calls for a unique set of skills: the ability to simplify without appearing condescending, the ability to think rapidly under pressure, the ability to capture and hold the attention of the judge and the jury, and stage presence (a trial is, after all, theater). These are the peculiar skills of the trial attorney, a much less numerous breed than the litigator. Meet the individuals who will actually present the case. Are they compelling? If they make their client drowsy, imagine what they will do to a jury (which probably doesn't want to be in the courtroom in the first place). Nothing is more disheartening than to see a good, well-prepared case lost through ineffective presentation at trial. Be certain that the litigation team includes a first-class trial attorney.

The Willow, Not the Oak

Patent infringement litigation is a lengthy process. It is, under the best of circumstances, exhausting and exasperating. Conflict with one's counsel can make it infinitely worse. Everything possible should be done to ensure that cordial working relations will be maintained. Such relations require compatible personalities and a reasonable degree of flexibility on the part of counsel.

The requisite flexibility will manifest itself in a number of ways. First, the chosen counsel must share the client's views and attitudes concerning the case to be litigated. This does not mean that the search is for a sycophant—to the contrary, counsel is most effective when espousing beliefs he shares; an attorney who will meekly adopt the views of the client will often, just as meekly, surrender critical issues to opposing counsel. Nevertheless, if one doesn't agree with counsel before the firing begins, the disagreements will only grow more acrimonious when the bullets begin to fly. (*Note*: If, after extensive searching, no competent counsel can be found with whom one agrees, one should consider the possibility that one has an unreasonable view of the matter or a poor case.)

Second, counsel should be willing to work not only *for* the client but also *with* the client. However diligent and expert the counsel, it is likely that the client will have better knowledge of all of the relevant facts and circumstances of the case. Moreover, as a case proceeds, lawyers tend to narrow their focus. It is incumbent upon the client to maintain a more global perspective, maintaining awareness of changing conditions in the industry and in the circumstances of the parties. Litigation should serve the client's needs, not drive them. An alert and participatory client can assure that tactics, and even strategy, are promptly and appropriately modified to meet changing circumstances. This requires that the client remain informed of all matters in the case and that the attorney is willing and able to accept changes to the battle plan during the heat of battle.

Virtually all counsel will promise to keep the client informed as to the developments in the case. Many, but not all of them, truly mean it. However, such promises mean different things to different people. Counsel should provide information in such a way that there is time to act upon it. Information received after the fact (i.e., copies of documents already filed) is of merely historical value. Ideally, preliminary drafts or outlines of briefs and motions should be provided, such that the client can effectively contribute to finalization of the document with minimal, if any, disruption. Similarly, plans and tactics for depositions should be discussed *before* the depositions are taken.

Attorney Costs

There are three basic approaches to attorney compensation (being professionals, attorneys are *compensated*, not "paid" for their services): fixed fees, time-based billing, and contingency fees. However, various combinations of these three approaches exist.

Fixed fees are best suited to matters where the amount of work to be done is highly predictable; for this reason, they are never encountered in patent infringement litigation.

Time-based billing, also known as hourly billing, is the approach most favored by patent litigators and, hence, is the approach most commonly utilized. Unlike contingency fees, hourly billing involves no risk to the law firm that it will not be paid for its services. At the same time, it allows the client to pay for only those services actually provided. Assuming that the client has the cash available to pay the (generally) monthly invoices from the law firm, time-based billing is probably the preferred compensation scheme for the client as well.

Time-based billing is, however, not without its drawbacks. Foremost among those drawbacks is the lack of incentive to work efficiently or otherwise minimize costs. If left unchecked, overstaffing and the use of senior-level people to do junior-level work may occur. These problems are most prevalent in larger firms. Indeed, after analyzing much empirical data, the following law of nature (modestly known as Lerner's Law) has been discovered:

- There is little relationship between price and quality.

- There is little relationship between the size of a law firm and quality.

- There is a significant relationship between the size of a law firm and the prices it will charge.

It is not to be concluded that large law firms are evil or dishonest; but size, beyond a certain point, imposes diseconomies of scale, as marketing and management become ever more important to the life of the firm (and the success of its members). In general, if counsel is to be retained on a time-based billing approach, it is best to retain a firm that is just large enough to handle the matter in question.

They Also Bill Who Only Stand and Wait

Another cost-containment measure is to insist upon detailed bills specifying the tasks performed by each timekeeper, each day, and the amount of time devoted thereto—so-called task-based billing. This billing format is available from all law firms. If one insists upon it, they will comply. The analysis of task-based bills can provide much useful information (there are firms, known as law-audit firms, which specialize in performing such analyses). In particular, task-based billing has the beneficial effect of restraining the tendency of law firms to overstaff (a practice formerly known as overmanning) a matter; for example, sending three attorneys to a deposition when only two would suffice. Also, by identifying the various timekeepers who are billing time to a matter, task-based billing highlights the introduction of new players to the team. This is important because new players must be brought up to speed— briefed on the facts and the status of the case, a process that is time-consuming (both the briefer and the briefee are billing their time) and, hence, costly.

The obvious goal is to involve the fewest possible people in the case. A client should be careful not to let lawyers use his case as a convenient account to which they can bill otherwise unbillable time (this practice should be familiar to anyone who has worked for a government contractor) nor allow the firm to use the case as a training vehicle for interns and new associates. Let them train their employees at someone else's expense. Moreover, law firms that know they are being monitored simply perform more efficiently.

Check on a firm's policy with respect to disbursements. Some firms take a surprisingly narrow view of what is covered by their hourly fees—virtually everything is a disbursement. One firm, in the authors' experience, charged a fee for the use of the firm's own library. Another firm (more aggressive than creative) simply tacked on a "Misc. fee." A surprising number of firms will mark up their disbursements, adding a profit margin. Sometimes this is disguised as an accounting fee or administrative fee. Such a markup is unethical if it is not disclosed to the client and tacky when it is. Some firms will add an overtime charge to a client's bill, reflecting additional compensation paid to support staff who may have worked late. Such charges may be acceptable when the overtime was necessitated by the demands of the case. They are clearly not acceptable when they result from poor scheduling or understaffing by the firm.

Read legal bills carefully, and do not hesitate to object to charges that may be improper or staffing practices that may be considered undesirable. Do this promptly (if 'twere done, 'twere best done quickly), before the amounts in dispute grow.

Finally, pay legal bills promptly. The law firm is not a banker and has not agreed to finance the litigation. A client that pays on time is in a much better position to win concessions from its law firm.

Sharing the Risks—And the Rewards

Contingency fees involve an agreement between the client and the law firm that the latter will be compensated solely out of the proceeds of the case. Some law firms will also advance the funds needed to litigate the case—the costs of litigation (e.g., filing and service fees, fees for expert witnesses and court reporters, and travel expenses); others will not. In either event, it is readily apparent that the law firm has accepted the risk that it will not be paid or that it will not be paid in full. If the law firm has advanced the costs of litigation, it runs the further risk of losing the funds it has advanced. To compensate for this risk, and also simply because they have the economic power to do so, law firms that undertake cases on a contingency basis typically demand a percentage of the projected recovery that would yield a fee three to four times the fee that would have been accrued on a time-based fee basis. Thus, it should be clear that the contingency fee arrangement is the most costly to the client and should be utilized only out of necessity.

It is commonly understood that lawyers undertaking a case on a contingency fee basis take a third of any recovery. This is a gross oversimplification. Like most things in life, lawyers' contingency fees are subject to negotiation. Even in a contingency arrangement, there should be a correlation between the effort expended and the reward reaped. Few patent infringement suits actually proceed through trial (only about 4 percent); most are settled. Settlement can occur at any point in the proceedings (although, most commonly, after the Markman hearing). It is this fact that provides the basis for negotiation. Often, the firm will agree to a graduated scale of recovery, with the rate tied to the stage at which the matter is concluded.

As might well be suspected, there are numerous possible combinations of the three basic fee approaches. Sometimes, such blended arrangements include a cap on any contingency fee, often coupled with a guaranteed minimum. The best arrangement is the one that best serves the needs of the parties. That being said, a fee arrangement preferred by the authors involves an equal mixture of time-based billing and contingency fee. The client pays the costs of litigation and one-half of the conventional time-based fee, and agrees to pay one-half of the conventional contingency fee. Since most law firms have an overhead rate of 40 to 50 percent, such an arrangement eliminates their risk in the matter— at worst, they will break even. At the same time, the sizable contingency provides motivation to succeed. If several firms reject such an arrangement or decline to take a case on a conventional contingency fee basis, it might be considered that they are, cumulatively, saying something about the perceived merits of the case (or lack of same).

Strategies and Tactics of Enforcement

Tactics is the plan for fighting a battle. *Strategy* is the plan for winning the war (i.e., reaching the specified objective).

Successful patent enforcement, like a successful military operation, often hinges upon the possession of intelligence (i.e., knowledge of the enemy). In business, intelligence gathering is called market research and competitive analysis. Gather as much intelligence as possible before embarking on a campaign of patent enforcement. Continue intelligence-gathering activities until the campaign has ended.

Note that patent enforcement is described in terms of a campaign. Patent infringement is, most often, not confined to a single offender. Frequently, it spreads across an industry. If an infringer is identified, investigate its competitors. It is likely that at least some of them are infringing as well. If such is the case, a program of patent enforcement becomes a campaign against an industry.

Choosing a Defendant

When gentle persuasion proves unsuccessful, it is time to take up the cudgel. Having identified multiple infringers, the first question that must be addressed is which infringer(s) to sue first. The recommendation is often made, more often by well-intentioned laypersons (here a euphemism for "idiot"; known to lawyers as "officious intermeddlers") than by experienced attorneys, to first tackle the biggest and strongest infringer. The theory here is that, after successfully defeating such an infringer, all others will fall into line, taking licenses without further fuss. *Do not listen to such people.* Such advice is tantamount to butting one's head against a wall in preference to opening a door and walking through. Choose the weakest opponent, not the strongest one; choose the one most likely to settle, not the one most likely (and able) to resist.

While there is invariably great reluctance on the part of most business executives to be the first to take a license under a patent or patent portfolio, there is much less reluctance to be the second. As the number of licensees grows, each successive license becomes easier to conclude. This being so, there is good reason to leave the most intransigent offenders to be dealt with last. Also, as the number of licensees grows, the cost of the licenses increases. Thus, the most difficult and recalcitrant infringers, dealt with last, generally pay the most—proving that there is some justice in the world.

Having decided to first harvest the low-hanging fruit, the question devolves to one of identification: Which infringers are least likely to mount an aggressive defense? This is an area where intelligence proves its worth. Corporations, like natural persons, have personalities—some are aggressive gamblers, others are risk-averse. Much can be learned from studying an infringer's past history. Does it litigate often? When it does litigate, does it settle early or fight to the bitter end? Publicly traded firms, managed by professional managers, tend to be more conservative than privately held concerns. Corporate managers fear shareholder reaction to a costly defeat. Small firms, where the founder is the president and owns all, or virtually all, of the equity, should be approached with particular care. Such leaders are often strongly opinionated and answerable to no one. Suing one of these companies is often akin to attacking a tar baby; even when victory is achieved, the costs may exceed the amount recovered.

Another factor to be considered when selecting a first target is the possibility of so-called *pendant claims*—claims, other than patent infringement, which arise out of the same activity of the defendant. For example, there may also be claims for trademark or copyright infringement, for breach of the obligations of a confidential disclosure agreement, or even for breach of a previously granted license agreement. The presence of such claims confers several advantages.

First, it sharply reduces the probability that the defendant will succeed in avoiding a trial. Most defendants initially react to a suit by loudly and belligerently asserting that the case is without merit—that the patent is invalid and, even if it is valid, it is not infringed—and that the court will dismiss the suit (in some cases, these assertions are actually made in good faith). If pendant claims are present, a defendant that succeeds in establishing patent invalidity or noninfringement is still faced with the prospect of trial with respect to the other claims. This factor alone may cause a defendant to consider settlement more seriously.

Second, it is obvious that the greater the number of claims presented, the greater the probability that the plaintiff will prevail with respect to at least one of them. Lastly, and perhaps most importantly, the presence of pendant claims may allow the plaintiff to introduce evidence casting the defendant in an unfavorable light. A trial (especially a jury trial) is, to a considerable extent, a morality play—an episode in the continuing struggle between good and evil. Quite early in a trial, a jury decides which party is the good guy and which is the bad guy. All evidence presented thereafter is considered, evaluated, and accepted or rejected in the context of this decision.

While a jury may not fully understand the finer points of patent law (who does?), it is comfortable with the more universal concepts of lying, stealing, and taking unfair advantage. It is on this basis that a jury will ultimately render its verdict. If one of the universe of potential defendants has engaged in extensive communications with the patentee, inquired about product enhancements or further developments, or inquired about a possible license, that is the defendant of choice. Stated succinctly, choose the defendant against which success is most likely.

Other infringers that should be considered as candidates for a starring role in early litigation are those undergoing reorganization—acquisitions, mergers, spin-offs, divestitures, leveraged buyouts, public offerings, and so on—where the risks and distractions of litigation would be particularly unwelcome. These conditions often motivate a defendant to settle. Similarly, companies in weak financial condition or those committed to risky and expensive projects may also be inclined to settle. However, it is extremely frustrating to prevail at trial or secure a favorable settlement only to have the victory obviated by the bankruptcy of the defendant. Weak is good; too weak is not good—another example of the value of good intelligence.

Like war, patent enforcement may be defensive or offensive in nature. Defensive patent enforcement is directed to the protection of the monopoly supposedly secured by the patent-in-suit. It seeks to eliminate infringers who are poaching in the patented preserve. Offensive patent enforcement is most often directed to the extraction of value from otherwise unexploited (noncore) patents. It seeks to recover royalties from those using the subject inventions. Less often, offensive patent enforcement comprises an attempt to break into a protected market by attacking and overcoming the guardian patent through a declaratory judgment action.

Developing a Strategy

Given that strategy is the plan for reaching an objective, the first step in developing a strategy is to clearly define the objective. Defining the objective too narrowly may lead to faulty strategy. For example, the objective of defensive patent enforcement may be to maintain an effective monopoly in the field of the patented invention. Obviously, obtaining a permanent injunction barring further infringement of the patent accomplishes this objective.

Consider, however, an infringer for whom use of this patented product is vital; for example, it is necessary for production of the infringer's only product. Imposition of an injunction, coupled with a refusal to subsequently grant a license in respect of the patent-in-suit, might well have a fatal impact on the infringer—it might put such an infringer out of business. Faced with such a catastrophic possibility, the infringer would have no choice but to fight to the bitter end. Such a reaction is clearly not to the advantage of the patentee. The infringer might succeed in proving the patent-in-suit invalid, unenforceable, or not infringed. Even if the patentee ultimately prevails in court, the costs of the matter may render the victory Pyrrhic at best.

If, however, the objective of the defensive enforcement is viewed not as securing an injunction but as profit maximization (the ultimate objective of all business strategies), a new solution is possible—namely, licensing the infringer. By adding to the infringer's cost, the patentee retains a competitive advantage in the relevant market and receives a royalty, while avoiding the costs and risks of litigation to the death. If such an objective is indeed viable, the patentee could pursue a more flexible strategy of litigating to the point of maximum advantage—the point beyond which the costs of further litigation exceed the benefits derived therefrom—and then settling.

Determining the point of maximum advantage requires a careful analysis of the value actually being derived from the patent monopoly. Often, the result of such an analysis is surprising. For example, where the patentee lacks the resources to completely satisfy the demand for the patented product or service and does not foresee obtaining those re-sources in the near future, the presence of another supplier in the market may not result in lost sales and, indeed, may not even result in any price erosion. In such event, it would be advantageous to convert an infringer to a licensee, rather than wasting resources in seeking an injunction. Similarly, it may be determined that the market for the patented product or service is segmented and that the infringer is positioned in a segment that is not presently addressed by the patentee nor likely to be so addressed in the near future. In such situations, the license will not only create a revenue source but, more importantly, may be used as a tool to prevent the former infringer from expanding into the market segment occupied by the patentee.

Patent Reexamination: To Reexamine or Not to Reexamine, That Is the Question

Patent reexamination is, in essence, a procedure for removing uncertainty as to the validity of claims of an issued patent. The procedure is available to all—patentees as well as third parties. The reexamination procedure allows a patent examiner to reopen the prosecution of the patent to consider prior art that had not been considered prior to issue.

Until recently, all patent reexamination was *ex parte*—anyone could initiate a reexamination, but only the patentee could communicate with the patent examiner after the process had commenced. This ability to respond to the examiner, indeed to bring substantial resources to bear, without any reply from a third-party petitioner, gave the patentees a decided advantage. As a result of these factors, approximately 70 percent of reexamined claims survived reexamination, without the need for any amendment.

More importantly, once prior art had been cited to the Patent Office as the basis for a reexamination and successfully overcome by the patentee, its value as a basis of attacking the validity of the patent at trial was, for all practical purposes, destroyed. If a patent examiner has found the patent valid a second time (a so-called twice-blessed patent), neither a judge nor a jury is likely to find to the contrary.

Thus, if on the eve of filing suit or (after suit has been filed) during pretrial discovery, potentially invalidating prior art is uncovered, what is to be done? Should reexamination be sought? The answer to that question (like many legal questions) is "It depends."

Given the aforementioned reexamination advantage, the patentee, under these circumstances, may well opt for reexamination. Indeed, where the defendant (or prospective defendant) is relying primarily on the defense of patent invalidity, a successful reexamination may induce settlement.

When the defendant asks the same question, the answer is not as clear. The facile response, of course, is that reexamination favors the patentee; it should not be sought by the accused infringer. In actuality, the decision is not quite so simple; it may well depend upon whether the accused has other, effective responses to the charge of infringement—invalidity due to prior sale or public use, failure to disclose the best mode of practicing the invention, lack of enablement, or noninfringement—which can be presented to a trier of fact. If such other defenses exist, the accused may well decide to accept the procedural handicap and present the highly technical, complex arguments as to invalidity to a patent examiner who is trained to understand them. If these arguments succeed and the patent claims are rejected as unpatentable in view of the newly cited prior art, the accused has prevailed. If the patent claims survive reexamination, the accused still may present to a judge or jury those other defenses that are more comprehensible to the layman.

There is a second type of reexamination that (in theory) will eliminate the advantage presently enjoyed by the patentee. The new form of reexamination, known as an *inter partes* proceeding, allows the reexamination petitioner (the party that initiated the reexamination) to participate in the reexamination. The new procedure is only available with respect to patents issued on applications filed on or after November 29, 1999.

This ability to participate is the good news for a defendant or prospective defendant. The bad news is that, having initiated an *inter partes* reexamination, the petitioner will be estopped (barred or prevented) from presenting, at a subsequent trial, any defense which was raised or *could have been raised* during the reexamination. It remains to be seen how serious an effect this provision will have. Indeed, at this point, the tactical implications of *inter partes* reexamination remain unclear.

Trial versus Settlement

Litigation involves risk—lots of it. Litigation, especially patent enforcement litigation, is very expensive. These are two good reasons to consider settlement rather than trial.

Historical data indicates that the odds are on the side of the patentee in a patent infringement suit. This is well and good; but, before drawing too much comfort from such data, you should consider the true nature of these statistics. They are an example of the law of large numbers. (For those who are mathematically challenged, the law of large numbers essentially states that as the number of events increases, the actual results will converge on the mathematically calculated results.) Thus, historical data provide a good prediction of the cumulative results of a large number of events. They do not provide nearly as good an indication of the result of the next single event. If a large number of cases are to be litigated, the results will likely approximate the historical statistics for such litigation. However, few patentees litigate a large number of cases. Most patentees will litigate one or, at most, a few cases. For these patentees, the historical data may have limited relevance.

For example, let us assume that one wishes to play Russian roulette (a good analogy to patent enforcement trials). Mathematics tells us that, in any single game, the odds are five to one that the hammer will fall on an empty chamber. If the game is played six times, the odds are that the player will only lose once. However, it is just as likely that the loss will occur in the first game as in the second game, or in the third game, or so on. A player who loses the first game never gets to play again.

The typical patentee, trying a suit for the patent infringement, is in much the same situation. If the patent is held invalid or unenforceable (i.e., dead), there will be no more trials. If the patent is found valid and enforceable but not infringed, the patentee may well lack sufficient resources (money) to try a second suit against a different infringer.

Most inventors are justifiably proud of their inventions. Some inventors are blinded by their pride. They will insist that a jury is certain to comprehend the merits of their inventions. *Do not listen to such people.* While it is true that historical data indicates that juries have somewhat of a pro-patent bias, juries are unpredictable. Post-trial discussions with jurors, or studies of so-called mock or shadow juries, consistently show that juries often reach their decisions based upon matters considered trivial or even irrelevant by both plaintiff and defendant. This is especially true when neither side can present a clearly more sympathetic image than the other and the case is to be decided upon purely technical (i.e., boring) grounds. If one can't entertain the jury or garner their sympathy, one can't count on their support. The same applies to judges. However well versed in the law, precious few judges ever studied the sciences or engineering. The more complex (incomprehensible) the technology of a case, the less likely the case will be decided on technological grounds. In many cases, going to trial is a poor (here, a euphemism for "dumb") risk-management technique.

Settlement avoids risk. It keeps the decision making in the hands of (supposedly) knowledgeable and educated executives rather than in the hands of 12 bored jurors who generally are angry that they have been dragooned into jury duty. Settlement saves costs and avoids the distractions engendered by litigation. More importantly, litigation has few possible outcomes, while settlements can be structured to meet the peculiar needs of the parties. Finally, settlement tends to bring an end to the hostilities engendered by litigation. Think carefully before deciding to roll the dice because, to an unhappy extent, that is what occurs at trial. If you wish to gamble, go to a casino, where at least the drinks are free.

Alternative Dispute Resolution: Blessed Are the Peacemakers

It should be apparent to the reader that patent enforcement litigation is, at best, costly, time-consuming, and distracting. (If it is *not* apparent, reread the "Patent Infringement" section of this chapter.) Fortunately, there are other avenues to the resolution of patent disputes, known collectively as *alternative dispute resolution.*

Although an infinite number of variations exist (and new ones are constantly being proposed), the different forms of alternative dispute resolution may be loosely categorized in three classes:

1. Mediation.

2. Arbitration.

3. Private trial.

Mediation involves the introduction of a neutral third party who seeks to facilitate agreement between the disputants. It is quick and inexpensive. Success at resolution through mediation, however, is largely dependent upon the interpersonal skills, experience, creativity, and professional stature of the mediator. While a mediator cannot force the parties to settle, a mediator whose opinions are highly valued and, hence, accepted by both disputants may succeed in bringing them to a resolution. In general, however, mediation is not highly regarded, as the success rate is low. It seems to work best when it is truly voluntary and when the participants have full settlement authority, including sufficient rank and discretion that they needn't subsequently explain themselves to others. If these twin conditions are not satisfied, what ensues is merely a conclave of sullen flunkies whose only goal is to gather intelligence concerning their opponent's case, while disclosing none of their own. Mediation may be sought at any time, even during litigation (most commonly after discovery has been completed). This is, in fact, encouraged by the courts (judges do not find patent infringement trials entertaining).

Like mediation, arbitration involves the introduction of a neutral third party (most often a group of three neutral parties) into the dispute. Yet, where a mediator seeks to facilitate resolution, an arbitrator imposes one. Arbitration is final in that it is, for all practical purposes, unappealable. Arbitrators are not required to state the reasons or basis for their decision, nor are they obligated to follow the law, either statutory or precedential, substantive or procedural (hence the term, an *arbitrary decision*). Thus, in many respects, arbitration is even more unpredictable than litigation. There seems to be, however, a noticeable tendency on the part of arbitrators to split the baby, giving something to each party. Finally, although arbitration is less costly and time-consuming than litigation, it is far from rapid or inexpensive. Arbitration does, however, often yield a certain equality—leaving both parties equally angry and frustrated.

Private trial is the least utilized and most varied category of alternative dispute resolution devices. At one extreme, the parties retain a retired judge, who tries the case exactly as if it were being prosecuted within the judicial system. Because the judge has only one case on his docket, the matter progresses much more rapidly than it would have had it been brought to court. At the other extreme, in the so-called minitrial, each side is given a limited period of time (commonly half a day) to present its case, after which the judge, or sometimes a panel of judges, renders a decision. Private trials offer the considerable advantage of a reasoned opinion. However, since the decision is unappealable, the possession of a written opinion may be of little consolation to the losing party. Private trials are comparatively quick and economical, especially the minitrial, although the degree of formality (along with the cost and duration) tends to increase in proportion to the stakes at risk.

An interesting combination of the private trial and mediation involves a minitrial attended by one or more executives from each of the disputing parties. At the close of the case, the judge attempts to mediate a settlement by the attending executives. Often, the minitrial hearing is the first time that senior executives have heard a full, uninterrupted, and unfiltered presentation of their opponent's case. Such a hearing may have a powerful impact on those who previously had been led to believe that the opposing case was meritless.

Whatever the approach selected, alternative dispute resolution can be tailored to meet the needs and desires of the parties involved. Moreover, it is private. It creates no transcript and no precedent (although documents produced may be subject to discovery in subsequent litigation).

Summary

A patent claim is infringed when each of the claim limitations is found in the accused device or process. Infringement may be either literal or under the doctrine of equivalents. Literal infringement occurs when the claim language literally reads on the accused device or process. If a claim limitation is not literally met, but the corresponding structure in the accused device performs substantially the same function, in substantially the same way, to achieve the same result, the claim may be infringed under the doctrine of equivalents.

One who actively induces infringement of a patent is liable as an infringer. One who sells a component of a patented invention, knowing the component to be a nonstandard item especially adapted for use in an infringement of the patent, is liable as a contributory infringer.

The chief limitation on the doctrine of equivalents is file wrapper estoppel, which prevents recapturing, through a broad interpretation of claim language, scope that was surrendered during prosecution of the patent application. The decision in the *Festo* case has retroactively eliminated all equivalents of any claim limitation that was amended during prosecution.

Patent litigation involves the risks that the patent(s)-in-suit will be found to be invalid, unenforceable, or not infringed. Moreover, it is possible that a prevailing patentee will recover less than the costs of the litigation.

Suit may only be brought in a court that has jurisdiction over both the subject matter of the litigation (subject matter litigation) and the person of the defendant (personal jurisdiction). Personal jurisdiction may be based upon the defendant's place of residence or, in some circumstances, upon the defendant's actions (long arm jurisdiction). In addition, suit may only be brought in the proper venue, which is that court or courts, among all those having jurisdiction, where the rules provide that the case may be heard. Choice of venue may have a significant impact on the cost and outcome of litigation.

Generally speaking, plaintiffs in patent infringement lawsuits should demand a jury, rather than a bench trial, as they thereby have a greater chance of prevailing.

A party that has standing may bring an action, called a declaratory judgment (DJ) action, seeking to have a patent held invalid, unenforceable, or not infringed. Standing is essentially a reasonable belief of an imminent suit for infringement by a patentee. Such a belief may arise out of communications from the patentee to a possible infringer.

A prevailing plaintiff in a patent infringement action may be awarded, as damages, either lost profits or a reasonable royalty. Lost profits are the incremental profits that would have been earned by the patentee if the patentee had made the sales that were, in fact, made by the infringer. A reasonable royalty is the royalty that would have been agreed upon, by a willing licensor and a willing licensee, at the time the infringement began.

A prevailing patentee should consider damages resulting from price erosion (i.e., the need to reduce prices to compete with an infringer). In addition, the effect of the infringement on the sales of associated products or services should be considered. Sales of these products or services are known as convoyed sales.

If sales of a product are driven by the inclusion of a patented improvement, the sale price of the entire product may be the appropriate basis for the calculation of damages for the infringement of the patent on the improvement. This is known as the entire market value rule (EMV rule).

Patent infringement litigation, like all civil litigation, is commenced by the service of a summons and complaint. Thereafter, the defendant files an appearance and an answer and, generally, files affirmative defenses and counterclaims.

Claim construction is now a matter of law to be decided by the trial judge at a so-called Markman hearing, which is most commonly held after the pleadings are closed and a limited amount of discovery, directed to claim construction, has been made.

Two of the most common responses to a charge of patent infringement are (1) "I invented the accused product myself," and (2) "I purchased the accused product from another." Neither response is legally sufficient.

Laches and estoppel are two commonly encountered legal defenses. Both relate to a failure to take reasonably prompt action against known infringers. Laches bars recovery of past damages. Estoppel, which involves an affirmative act by the patentee that leads the accused infringer to believe it will remain unmolested, bars any recovery by the patentee.

When seeking legal representation, a law firm should be selected on the basis of its quality, flexibility, and price.

There are three basic approaches to attorney compensation: fixed fees, time-based billing, and contingency fees. Fixed fees are virtually never found in patent infringement cases. When using time-based billing, insist on detailed bills specifying the tasks performed, the amount of time devoted to each task, and the timekeeper(s) who performed each task (so-called task-based billing). Contingency fees are often subject to negotiation.

Patent enforcement is often a campaign against an industry. In such cases, a first defendant must be selected. Several factors should be considered when making this selection: a party's strength and ability to mount a strong defense; a party's past history—whether they settle or fight vigorously; the presence of so-called pendant claims—claims, other than patent infringement, which arise out of the same activity by the party; and a party's engagement in activities such as mergers, acquisitions, spin-offs, divestitures, and so on, which would constitute a distraction and might incline the party to settle any litigation.

Litigation requires a strategy, which in turn requires a clearly defined objective. Defining the objective too narrowly can result in faulty strategy by foreclosing otherwise advantageous resolutions or settlements.

Reexamination of a patent is a procedure whereby prosecution is reopened to allow the patent examiner to consider prior art not considered during the original prosecution. Uncertainty as to the validity of a patent, in light of newly discovered prior art, can often be resolved by reexamination.

The risks and costs inherent in litigation may be avoided by settlement. Additionally, the parties may structure a settlement to meet their peculiar needs.

In lieu of litigation, the parties may elect alternative dispute resolution. The various types of alternative dispute resolution may be divided into three loose categories: mediation, arbitration, and private trials.

CHAPTER 9

The Fundamental Things Apply, As Time Goes By: Intellectual Property in Cyberspace

After reading this chapter you will be able to:

- Understand the special problems posed by business method patents and e-commerce.
- Understand the relation of domain names to trademarks.
- Understand the particular copyright problems presented by the Internet.

Business Method Patents and E-Commerce

Intellectual property in cyberspace is, essentially, the same as intellectual property in the real, brick-and-mortar world, where corporations are managed by adults and have earnings. The reader need not fear—everything (hopefully) learned from the preceding chapters and (again, hopefully) to be learned from the succeeding ones also applies to the new economy. A patent is still a patent. A trademark is still a trademark, albeit issues may arise with respect to conflicting domain names. And a copyright is still a copyright (much to the chagrin of the folks at Napster).

167

It had long been considered axiomatic, by patent attorneys and agents, that neither algorithms nor methods of doing business were patentable. This belief, which was surprisingly lacking in precedential support, was laid to rest by the Court of Appeals for the Federal Circuit (CAFC) (*State Street Bank & Trust Co. v. Signature Financial Group, Inc.*, 149 F.3d 1368 [Fed. Cir. 1998]). Now business methods are (theoretically) patentable (see Chapter 11, the section on *Bilski*), although no one seems able to agree upon a definition of the term, least of all Congress. The American Inventors Protection Act gives the public certain prior-use rights with respect to business method patents, without precisely identifying those patents to which it applies (see Exhibit 9.1). Basically, however, the term encompasses three broad categories:

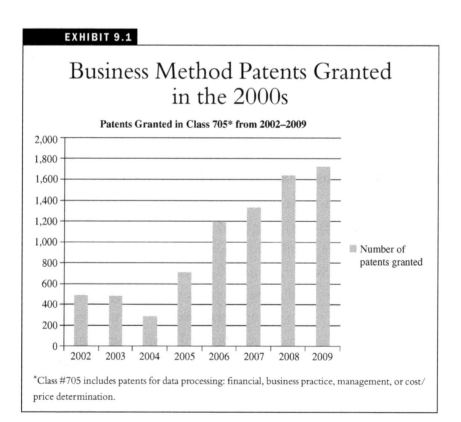

EXHIBIT 9.1

Business Method Patents Granted in the 2000s

Patents Granted in Class 705* from 2002–2009

*Class #705 includes patents for data processing: financial, business practice, management, or cost/price determination.

1. Patents directed to the use of computers to perform traditional business functions.

2. The so-called e-commerce category—patents directed to inventions pertaining to the Internet and electronic commerce.

3. Patents directed to new methods of doing business that do not necessarily involve the Internet.

Tradition, Tradition!

Traditionally, scientists and engineers who had become familiar with the patent system's requirements as to the best mode and an enabling disclosure (through continued exposure to the patent system) were the ones who created patentable inventions. (If the terms *best mode* and *enabling disclosure* seem unfamiliar, see Chapter 1.)

These scientists and engineers generally were familiar with the pertinent prior art. Often, they were employed by business organizations that had created forms and procedures for disclosing new inventions; sometimes, these organizations even had an in-house patent department. Almost invariably, the inventors were able to provide plans, drawings, circuit diagrams, chemical formulas, and so on to an attorney charged with preparing a patent application. Not uncommonly, prototypes had been built and test results were available. All of these factors combined to maximize the quality of the resultant patent applications, while facilitating their preparation and, hence, minimizing their cost. None, or few, of these factors are present with respect to business method inventions.

Business method inventions are frequently created by first-timers—people, such as computer programmers, salespeople, and marketing personnel, who have not previously had any contact with the patent system. Often, they are employed (*if* they are employed) by organizations that are themselves first-timers and that can provide no institutional support. The inventors of business method inventions seem always to be in a hurry. Rather like Alice's rabbit, they are in much too much of a hurry to stop and describe their invention to an attorney. They don't know, or can't be bothered to describe, the prior art (no invention is an island—there is *always* prior art). They really haven't worked out all the details of their invention (these are generally big-picture people), but they assume that a few words and perhaps a sketch will suffice. Often, it does suffice—the attorney spins straw into gold and completes a patent application. Such spinning, however, is time-consuming and, therefore, costly (again, if this doesn't sound familiar, reread Chapter 1). The cost of preparing a business method patent application is typically about $15,000 (not including filing fees, amendments, issue fees, maintenance fees, automatic transmission, or white-wall tires).

Problems, Problems, Problems

One of the first, and arguably the most important, steps in the examination of a patent application is the patent examiner's search for pertinent prior art. It is this prior art against which the examiner will assess the novelty and nonobviousness of the claimed invention. To find these documents, examiners rely on the Patent Office search files—a voluminous collection of documents carefully arranged according to subject. Because they are in a convenient format and are already categorized in accord with the Patent Office system, the vast majority of the documents in the search files are earlier-issued patents. Thus, as a practical matter, the examiner's search, with respect to an application undergoing examination, is a search for previously issued patents in that field of technology.

Generally, the system functions well, but not in the case of business method patents. Until a decade or so ago, there *were* no business method patents. Hence, there were no earlier-issued ones in the search files when the examiners performed their searches. The result: The earliest applications for these patents, filed after the *State Street Bank* decision opened the floodgates, sailed through the Patent Office to issue. Many of these patents are, to say the least, of questionable validity (a fact known to many in the industry). The Patent Office, having recognized the problem, has taken substantial steps to address it. A database has been created of various nonpatent documents, such as technical reports, product literature, and papers presented at meetings of professional associations pertaining to this field, and applications for business method patents are now examined twice. Yet even these efforts have only ameliorated but not solved the problem, because much of what was previously done was never openly documented. Since business methods were believed to be unpatentable—and at the time, they were—no one bothered to record and publish the results of their labors. Thus, the problem persists, albeit in a somewhat reduced degree, and criticism continues to be leveled at business method patents.

Another problem pertains to the scope of the patents. Even if (a very big *if*) they are valid, they are often narrow in scope. To a great extent, this is because many (if not most) business method patents rely on computer processing: Steps are performed by computers, which can, at very little cost, be reprogrammed so as to achieve substantially the same result through an entirely different procedure. Not only does this weakness reduce the value of the patent as a tool for securing a marketplace monopoly, it also limits the value of the patent as a tool for securing royalties through licensing to others. The cost of designing around the patent sets an upper limit on the amount of royalties a licensee would be willing to pay.

Ironically, another problem may arise if the patent *does* enable its owner to completely dominate a particular technology. The nature of e-commerce is such that the profitability of participation in a market is sometimes dependent upon the efforts of others who develop and make available to consumers additional applications and variations of a basic technology. If a patentee exercises too much control of a technology, these others may simply turn to an alternate technology, leaving the patentee to dominate a barren and dying market. It has, for example, been suggested that Sony exercised too much control over the Beta vid-eotape technology, causing its competitors to turn to the alternate VHS. In the end, the more widely available VHS became the popularly accepted standard, while Beta lapsed into obscurity. Similarly, a newly developed computer system is unlikely to be widely purchased unless and until there is a broad variety of compatible software available. These considerations must be borne in mind when licensing strategies are being developed.

If business method patents are so expensive and suffer from such infirmities, why are they so popular? The answer, again, rests largely on the nature of e-commerce, populated as it is by many fledgling busi-nesses (is that a proper description for an activity with no revenues?) with no assets beyond an idea or a concept. If such businesses (hobbies, social clubs?) are to raise capital, it can only be on the basis of their intel-lectual property. There must be a patent or a pending patent application to exhibit to venture capitalists or prospective shareholders. Indeed, given the short life span of such technologies, and the long periods of pendency in the Patent Office (currently well in excess of three years for business method patents), patent applications may be nearly as valuable and effective as issued patents.

Finally, for all its shortcomings, a business method patent does confer a first-mover advantage. Even if it can be circumvented or ulti-mately shown to be invalid, it may secure for the patentee a window of opportunity in which to establish itself in the marketplace.

Trademarks and Domain Names

Domain names are, in simple terms, the telephone numbers of the Inter-net. They allow us to send and receive messages (e-mail) and to reach desired web sites (information, products and services, advertising, games, and so on). Like telephone numbers, domain names must be unique. However, unlike telephone numbers, domain names are not a standard number of digits (ten, including the area code) assigned, seemingly at random, by the local telephone company. Rather, a company or other user chooses a name and applies to the Internet Corporation for Assigned Names and Numbers (ICANN) for registration. Unless the identical (and we do mean *identical*) name is already registered, the application will be granted.

Given virtually complete freedom to choose a domain name, most individuals and organizations select names that are easy to remember and are readily identified with their owners. Businesses, in particular, often choose names that constitute or incorporate their best-known trademarks or service marks. Sometimes, however, a business notices, to its chagrin, that its mark, or one confusingly similar thereto, has already been used in a domain name registered to another. Occasionally (actually, rarely) this is mere coincidence. More often, it is the prelude to what amounts to an attempt at extortion, when the registrant offers to sell the registration (prices in the range of $10,000 to $50,000 have been typical).

This type of activity, known as cybersquatting, is prohibited by the Anticybersquatting Consumer Protection Act (ACPA), which bars the registration, transfer, or use of a domain name that is identical or confusingly similar to the trademark of another, or which dilutes a famous mark, when such activity is done in bad faith. Those who believe that they are the victims of cybersquatting can have recourse to the federal courts, where they may seek to recover the domain name owner's profits, actual damages, and costs. The act does, however, also include an interesting antibullying provision. If a trademark owner knowingly misrepresents that a domain name is infringing or diluting its mark, the trademark owner may be held liable for resultant damages suffered by the domain name owner. To facilitate the resolution of disputes, ICANN has instituted an arbitration procedure whereby a trademark owner may object to the registration of a domain name by another; when successful, the contested domain name registration is canceled or assigned to the trademark owner.

Copyright and the Internet

In our legal system, *the law* comprises not only statutes but also the decisions of the various courts that have applied the statutes to the facts presented by cases being heard (*stare decisis*). Each succeeding court decision, interpreting and defining the statutes or previous court decisions, in turn becomes part of the body of the law. Court decisions are constantly adapting the law to meet the needs of our ever-evolving world. Nowhere is this practice more visible than in regard to the application of the copyright law (Title 17, U.S. Code) to the new, exciting (lawyerspeak for "opportunity to charge a lot"), and challenging (lawyerspeak for "opportunity to *really* charge a lot") problems presented by the Internet.

Copyright and Web Pages

As the reader should expect, web pages, like any original work of authorship, are protectable under the copyright law. Every time a page is downloaded from a web site, a copy of it is made in the user's computer. Permission of the copyright holder is required before this can be done. The problem of securing such permission is compounded by the fact that a single web page may include articles (works) by different authors; hence, there are often several copyright holders from whom authorization to copy may be required. Arguably, when material is placed on the Web, webmasters intend that it should be downloaded, even if this is not explicitly stated. Such an intent may evidence an implied license to download. Nevertheless, who wants to rely on "may," especially when it is not clear that the webmaster had the authority to give such permission in the first place?

While most web site owners would complain about copying, others may complain about linking because it burdens their servers. Does placing of a link from one site to another constitute copyright infringement? Although the law is still unclear on this issue, it seems to be moving toward "yes." Although most links are unlikely to arouse the wrath of the copyright owner, several caveats are warranted.

Direct links to content that would normally be framed elsewhere are apt to cause objections. At present, there is little precedent on this issue because the few parties involved in such disputes have settled them. Still, if a linking page surrounds another's material with its own ads, cuts out another's ads, or makes it appear that the linking site is the source of the linked material, trouble is likely. Moreover, consider situations where linked material infringes another's copyright. Most commonly, a copyright holder would act (threaten, sue, assault) against only the party responsible for the directly infringing page; others linked to the infringing page would remain unaffected (probably even unaware of the infringement). However, where a direct infringer is beyond the effective reach of local courts, and particularly where a site owner actively encourages use of an offending page, there may well be action taken against the owner of the linked site.

Copyright and Video Streaming

Copyright protection has long been the anchor that justified the billions of dollars spent to produce movies, television shows, and just about anything else involving video programming. Now the ability to turn anything into a digital video file means that anyone can create a perfect copy, throw it onto the Internet, and become a global pirate. The situation, which some claim could ruin the business model that makes all of this content possible in the first place, has already proven vexing.

Music royalties can be broken down into two primary types: performance and mechanical. Performance royalties are paid into a copyright pool when, for instance, a song is played in a public place such as a bar or restaurant. But mechanical royalties go directly to artists and record companies based on actual product sales.

How will cable operators and programmers divide licensing fees and advertising revenue in the Internet age, much less figure out copyright issues?

These central questions surround any type of digital streaming of content. For now, it's an issue of the PC versus the TV. But in the future, copyright royalty collection will become even more complicated as interactive TV platforms proliferate.

Copyright and Music on the Internet

The rapidly advancing technology of the Internet has spawned a plethora of legal entanglements as users explore the limits of the medium in the purchase and exchange of music. The latest war being raged in this arena is that over the MP3.

MP3 stands for moving picture experts group 1 (MPEG1), audio layer 3, and is a technique designed to compress bulky files of digitized music to facilitate ease of download and storage for bandwidth- and disk-space-starved music fans. Unlike its precursors, such as RealAudio, MP3 compression technology allows one to quickly download near–CD quality digitized sound recordings and to store them using minimal disk space. To copyright holders, this technology presents the threat of users being able to compile enormous libraries of pirated songs and to store them indefinitely, using only a small fraction of their hard drives. The files can also be easily attached to e-mail and sent to any number of friends or uploaded to other web sites.

The real threat to the recording industry, as the issue has been cast thus far, is that each successive copy is *identical to the original*; there is no loss in fidelity no matter the generation of the copy. It was precisely for this reason that the recording industry so vehemently opposed the introduction of DAT technology in the late 1980s and succeeded in the passage of the Audio Home Recording Act of 1992. Back in the days when the worst damage a wannabe music pirate could inflict was to dub his Aerosmith cassette and make copies for his friends, the industry did not worry as much about serial copying of copyrighted music. The marginal cost of making copies was constricted by the price of cassette tapes—not expensive, but enough to limit truly mass-scale copying for all but the most dedicated—and each successive copy was of poorer quality than the last. There was little market for a second-, third-, or fourth-generation scratchy home recording.

With the advent of MP3 and related technologies, that has all changed. Granted, making and listening to MP3s requires a computer and software, but the software is available for download from the Internet for free, along with simple instructions for its use. In addition, there is no shortage of affordable, portable MP3 players that can be used to play the music anywhere, eliminating the need to sit at one's computer in order to listen to the music.

Largely due to this ease of transmission and use, an underground movement in pirated MP3s has grown exponentially. As of January 2009, a music industry report claimed that 95 percent of music downloads were obtained without the copyright owner's permission. The industry has responded by waging an all-out war on MP3s, constantly monitoring the Web for signs of insurgence and sending cease and desist letters to the operators of infringing sites.

This war has largely been cast as a battle between the industry on one side and the artists and their fans on the other. Artists claim that the current system whereby they receive only pennies on the dollar for CD sales is archaic and that the Internet now provides a distribution medium that allows them to distribute their songs directly to their fans, cutting out the middleman. Music fans insist that paying $17.99 for a CD, which costs a small fraction of that to make, is a rip-off, and they cite the low royalties to artists as another reason for their ire. In some convolution of logic akin to a shoplifter's justification of only stealing from big businesses, they seem to be saying that it is okay to take the music because the sellers are making too much money from them.

IN THE REAL WORLD

The Cost of Free Music

In elementary school and Sunday school, we were repeatedly instructed that it was good—maybe even a religious obligation—to share what we had. Unfortunately for Jammie Thomas-Rasset, the federal court in Minnesota took a decidedly different view (*Capitol Records Inc. et al. v. Thomas-Rasset*).

A jury found the defendant guilty of illegally downloading 24 songs (I use that term advisedly) and assessed damages of $222,000. On appeal, Thomas-Rasset was awarded a new trial. The second jury again found her guilty, awarding $80,000 per song, or $1.92 million (yup, almost two million bucks) in damages. Then the chief judge described the second verdict as "monstrous and shocking" and ordered it reduced to $54,000. The plaintiffs rejected this amount and the case is now scheduled for a third trial.

The foregoing synopsis is presented as background to the more recent cases—yes folks, *two cases*—alleging similar nefarious conduct by one Joel Tenenbaum: *Sony BMG Music v. Tenenbaum* and *Capitol Records Inc. v. Alaujan* (Tenenbaum is a co-defendant with Alaujan).

In the Capitol Records case, a jury found Tenenbaum guilty of illegally downloading 30 songs and assessed damages of $675,000 (for those readers lacking ready access to a calculator, that's $22,500 per song). In post-trial motions, his attorney—a Harvard Law School professor—argued that the proper amount of damages was only about $21 (yes, twenty-one dollars) and that the jury's verdict was so excessive as to be unconstitutional. (Law professors *always* argue constitutionality.) In response, the judge noted that there was a legal question as to whether the professor had properly preserved the right to challenge the instructions given to the jury. Meanwhile, raising a constitutional challenge caused the government to intervene in the lawsuit to defend the constitutionality of the Copyright Act.

The lesson to be learned? Save yourself untold grief and expense and pay the 99 cents per song to download music from iTunes.

Summary

Intellectual property in cyberspace is much like intellectual property in more traditional businesses. Many of the problems associated with business method patents arise out of the fact that the prior art in this field was never documented and is not available to patent examiners during examination of business method patent applications. Although this problem has been somewhat ameliorated, many of the earliest-issued business method patents are of questionable validity.

Domain names are the telephone numbers of the Internet. Most individuals and businesses choose names that are readily identified with their owners. Some unscrupulous individuals seek to extort money by obtaining domain names that would be associated with famous individuals or businesses, a practice known as *cybersquatting*. Statutes have been enacted to prevent this. Copyright law is constantly evolving in response to new problems presented by the Internet. Partly as a result, the law in this area is rather unsettled.

CHAPTER 10

The Patent Portfolio and Its Effect on Stock Price

After reading this chapter you will be able to:

- Identify those firms in an industry that are likely to experience the greatest increase in value.

- Recognize three *figures of merit* useful in analyzing patent portfolios and their potential impact on stock price.

It is generally believed—or hoped—that research and development (R&D) expenditures by a business corporation will lead to increased profits and, ultimately, to an increase in the value of the corporation and the price of its stock. Empirical research tends to support this belief. It should be apparent, however, that all such expenditures do not produce equal results. Some R&D programs are technologically successful, while others are not. Some programs are focused on areas of declining interest or value, producing only incremental improvements to mature technologies, while other programs are pioneering efforts in promising new fields. Some otherwise successful R&D efforts result in products that are market failures.

The task, therefore, is to ascertain the value, as opposed to the cost, of a firm's intellectual assets, in such a manner as to provide an indicator of future stock appreciation. If this can be done, based upon publicly available information (the SEC is really cracking down on insider trading), one can attempt to forecast future stock performance and pick the winners. (*Question*: How can one leave Wall Street with a small fortune? *Answer*: Enter Wall Street with a large fortune.) Somewhat surprisingly, the necessary information is at hand, although it requires a little familiarity with patents and a considerable amount of compiling and massaging.

A very good picture of an organization's intellectual assets may be derived from an examination of its patent portfolio. By now, the reader should be aware that this information can be compiled either from public records of the Patent Office or online. The question, therefore, reduces to one of analyzing patent portfolios to determine which firms will experience the greatest increase in stock price. In essence, we need to identify some predictive portfolio characteristic or quality, so-called *figures of merit*. Fortunately, several such figures of merit have been developed and empirically tested by Baruch Lev, professor at the New York University Stern School of Business, and others. These portfolio characteristics include patent count, citation impact, and science linkage.

Patent Count

As the reader is undoubtedly aware, all patents are not equal. Some are much more valuable than others. Nevertheless, individual differences tend to be of less importance as the size of a portfolio increases (the law of large numbers rears its head once more). Thus, the number of patents in a firm's portfolio, the patent count, may be taken as an indicator of the intensity and the success rate of the firm's R&D activities. Within an industry, the relative size of a firm's patent portfolio, as compared to other firms in the same industry, has been found to correlate well with that firm's future ratio of stock price to book value (the SP/BV ratio).

Within an industry, the firms that have the greatest number of patents tend to have the highest SP/BV ratio. With over 30,000 patents in its portfolio, IBM holds the title as the world's largest single patent holder.

Citation Impact

Accepting that some patents are more valuable than others, in terms of their potential impact on future profitability, how do we identify these more valuable patents? The short answer to this question is that others have already identified them for us.

On the cover sheet of each United States patent is a listing of the prior art references cited during the course of the patent's prosecution. These references are categorized as U.S. patents, foreign patents, and nonpatent publications. By examining these citations, which may now be done by computer, it is possible to determine whether (or how often) a patent of interest has been cited as prior art with respect to a succeeding patent. The presence of such citation suggests that the citing patent pertains to technology that, in some way, is an improvement or refinement of the technology of the cited patent.

The existence of a number of patents wherein the patent of interest is cited as a prior art reference suggests that (1) the cited patent pertains to a basic invention, and (2) that this basic invention is in a field that is of significant interest to others in the industry. Indeed, it may well be that the cited patent dominates some or all of the citing patents. Remember the red fire engine. The more often a patent is cited as a prior art reference in later-issued patents, the greater the probability that the cited patent is a basic and, hence, valuable patent. We may therefore take it as a sign of merit or predictor of relative future profitability when the patents in the portfolio of one firm are more often cited in later-issued patents than are the patents in the portfolios of other firms in the same industry. In other (simpler) words, the firm whose patents are cited as prior art most often is likely to be the most profitable in the future.

Science Linkage

In citation impact, we are concerned with forward citation, which is the citation of the patent of interest as a prior art reference in later-issued patents. Science linkage is a tool that employs backward citation, which is an examination of the prior art references cited in the patent of interest.

It is generally accepted (a phrase used in academia meaning "you'll have to trust us on this, because we can't prove it") that basic research yields a higher return than product development (up to three times as high). How, then, does one determine whether a patent pertains to a basic research invention or a (probably less valuable) product development invention? An imperfect but workable solution is to count the number of scientific papers cited as prior art references. The underlying theory is that the greater the number of such citations, the closer the patented invention is to basic science (whatever that is). Thus, if the patents in the portfolio of one firm have, on average, more citations to nonpatent scientific papers than the patents in the portfolios of other firms in the same industry, it is likely that that firm will exhibit greater profitability, in the future, than the industry average.

There are, of course, significant limitations to the use of the foregoing figures of merit. They are only applicable to firms that have patent portfolios of statistically significant size—probably a minimum of about 40 patents. Also, they are suitable only for comparison of firms within a single industry. They do not provide meaningful results in comparing firms in different industries. Nevertheless, they do constitute a means of ranking the firms in an industry with respect to their projected relative profitability.

Summary

Corporate research and development efforts, if successful, lead to an increase in value of the corporation and the price of its stock. However, not all research efforts are successful or of equal impact on a firm's future earnings. Empirical data supports the use of three figures of merit as valid predictors of future profitability of a firm as compared to others in the same industry.

Patent count, which is the relative size of a firm's patent portfolio as compared to other firms in the industry, has been found to correlate well with that firm's future profitability.

Current impact, which is a measure of the frequency with which the patents of one firm are cited in later issued patents of others, is an indication of how basic the firm's technology is. The more often its patents are so cited, the more basic and valuable its technology is likely to be.

Science linkage is a measure of the frequency with which scientific articles are cited as prior art in a firm's own patents. The higher a firm's science linkage, the closer its technology is to basic research, as opposed to product development. Patents pertaining to basic research are generally more valuable than patents on product developments.

CHAPTER 11

How the Courts Have Changed the Patent Law

After reading this chapter you will know:

- How landmark legal decisions in individual lawsuits change patent law, as it is actually practiced, more often than amendments to actual patent law statutes.

- The basics of the *Bilski* case and how it raised issues of patentability.

- How the *eBay* case made it much more difficult for a nonpracticing entity to obtain a permanent injunction against an infringer.

- The background of several other major cases that changed patent law with regard to willful infringement, false patent marking, declaratory judgment actions, and many more facets of intellectual property law.

*P*lus ça change, plus c'est la même chose: The more things change, the more they remain the same.

At least with respect to the patent law, the French got it wrong—although what can you expect from people who consider Jerry Lewis a comic genius? When the patent law changes, it really *changes*.

In the United States, the law is composed of statutes and the court decisions that *define* and *simplify* (legal euphemisms meaning "confuse" and
"alter") them. The statutes are relatively few in number and rarely amended
(more on this later). The court decisions, however, just keep coming.
Among the most significant of the recent decisions are the following:

- *Bilski,* which relates to business method patents.

- *KSR,* which relates to the obviousness (patentability) of an invention.

- *Muniauction,* which relates to method claims.

- *Sandisk and MedImmune,* which relate to declaratory judgment
  actions.

- *Seagate,* which relates to willful infringement.

- *eBay,* which relates to permanent injunctions.

- *Egyptian Goddess,* which relates to infringement of design patents.

- *Aristocrat,* which relates to adequacy of disclosure of the invention.

- *Forest Group,* which relates to false marking.

(Keep in mind that the name of the case, or even just one of the
parties to the lawsuit, becomes a keyword for an entire thicket of thorny
legal issues—so, for example, patent attorneys are conditioned to begin
arguing the merits of business method patents at the mere mention of
the word *Bilski.*)

In this chapter we take a look at each of these landmark cases and
their significance to patent law. First, let's examine the case that had patent attorneys nervous for nine months: *Bilski v. Kappos.*

*B*ilski: Nine Months' Gestation But No Birth

The *Bilski* decision is to patent attorneys what politics is to late-night
television—an unending source of material. Strictly speaking, this case
relates to the scope of patentable subject matter (i.e., what types of inventions can be patented). As a practical matter, its greatest impact is on
so-called business method patents.

For a long time (actually until 1998), "methods of doing business" were legally deemed ineligible for patent protection. Then came the decision of the Court of Appeals for the Federal Circuit (CAFC) in *State Street Bank*, which held that "business methods" *are* patentable subject matter.

The *State Street Bank* decision resulted in the issuance of patents directed to all manner of processes or methods with little or no technological content. Although immensely popular with inventors, such patents drew the ire of much of the business community (mostly those businesses accused of infringement). The stage was thus set for a judicial reevaluation of the standard or test for patentable subject matter.

This reevaluation was effected by the CAFC in the seminal (lawyer-speak for "really, really important") *Bilski* decision, wherein they held that to constitute patentable subject matter, an invention must (1) "transform an article into a different state or thing," or (2) be "tied to a particular machine or apparatus." Unfortunately, several key terms, such as *transform*, *article*, and *particular machine or apparatus* were left undefined. The district courts then acted to correct this omission.

Cybersource Corp. v. Retail Decisions, Inc. dealt with a reexamined (pre-*Bilski*) patent directed to a system and method for detecting fraud in a credit card transaction conducted on the Internet. The court, in the Northern District of California, affirmed that an "electronic signal representative of a physical object or substance" *could*—under proper circumstances—constitute an "article," but that "manipulation" of such a signal *would not* constitute the requisite "transformation." The court then went on to hold that "the Internet" *is not* a "particular machine or apparatus." Bye-bye, patent.

Versata Software, Inc. et al. v. Sun Microsystems Inc. dealt with two software patents that allowed consumers to select from a variety of configuration options when ordering a product online. The software allowed the consumer to select only those combinations of options that would yield a workable product. The defendant argued that the claimed inventions did not satisfy the "transformation" prong of the *Bilski* test and that the limitation that the process be performed on a computer was insufficient to tie it to a "particular machine." The court, in the Eastern District of Texas, held *Bilski* specifically stated that it should not be taken as broadly applying to software. The patents-in-suit lived to be litigated another day.

Yet another district court decided that a *system claim* was unpatentable subject matter in view of *Bilski*, ruling that "simply because the process at issue requires machines or computers to work . . . does not mean that the process or system is a machine." The court went on to hold that the subject claim was "a mathematical algorithm [that] uses machines for data input and data output and to perform the required calculations. Those machines do not, however, impose any limit on the process itself. The involvement of the machine in the process is insignificant extra-solution activity . . . " (*Every Penny Counts Inc. v. Bank of America Corp. et al.*).

Moving even further afield, a district court in Arizona applied the CAFC's *Bilski* decision to an *apparatus* (*Research Corporation Technologies, Inc. v. Microsoft Corp.*).

One of the patent claims-in-suit was directed to "an apparatus . . . comprising a comparator for comparing . . . a plurality of color planes . . . against a . . . mask." The patent drawings included a figure illustrating the comparator as an electronic device comparing two input signals.

The court, apparently not deterred by the presence of the word *apparatus*, construed this claim to be a process claim. The court went on to hold that a comparator is *not a machine* but is "a collection of operations that performs an algorithm." It is "a device that compares numbers . . . 'device' is not synonymous with machine."

While all of this was occurring, Bilski appealed to the Supreme Court, which accepted the case. On June 28, 2010, the Supreme Court handed down its long-awaited decision. After *looooong* deliberations, it decided, basically, *nothing*. It held that the aforesaid "machine-or-transformation" test—affectionately known by us patent professionals as MORT—is a "useful and important clue, an investigative tool for determining whether some claimed inventions are [patentable] processes" but it "is not the sole test for deciding whether an invention is a patent-eligible process."

So, what *is* the proper test? It's not saying. The Court declined to adopt "categorical rules that might have wide-ranging and unforeseen impacts." All that it did say is that "laws of nature, physical phenomena, and abstract ideas," which have always been deemed unpatentable, *are* unpatentable.

Clearly, the matter is being left to the CAFC, which has already told us what *it* thinks. In the meantime, the USPTO has issued interim guidelines for examination of method patent applications: "[I]f a claimed method does not meet the machine-or-transformation test, the examiner should reject the claim . . . unless there is a clear indication that the method is not directed to an abstract idea. If a claim is rejected . . . the applicant then has the opportunity to explain why the claimed method is not drawn to an abstract idea."

KSR: How Obvious Is Common Sense?

The reader should remember from Chapter 1 that, in order to qualify for a patent, an invention must be nonobvious, which is to say that the invention must not be merely a combination of elements of prior works, such as would be apparent to a "person of ordinary skill in the art" (known as a *POSA* to us IP professionals). The critical question, of course, is what combinations would be obvious.

Heretofore, the CAFC employed a "teaching, suggestion, or motivation" (TSM) test, under which a patent claim is only proved obvious if the prior art itself, the nature of the problem, or the knowledge of a POSA contained some motivation or suggestion to combine the prior art teachings. This test was, in practice, applied rather strictly, the effect being to limit the number of permitted combinations. Well, no more! (*KSR International Co. v. Teleflex Inc. et al.*)

KSR produced certain adjustable gas pedal assemblies for the automobile companies. When Teleflex sued for patent infringement, KSR moved for a summary judgment that the patent-in-suit was obvious and, hence, invalid. The District Court granted the motion. Patent invalid.

Teleflex appealed to the CAFC, which reversed, holding that the District Court had not applied the TSM test *strictly enough*. Only prior art references that addressed the precise problem that the patentee was trying to solve could be combined to establish obviousness. Patent valid.

KSR appealed to the Supreme Court, which reversed, holding that the CAFC had applied the TSM test *too strictly*. "Under the correct analysis, any need or problem known in the field and addressed by the patent can provide a reason for combining [references] . . . [t]he obviousness analysis cannot be confined by a formalistic conception of the words teaching, suggestion, and motivation or by overemphasis on the importance of published articles and the explicit content of issued patents." Once again, patent invalid.

If the reader finds this new standard vague and confusing—well, so does everyone else. Much has been written about this decision. Unfortunately, much of this writing is philosophical blather that only serves to obfuscate the case holding. A recent decision of the CAFC, *Perfect Web Technologies, Inc. v. InfoUSA, Inc.*, however, may provide some much-needed clarification.

The patent-in-suit was directed to methods of managing bulk e-mail distribution to groups of targeted consumers. Advertisers wished to guarantee that at least a specified number of group members actually received a given message. For various reasons, some messages were undeliverable. However, due to cost considerations, the advertisers wished to meet their delivery goal while sending as few messages as possible.

Each of the asserted claims comprised four steps. The first three of these steps essentially involved transmitting a set of messages to targeted recipients and calculating the number of such messages that were successfully received. It was, ultimately (lawyerspeak for "because they had no choice"), acknowledged by the patentee that these steps were disclosed by the prior art. If the number of successfully received messages was less than the desired minimum number, the fourth step involved repeatedly transmitting more messages until the desired minimum was met.

Citing *KSR*, the trial court held that a " . . . person of ordinary skill is also a person of ordinary creativity . . . " The court went on, "the final step is merely the logical result of commonsense application of the maxim 'try, try again.'"

Perfect Web argued that "common sense must be rooted in evidence and factual findings." (Pay close attention here—the following is the point of citing this case.) The court disagreed—repeatedly—holding that "use of common sense does not require 'a specific hint or suggestion in a particular reference,' only a reasoned explanation that avoids conclusory generalizations . . . [and] common sense of those skilled in the art demonstrates why some combinations would have been obvious where others would not."

Applying the foregoing logic, the court held that "this last step, and the claim as a whole, simply recites repetition of a known procedure until success is achieved."

The bottom line? Now that the courts are directed to be logical, the requirement that a patented invention be nonobvious has become more difficult to satisfy.

Muniauction: Step by Step—It's All About Control

As mentioned earlier in the section dealing with the *Bilski* case, a *process* or *method* patent is one directed (not surprisingly) to a process or method for doing something. The claims of such a patent set forth a number (a plurality, in lawyerspeak) of steps. Infringement of a process or method occurs when a single party (i.e., an infringer), without permission, performs all of the steps of at least one of the claims of the patent. The question remains, however, whether the patent is infringed when some of the steps are performed by one party and the remaining steps are performed by another party. In other words, when all of the claim steps have been performed by unlicensed parties but not all of the steps were performed by a *single* party, is the patent infringed? The answer, as the reader may have guessed, is: "It depends."

The applicable legal principle—yes, lawyers, or at least some of them, have principles—is that a defendant cannot avoid liability for infringement by having someone else carry out one or more of the claimed steps on its behalf. Accordingly, where the actions of multiple parties combine to perform every step of a claimed method, the claim is infringed only if one party exercises "control or direction" over the entire process such that every step is attributable to the controlling party. The controlling party is known—not surprisingly—as the "mastermind" (this is the legal term—I am not making this up). Mere "arm's-length cooperation" (another legal term) will not give rise to infringement by any party. Is that clear? The question, therefore, is what constitutes control or direction.

Fortunately, the reader need not lie awake at night pondering this question. The Court of Appeals for the Federal Circuit (the patent appeals court, known to us insiders as the CAFC) has recently given us the answer in *Muniauction, Inc. vs. Thomson Corporation*, 532 F.3d 1318; 2008 U.S. App. LEXIS 14858; 87 U.S.P.Q.2D (BNA) 1350: "The control or direction standard is satisfied in situations where the law would traditionally hold the accused infringer vicariously liable for the acts committed by another party that are required to complete performance of a claimed method." Is *that* clear? Hopefully, it is, because the Supreme Court declined to hear an appeal of this decision. Hence, the foregoing is now the undisputed law on the issue.

Why should the reader care about this when there are truly important issues to consider, like the likelihood of increased taxes, resulting in higher prices for bourbon? Inventions of the type considered in the *Muniauction* case—where different process steps are performed by different parties—are particularly common with respect to processes or methods involving use of the Internet, such as order processing, auctions, or providing for secure transactions between buyers and sellers or between clients and financial institutions. For the compulsively curious, or the truly masochistic, we reproduce here claim 1 from the Muniauction patent, which is directed to a method of selling bonds through an online auction. The parties performing the various claim steps are indicated thereon in brackets.

> In an electronic auction system including an issuer's computer having a display and at least one bidder's computer having an input device and a display, said bidder's computer being located remotely from said issuer's computer, said computers being coupled to at least one electronic network for communicating data messages between said computers, an electronic auctioning process for auctioning fixed income financial instruments comprising:
>
> - THE BIDDER inputting data associated with at least one bid for at least one fixed income financial instrument into said bidder's computer via said input device;
> - THE AUCTIONEER'S SYSTEM automatically computing at least one interest cost value based at least in part on said inputted data, said automatically computed interest cost value specifying a rate representing borrowing cost associated with said at least one fixed income financial instrument;
> - THE BIDDER submitting said bid by transmitting at least some of said inputted data from said bidder's computer over said at least one electronic network; and
> - THE AUCTIONEER'S SYSTEM communicating at least one message associated with said submitted bid to said issuer's computer over said at least one electronic network and displaying, on said issuer's computer display, information associated with said bid including said computed interest cost value;

- INDETERMINATE wherein at least one of the inputting step, the automatically computing step, the submitting step, the communicating step and the displaying step is performed using a web browser.

If you have invented a process of this sort, rather than worry about "vicarious liability" (however *that* may be defined), draft patent claims (or better yet, have your patent professional draft them) so that all of the steps recited in a given claim are performed by a single party.

A final question to be addressed is whether a method claim, directed to a computer-implemented invention, is infringed through domestic use, when the host servers are offshore. The answer is no (bad news for patentees)—see *Renhcol Inc. v. Don Best Sports, et al.* To infringe a method claim of a U.S. patent, all of the steps must be performed in this country.

However, the same use was held to constitute infringement of *article* claims in the same patent (good news for patentees). Don't let some slimeball avoid infringement by moving its server offshore. Patents directed to computer-implemented methods should include both article (system) claims and method claims.

*M*ed*Immune* and *SanDisk*: Making Lawsuits More Likely

Just as the affronted gunfighter of yore offered his foe the choice to "get out of town" (said with a snarl) or "meet me in the street at high noon," so might the white-hatted patent owner have offered a choice to a black-hatted, dastardly infringer, contacting the swine and offering a license before initiating suit for patent infringement. Well, no more, thanks to *MedImmune, Inc. v. Genentech, Inc.*!

Genentech entered into a license of certain MedImmune intellectual property, among which was a pending patent application. Subsequently, the application matured into a patent. MedImmune informed Genentech that a new Genentech drug, Synagis, was covered by the newly issued patent and, hence, was subject to the payment of royalties. Genentech professed to consider that the patent, known as Cabilly II, was invalid, unenforceable, and not infringed. However, Genentech also professed to consider MedImmune's communication "a clear threat to enforce the patent, terminate the license agreement, and bring a patent infringement action if [Genentech] did not pay."

These competing considerations left Genentech in a quandary. On the one hand, if it refused to pay the royalties *and* MedImmune sued, *and* MedImmune won, Genentech could be subject to treble damages, attorneys' fees, and an injunction barring the sale of Synagis—which accounted for more than 80 percent of Genentech's sales revenue. On the other hand, Genentech didn't wish to pay royalties in respect of Synagis. What to do?

Genentech paid the royalties "under protest and with reservation of all rights," then filed a declaratory action against the Cabilly II patent. The district court, adhering to long-established precedent, dismissed the action on the grounds that a patent licensee in good standing could not establish the requisite "case or controversy." The appellate court, relying on *its own* precedent, affirmed the dismissal.

Enter the Supreme Court, which reversed, holding that "[b]asically, the question in each case is whether the facts alleged, under all the circumstances, show that there is a substantial controversy, between parties having adverse legal interests, of sufficient immediacy and reality to warrant the issuance of a declaratory judgment." Good-bye clear precedent, hello uncertainty. And what about the fact that Genentech had continued to pay royalties? Well, that didn't matter because it was "coerced" and, besides, in the license agreement, Genentech had never promised *not* to sue for declaratory judgment.

As if the declaratory judgment flood gates had not been opened wide enough by the Supreme Court's *MedImmune* decision, the CAFC, shortly thereafter, handed down its decision in *SanDisk Corp. v. STMicroelectronics, Inc.*

ST and its competitor, SanDisk, had correspondence and meetings directed toward the possibility of a cross-license of their respective technologies. In the course of these communications, SanDisk wrote of its "understanding that both sides wish to continue . . . friendly discussions." ST responded that it was "look[ing] forward to open and frank discussions with SanDisk concerning fair and reasonable terms for a broad cross-license agreement." At a meeting between the parties, SanDisk requested that the discussions be treated as "settlement discussions" under the federal rules of evidence (that's FRE 408 for you nitpicky types). At the end of the meeting, ST told SanDisk that "ST has absolutely no plan whatsoever to sue SanDisk." Six weeks later, SanDisk sued for a declaratory judgment that *each* of the 14 (yes, 14) ST patents, which had been discussed, was invalid and not infringed by any SanDisk product.

The district court granted ST's motion to dismiss, holding that no actual controversy existed because, under the circumstances, SanDisk did not have an "objectively reasonable apprehension of suit." SanDisk appealed to the CAFC, which began its analysis by noting that "the Supreme Court's opinion in *MedImmune* represents a rejection of our reasonable apprehension of suit test." Proceeding in an apparent effort to muddy the waters even further, it went on to hold that "[w]e need not define the outer boundaries of declaratory judgment jurisdiction, which will depend on . . . the facts and circumstances of each case."

So now the rule is that there is no rule. Nevertheless, it is clear that neither a promise not to sue nor the grant of a license will insulate a patentee from declaratory judgment actions.

Following the *MedImmune* and *SanDisk* decisions, great care was required to offer a license to an infringer without conferring standing to bring a declaratory judgment action. It was difficult, but it could be done. In any event, all patent owners suffered under the same oppressive rule. Well, no longer. Now, if you happen to be an NPE (a nonpracticing entity or, pejoratively speaking, a troll), the rule just got worse. The courts are now discriminating against NPEs (*Hewlett-Packard Company vs. Acceleron LLC*).

Acceleron is an NPE—a fact that will prove to be of supreme importance. In May 2007 Acceleron acquired the '021 patent and, four months later, wrote to Hewlett-Packard (HP). The letter called the '021 patent to HP's attention and requested that all information exchanged between the parties not be used for litigation purposes.

Two weeks later, HP responded, offering a mutual standstill agreement. Acceleron rejected both the standstill agreement and, seemingly, a confidentiality agreement. Two weeks thereafter, HP filed its declaratory judgment action. Acceleron moved to dismiss this action, claiming HP lacked standing, as it had not been threatened.

The trial court observed that Acceleron had failed "to specifically request a confidentiality agreement" and accept HP's proposed standstill agreement. Despite taking into consideration Acceleron's business model as an NPE, the trial court held that any threat of litigation against HP was "too speculative a prospect to support declaratory judgment jurisdiction" as the Acceleron correspondence lacked "a statement of infringement, identification of specific claims, claim charts, prior pleadings or litigation history, or the identification of 'other licensees.'"

HP appealed. The CAFC began by noting that "a communication from a patent owner to another party, merely identifying its patent and the other party's product line, without more, cannot establish adverse legal interests between the parties, let alone the existence of a 'definite and concrete' dispute." So far, so good for the NPE. However, the appellate court went on to declare that "[t]he purpose of a declaratory judgment action cannot be defeated simply by the . . . stratagem of a correspondence that avoids the magic words such as 'litigation' or 'infringement.'" Like the trial court, it noted that Acceleron failed to propose a confidentiality agreement and failed to accept the proposed standstill agreement.

Here is where it gets interesting. The CAFC held that "the receipt of such correspondence from a non-competitor patent holding company . . . may invoke a different reaction than would a meet-and-discuss inquiry by a competitor, presumably with intellectual property of its own to place on the bargaining table." Further, "we observe that Acceleron is solely a licensing entity, and without enforcement it receives no benefit from its patents. This adds significance to the fact that Acceleron refused HP's request for a mutual standstill." Finally, "Acceleron took the affirmative step of twice contacting HP directly, making an implied assertion of its rights under the '021 patent." Note the presence of "may invoke," "presumably," and "implied" in the foregoing quotes. Nevertheless, the CAFC—the so-called "Patent Court"—reversed the dismissal of HP's declaratory judgment action, admitting that "[o]ur decision in this case undoubtedly marks a shift from past declaratory judgment cases."

No more Mr. Nice Guy. Sue first, talk later, especially if you're an NPE.

In Re Seagate Technology, LLC: Holding Willfulness to a Higher Standard

It's great when you sue for infringement of your patent and win. It's even better when the infringement is found to be *willful*, opening the door to possible *treble damages*. Well, friends, thanks to the CAFC—the so-called patent-friendly court—your chances of hitting this home run have been substantially diminished.

The key question, obviously, is what constitutes willfulness? Heretofore, the threshold for willful infringement was essentially a finding of negligence. Lest the reader—who presumably is unfamiliar with legal terminology—fail to appreciate the humor in this, we note here that *negligence* is a failure to exercise the level of care and caution normally expected of a reasonable person in like circumstances. As if infringers were ever "reasonable." Fortunately for plaintiffs (the good guys), negligence was not *too* hard to prove. Indeed, a failure to obtain (lawyerspeak meaning "buy") an exculpatory opinion of counsel was deemed to create an inference of negligence. Well, no more.

The negligence standard has been expressly overruled. Now, "proof of willful infringement permitting enhanced damages requires *at least* a showing of objective recklessness" (emphasis added). "[T]o establish willful infringement, a patentee must show by clear and convincing evidence that the infringer acted despite an objectively high likelihood that its actions constituted infringement of a valid patent." The state of mind of the accused infringer is not relevant to this objective inquiry and the patentee must also demonstrate that this risk was either known or so obvious that it should have been known to the accused infringer. As if this wasn't damaging enough, the court reemphasized that "there is no affirmative obligation to obtain opinion of counsel."

Before *Seagate*, the award of enhanced damages was relatively rare. Now it's an endangered species.

eBay: From No Question, to Four Questions, to Only One Question

Plaintiffs in patent infringement lawsuits invariably seek a permanent injunction—a court order barring the defendant from future infringement of the patent or patents in suit. Until recently, such an injunction was granted automatically to a prevailing plaintiff—no question.

In 2006, the Supreme Court, in *eBay Inc. v. MercExchange, LLC,* again overturned a substantial body of precedent (the decision, although surprising, is mercifully brief), deciding that the award of an injunction should be governed by the "traditional four-factor test applied by courts of equity." Under this test, the plaintiff must demonstrate:

1. That it has suffered an irreparable injury.

2. That remedies available at law are inadequate to compensate for that injury.

3. That considering the balance of hardships between the plaintiff and defendant, a remedy in equity is warranted.

4. That the public interest would not be disserved by a permanent injunction.

Thus we've gone from no question to four questions. Since *eBay*, however, the district courts and the CAFC have effectively distilled the four-factor test down to *one* question—a single factor, which is whether competition exists between the plaintiff and the infringer. If you don't compete with the infringer, forget about a permanent injunction.

As usual when the Supreme Court renders a decision in a patent case, a portion of the IP community screams that the world—more particularly, *their* portion of the world—is ending. So how much of a change has this case caused? The answer, according to a survey of decisions in trials subsequent to *eBay*, is *not much*, at least if you're not an NPE.

If you are practicing the patented invention, and especially if you compete with the infringer, *eBay* didn't effect much of a change. If you're an NPE, the news is not so good. Unless you are a research organization that is funded by royalties, or you are an indirect competitor of the defendant, you won't get an injunction. However, the ever-resourceful NPEs are now developing a new weapon: the ITC exclusionary order, which is an order of the International Trade Commission barring the importation into this country of goods found to infringe the complainant's patent(s).

One of the requirements for bringing an action in the ITC is that the complainant must prove the existence of a domestic industry related to articles protected by the intellectual property at issue (not surprisingly, known as the *domestic industry requirement*). The question is, what constitutes a domestic industry?

The law provides (19 USC §1337 [a][3]) that " . . . an industry . . . shall be considered to exist . . . with respect to the articles protected by the patent" if there is "substantial investment in its exploitation, including . . . licensing." Thus, "[t]he domestic industry requirement can be satisfied solely based on complainant investing a *substantial* amount of money in a licensing program to exploit the patent, even if complainant does not manufacture the product" (emphasis added). Fine, so what constitutes "substantial investment"?

Ever determined to keep things vague—lawyers have to make a living, too—the ITC has held that there is no bright-line test to determine what constitutes a substantial investment in the licensing of patents. It did note, however, that "[p]roof of substantial investment could include factors such as the number of companies that are licensed, licensing revenues, licensing costs, the number of employees involved in the licensing process, legal fees, and whether licensing activities are active and ongoing." Nevertheless, the ITC has made clear investments and/or licensing efforts that fail to result in any license agreements are likely insufficient to be considered a substantial investment. Putting it more bluntly, it noted that "there is no Commission precedent for the establishment of a domestic industry based on licensing in which complainant did not receive any revenue from the alleged licensing activities." This last position is now being challenged.

So, if you are an NPE and you have *already* licensed your patent(s), maybe you can pursue foreign infringers in the ITC (or hire the A-Team).

Egyptian Goddess: Taking Design Patents a Step Back in Time

This is a case where the CAFC changed what we know, going back to what we formerly knew (*Egyptian Goddess, Inc. et al. v. Swisa, Inc. et al.*).

Heretofore, the test for infringement of a design patent was in two parts. The plaintiff was required to prove (1) that the accused device is substantially similar to the claimed design under what is referred to as the "ordinary observer" test, and (2) that the accused device contains "substantially the same points of novelty that distinguished the patented design from the prior art." Well, no more.

The court went back to the ordinary observer test, holding that " . . . the 'point of novelty' test should no longer be used in the analysis of a claim of design patent infringement. Instead . . . the 'ordinary observer' test should be the sole test for determining whether a design patent has been infringed." This, of course, has had the effect of substantially *broadening* the scope of protection of design patents—one of the few times the courts have done any favors to patentees of late.

Note that the new test relates only to infringement. The effect of this decision, if any, on the issue of *patentability* of a design remains unclear.

*A*ristocrat: Justifying the Means

Many self-proclaimed inventors seem unable to fully comprehend the distinction between a *concept* and an *invention*. This failure is most commonly seen in patent applications—often filed *pro se*—directed to computer-implemented processes. The patent application for such an invention typically *recites* one or more system components without actually *disclosing* a corresponding algorithm. The CAFC has clearly decided that such a failure is fatal to patentability (*Aristocrat Techs. Austl. Pty Ltd. v. Inter. Game Tech.*).

Aristocrat sued its competitor, IGT, alleging infringement of a patent directed to an electronic slot machine that allows a player to select winning combinations of symbol positions. This, of course, was a tremendous technological leap from the cherries, lemons, and so forth found in *old-fashioned* slot machines. All of the claims of this patent were written in *means-plus-function* form. Such claims recite a means—in this case, *control means*—and one or more functions performed by the means, but do not recite the structure that actually performs these functions.

The said control means of the Aristocrat patent performed three functions: (1) controlling the images displayed on a screen; (2) paying a prize when a predetermined combination of symbols appeared on the screen; and (3) determining the "pay lines" for the combinations of symbol positions selected by a player (read: "chump"). Patent Office rules require that the corresponding structure be disclosed in the specification.

How did Aristocrat describe the control means in the patent specification? It merely disclosed a general purpose, programmable microprocessor with appropriate programming.

Not good enough, ruled the court. "[I]n a means-plus-function claim in which the disclosed structure is a computer or a microprocessor programmed to carry out an algorithm, a corresponding structure must be a specific algorithm disclosed in the specification, rather than merely [reciting] an algorithm executed by a computer." There was no adequate disclosure of structure in the specification to perform these functions. "Merely stating that a standard microprocessor is the structure without more is not sufficient . . . because it does not set forth any specific algorithm for performing the recited function." Lest this point somehow be overlooked, the court repeated it a half-dozen times. Apparently, however, some people have not gotten the message. Making the point yet again, the Patent Office Board of Patent Appeals and Interferences (BPAI) has repeated it (*Ex parte Rodriguez*).

In the Rodriguez application, generic block diagrams were used to describe various system components, namely "a system configuration generator," "a system builder," and "a system verification environment," each of which was described and claimed as "configured to . . ." The specification of the patent application stated that "appropriate software coding can readily be prepared by skilled programmers based on the teachings of the present disclosure."

The BPAI held that the claims reciting the aforesaid system components were in "means-plus-function" form. " . . . [We] must determine whether the term [used to identify the system components] is one that is understood to describe structure, as opposed to a term that is simply a nonce word [we are not making this up] or a verbal construct that is not recognized as the name of structure and is simply a substitute for the term 'means for' . . . [we] have looked to both general and subject matter specific dictionaries and we find no evidence that any of these terms have achieved recognition as a noun denoting structure." Not surprisingly, they found that none of the terms had achieved such recognition. Therefore, the applicants had "failed to adequately describe sufficient structure for performing the functions recited in the means element contained in [the claim of the application] so as to render the claim definite. Accordingly, [the] claim is unpatentable . . . as indefinite."

If you're going to claim a computer-implemented system component, you've got to disclose an algorithm for performing the function; if an invention is worth patenting, it's worth paying a patent professional to do it right.

Forest Group: False Marking, True Opportunity?

False marking or mismarking claims is an exciting (lawyerspeak for "potentially lots of money to be made") new area of the law.

False marking is the intentionally deceptive representation that a product is covered by a patent or patent application. This may occur when a manufacturer marks a product with the number of a patent that doesn't cover the product, or has been found—by a court—to be invalid or unenforceable, or, more commonly, a patent that has expired. At present (although this seems to be changing), an action for false marking may be brought by anyone. There are no statutory limitations imposed on plaintiffs—any money grubber qualifies. A successful plaintiff gets to keep half of any recovery; the other half goes to the government.

The penalty for false marking is up to $500 for each such offense. The critical question is the meaning of the phrase "each such offense." Assume, for example, a production run of 10,000 widgets that are mismarked. Is this one offense—one production run—or 10,000 offenses? If the former, the potential recovery is no more than $500, of which half goes to Uncle Sam. Clearly, no self-respecting troll—an oxymoron if ever there was one—would be interested. If the latter, however, the potential recovery is $5 *million*, a much more enticing amount.

A century ago, the First Circuit Court of Appeals (this was before the creation of the CAFC) held that the false marking statute should be interpreted to impose a single fine for continuous false marking. Over the years, a number of district courts followed this precedent. Well, no more! In late 2009, the CAFC ruled that *each mismarked article* is an "offense" (*Forest Group, Inc. v. Bon Tool Co.*). The result? More than 180 false marking cases were filed by mid-May 2010. Clearly, someone saw an opportunity here.

The New Trolls

Patent trolls allegedly buy patents with the sole purpose of enforcing them. Well, now there is a new kind of troll, the marking troll, who doesn't even have to buy a patent! The marking troll sues companies that *mismark* their products—mark them with the number of a patent that doesn't actually cover the product or, more often, the number of an expired patent. As mentioned earlier, the plaintiff in such an action (for arcane reasons known as the *relator*) may recover *up to* $500 per mismarked item but has to split the take with the federal government. The profit potential of such lawsuits is obvious and the number being filed is increasing daily. Indeed, some relators, such as Patent Compliance Group, Inc., and Bentley A. Hollander, have already filed multiple suits.

Patent Compliance Group, whose name makes it sound like it's some sort of public service watchdog, filed three separate suits in one day. The company appears to have developed a boilerplate form of complaint to facilitate filing, wherein it asserts that the defendant "knew or reasonably should have known" that their mismarking "violated Federal patent marking laws" and that they "intended to deceive the public."

Hollander, who has filed eight suits at last count, has similarly standardized his complaints. In one case, however, he added an interesting twist (*Hollander v. B. Braun Medical, Inc.*). He alleged that "Braun has taken steps to withdraw its mark from certain products when the patent expired, providing clear evidence that Braun knows the law and requirements that bear on the marking of products and the obligations on a product manufacturer not to falsely mark a product." Yes, indeed, he points to Braun's efforts to comply with the law as evidence of its evil intent. You've got to give Hollander credit for chutzpah, if not for logic.

Of All the Nerve

Every excess provokes a reaction, and the recent plague of false marking suits is no exception to this rule. Courts now are requiring evidence that the defendant *intended* to deceive the public. They are also—granted, it's *dicta* (gratuitous statements)—raising questions as to whether a plaintiff must demonstrate it has been harmed by the alleged mismarking as a requisite for standing to sue. As a practical matter, of course, this would require that the plaintiff and the defendant be competitors. Indeed, the proposed patent reforms include a provision that would make this a statutory requirement. Clearly, the pendulum has swung, but not everyone has gotten the message: *Heathcote Holdings Corp., Inc. v. Maybelline LLC et al.*

Heathcote sued Maybelline and L'Oréal (the "et al."), alleging that they had marked various eyeliner products with the numbers of long-expired patents. Heathcote does not compete in the eyeliner market and, to our knowledge, produces nothing other than lawsuits.

To establish intent, Heathcote alleges that "Defendants are sophisticated companies with many decades of experience applying for, obtaining, and litigating patents, and there knows [sic] that patents do not have unlimited scope, but rather, have a scope limited to that which is claimed."

As to standing (which, admittedly, has not *yet* been held to be a requirement for standing to sue), Heathcote alleges that "[e]ach false marking on the products . . . is likely to, or at least has the potential to, discourage or deter persons and companies from commercializing competing products." Apparently, Heathcote would have the court—including a jury—believe that it brought this suit not as a cheap effort at extortion but as a public-spirited effort to maintain freedom of entry into the critical eyeliner market.

Not content with damages based upon the number of (allegedly) mismarked products, the civic-minded Heathcote is seeking to *expand* the scope of the mismarking statute by requesting that *each* expired patent (there are five of them) on each package be treated as a separate offense. Given the current judicial and political climate, you have to admire their nerve, if not their smarts.

Summary

The patent law statutes may be amended only rarely, but practically speaking, patent law changes fairly often as a result of court decisions in major patent infringement cases. This chapter discussed several key court decisions and their effect on patent law. For example, the famous *Bilski* case concerned whether business methods should be patentable but also had broader implications for software patents. The case made it to the U.S. Supreme Court, which, after nine months of deliberations, upheld the status quo and left the question of "what is patentable" for another day.

Other examples of lawsuits that changed patent law include *eBay*, which raised the question of whether a nonpracticing entity (NPE) has the right to a permanent injunction after prevailing in a patent trial; *Seagate*, which made it more difficult to obtain a finding of willful infringement in a patent suit (and, thus, the award of treble damages that may accompany such a finding); and *KSR*, which raised the question of how to determine whether a patent is obvious (which would render it invalid). *Egyptian Goddess*, a case concerning the infringement of a design patent, broadened the scope of protection afforded by design patents; and *Forest Group* opened a whole new field of legal enterprise based on a new and lucrative measure of damages for false marking.

Although the cases and court decisions detailed in this chapter had the effect of making major changes to patent law as it is practiced, further changes will result if Congress eventually manages to pass a Patent Reform Act. That legislation, which has been in the works for a few years as of this writing, is the focus of Chapter 12.

Patent Reform

After reading this chapter, you will understand:

- Several facets of the proposed patent reform legislation and their potential impact on inventors and businesses.

- How some of the proposed reforms have been effectively implemented by the courts already through precedent-setting rulings in recent lawsuits.

- Why a finding of *willful infringement* will be harder to come by.

- The reason for the boom in *false marking* lawsuits and how the courts are limiting them by insisting on proof that the defendant's mismarking of products with expired patent numbers was intentional.

- The difference between a *first-to-file* patent system and a *first-to-invent* patent system, and why it matters to individual inventors and small businesses.

- What *inter partes* and *ex parte* patent reexaminations are, how they are currently used, and how *post-grant review* (one of the proposed reforms) might benefit infringers.

I n the previous chapter, we discussed several precedent-setting patent infringement cases. Now we turn our attention to the Patent Reform Act of (2007, 2009, 2010 . . . insert year—Congress has been busy with this for quite some time now) and the changes it would make to patent law. But as you'll see, in many cases, the courts themselves have already effectively implemented some of the reforms through their rulings.

Much has been written about patent reform—the Patent Reform Acts of 2007, 2008, and 2009 (never passed), the Patent Reform Act of 2010 (currently being debated, as of this writing), and the Patent Reform Act of 2011 (which will almost certainly follow if the 2010 act doesn't pass). The problem with writing about patent reform is that it is a moving target. Regardless of which particular reforms are in the proposed legislation at the moment and which have been removed, any change that has been discussed in the past is liable to come up again in the next iteration of the Patent Reform Act—and new reforms may be added that aren't even on the table yet. For example, the recent boom in false marking cases—which are easy to file and could be devastating to businesses—may necessitate some changes in the laws regarding patent marking even though these issues are not a part of the current Patent Reform Act. Therefore, this chapter discusses various proposals, some of which may or may not be enacted and some of which have already been mooted by the courts.

Most pundits (newspaper lingo for "someone who doesn't really know much about a topic but is nevertheless willing to opine on it") agree that any reform that actually is enacted will likely include some or all of the following features:

- First-to-file.

- Willful infringement.

- Post-grant review.

- Litigation venue.

Lest anyone worry whether patent reform will actually be enacted, relax! Enactment, if it ever occurs, will have little effect, for the simple reason that, while Congress *debated*, the courts *acted*. The courts have *already* implemented some of the proposed reforms. Once again, Congress is leading the charge from the rear.

Litigation Venue

Currently, a plaintiff can select the venue (court) in which to file suit with very few limitations. The proposed patent reform legislation would require patent infringement suits to be filed where the defendant has its offices, is incorporated, or has committed "a substantial portion of the acts of infringement" and "has a regular and established physical facility that it controls." This change to patent law would allow district courts to reassign a case to a forum that has a greater connection to the infringement claim.

Why is this change necessary? While it would seem to make sense to file suit on your home turf, historically, some courts have been much friendlier to patent owners bringing infringement lawsuits than have others. One such venue is the Eastern District of Texas (EDTX)—a place known to be friendly to patent owners, whether the owner practices the patent (uses it to manufacture a product) or is a nonpracticing entity (NPE).

The Eastern District of Texas has long been the venue of choice for plaintiffs in patent infringement cases, so much so as to spur the cry for choice of venue provisions in the proposed patent reform. The local juries have consistently recognized the merits of plaintiffs' cases and routinely awarded generous damages. Moreover, the Eastern District was like Las Vegas (albeit without Wayne Newton and free drinks): Whatever case was brought in the Eastern District *stayed* in the Eastern District. And none of those fancy summary judgments or judgments as a matter of law (JMOL) for defendants—a case that didn't settle went to the *jury* for *trial*. Well, those days may be over.

The Court of Appeals for the Federal Circuit (CAFC) recently ruled that a refusal by an EDTX judge to transfer a patent infringement case to a "more convenient forum" was a clear abuse of the judge's discretion (*Lear Corp. v. TS Tech Co.*). So now it appears that the Eastern District may be forced to follow the same venue rules as the rest of the country—rules much more palatable to defendants. As if that wasn't enough, the Eastern District has begun granting judgments as a matter of law to defendants. Of late, even the juries in the EDTX have found for defendants.

Finally, as if to add insult to injury, the time from filing suit to trial, once only slightly more than a year, has now stretched to about two and a half years. The Eastern District is no longer a rocket docket.

Damages

One of the most contentious provisions of the proposed Patent Reform Act pertains to the manner in which damages are to be determined. At one point, the proposed Senate bill would have required that a "reasonable royalty" be applied "only to the portion of the economic value of the infringing product or process properly attributable to the claimed invention's specific contribution over the prior art."

Now, after much self-serving testimony from both sides of this controversy, the Senate Judiciary Committee has changed tacks and advocates a so-called gatekeeper function for the court (meaning the judge) to determine whether damages theories and contentions offered by the damages experts are legally sufficient before they are presented to the jury. This sounds a lot like the Daubert rule, whereunder the court examines the technical theories and contentions of technical experts and determines their sufficiency before they are presented to the jury. (You gotta love the Judiciary Committee—they recycle.)

While all of this debate swirled about, the courts decided, inter alia, the case of *IP Innovation, LLC v. Red Hat, Inc. et al.*

IPI sued Red Hat, alleging that its Linux-based operating systems' multiple virtual workspaces and workspace switching features infringe the patents-in-suit. IPI's damages expert invoked the entire market value rule (EMV rule, described in Chapter 8) and included *all* of Red Hat's revenues from sales of subscriptions to the accused operating systems in his proposed royalty base.

The court—and this was in the Eastern District of Texas, where the spaces are wide open and the damages are sky-high—rejected this proposed damages model for several reasons. First, it found that "the workspace switching feature represents only one of over a thousand components included in the accused products . . . [and] the workspace switching feature's small role in the overall product is further confirmed when one considers the relative importance of certain other features such as security, interoperability, and virtualization." It went on to hold that "this proffered evidence has no economic foundation," in part because there was no evidence in the record that would suggest that users buy the accused system for the workspace switching feature.

Warming to the subject, the court went on, "the record shows that some accused operating systems are sold to the public with a default setting that does not enable the workspace switching feature." The expert (we use this term advisedly) "made no effort to even discern the percentage of users who would never enable or use the claimed feature . . . [and] never accounts for the record evidence that most users of the accused operating systems do not seem to use the workspace switching feature at all." The court went on, "[i]n sum, this stunning methodological oversight makes it very difficult for this court to give any credibility to [the so-called expert's] assertion that the claimed feature is the basis for customer demand."

Having demolished the proffered royalty base, the court turned to the proposed royalty rate. As an opening shot, the court castigated the expert because "he arbitrarily picked a royalty rate that is much higher than the existing royalty rates for licenses to the patents-in-suit." As a starting point, the expert turned to two surveys of royalty rates conducted in 2004—the case at bar was filed in 2007 and was being argued in 2010. "Instead of relying on these studies, [the expert] should have at least inaugurated his analysis with reference to the existing licenses to the patents-in-suit."

Not surprisingly, the expert was precluded from testifying at trial or otherwise presenting his opinions on the issue of damages based on his current expert report. Two strikes and he's out.

In another case, Cornell University sued Hewlett-Packard for infringement of a patent directed to a component of a computer processor. The processor, in turn, is inserted into a server. The trial judge repeatedly warned Cornell that he expected "well-documented economic evidence closely tied to the scope of the claimed invention." Apparently, Cornell could not take a hint. It sought damages based upon the sales of all Hewlett-Packard server and workstation systems in which the patented components were incorporated. The jury obliged, awarding damages of $184 million, based upon $23 billion in sales (that is a royalty rate of 0.8 percent).

The trial judge, who gets the last word in such matters, then entered a judgment as a matter of law, reducing the damages to a measly $53.5 million because Cornell had attempted "to show economic entitlement to damages based on technology beyond the scope of the claimed invention." While the EMV rule permits damages on technology beyond the scope of the claimed invention, application of the rule requires proof that the patented component offers a significant competitive advantage and is the main reason for the consumer demand. The court found that Cornell failed to provide such proof. Indeed, Cornell failed to offer any evidence of a connection between the patented invention and consumer demand for the servers and workstations (where were all the Cornell economics majors?).

False Marking

What the court giveth, the court may take away. *Dicta* (gratuitous statements) in recent cases and questions posed by judges during oral arguments suggest that the false marking landscape may soon change.

Courts are requiring *proof* that mismarking was intentional, and some judges are apparently considering what the standard of such proof should be. Presently, it is the "mere preponderance of the evidence" standard of civil litigation; but, perhaps, it should be the "proof beyond a reasonable doubt" standard of criminal cases? (This would afford those accused of false marking the same rights as accused serial killers and child molesters.)

In addition, the courts are beginning to focus on the prophylactic purpose of the false marking statute (35 USC 292). This statute was intended, in the view of some jurists—and many patentees—to prevent acts that would "deter innovation and stifle competition in the market-place" and "cause unnecessary investment in design around or costs incurred to analyze the validity or enforceability of a patent whose number was marked upon a product"—in other words, to protect competitors of the accused perpetrator of false marking. Adoption of such a standard would severely reduce the population of potential plaintiffs.

The proposed false marking reform would limit plaintiffs to those who have "suffered a competitive injury as a result of" false marking. We support this proposed legislation, in part because it will eliminate meritless claims against the ever-decreasing number of firms actually manufacturing something, and in part because it is one of the few pieces of proposed legislation that would not increase the national debt.

Willful Infringement

Congress, no friend of the small inventor and small patent owner, seems determined to codify the holding in *Seagate* (see Chapter 11), as if that now made a difference. The proposed statute would specify that knowledge alone—of the infringed patent by the accused infringer—is not sufficient support for a finding of willful infringement and (just to drive the last nail in the coffin) any close case should be decided against willfulness.

First-to-File

What happens when two individuals, independently and without knowledge of each other, create substantially the same invention at about the same time? Assuming that the invention is patentable, which one is entitled to a patent—the one who made the invention first or the one who was first to file a patent application?

In the United States, the patent would be awarded to the one who *invented* first. Not surprisingly, this is known as the *first-to-invent* system. In the rest of the world, however, the patent would be awarded to the inventor who won the race to the patent office—the *first-to-file* system. If Congress has its way, the United States will join the rest of the world, at least in this regard.

Of all the proposed reforms, the change to a first-to-file system has earned the most comment—and the most vociferous. In all probability, it will have the least practical effect. A change of this type in Canada in 1989 produced no noticeable effect.

Post-Grant Review

Among the tactics that can be employed by an infringer is the re-examination. Any party believing a patent to be invalid may petition the U.S. Patent and Trademark Office (USPTO) to reexamine said patent. Accompanying the petition is the statutory fee—a not insubstantial amount—and prior art that in the self-serving opinion of the petitioner, presents a "substantial new question of patentability." The Patent Office can either grant the petition and reexamine the patent or deny the petition and return the fee (as if that's likely to happen).

Reexaminations are of two types: *ex parte*, where the petitioner does not participate, and *inter partes*, where the petitioner does participate—joining with the patent examiner to gang up on the poor patentee.

Inter partes reexamination is a relatively new creature. It was intended to provide a quick and inexpensive way for those accused of infringement to defeat meritless claims. While it is true that *inter partes* reexamination costs less than litigation, it is, nevertheless, costly and time-consuming and hence places a considerable burden on small patentees. Despite the advantage this confers on large, well-financed infringers, *inter partes* reexamination has not proven very popular. Relatively few have been filed.

In furtherance of their apparent goal of destroying small patentees and eliminating any incentive for them to patent their inventions, Congress is now proposing to add *post-grant review* to the infringer's arsenal. Although the exact nature of such post-grant review is not yet clear, it is likely to be costly and time-consuming—a handicap for the small patentee.

Best Mode Requirement

For the benefit of the reader who skipped or doesn't remember the "What You Don't Tell" section in Chapter 1, the *best mode* requirement pertains to those situations where, at the time of filing a patent application, the inventor is aware of more than one way (or *mode*) of practicing the claimed invention. In such event, the inventor is obligated to disclose the *best* mode (see 35 USC 112, first paragraph). Failure to do so renders a patent invalid. Clearly, this is yet another weapon in the infringers' arsenal.

Although "failure to disclose the best mode" is raised by virtually every infringer as part of his or her laundry list of defenses, it is not often effective. It does, however, have the effect of slowing litigation and increasing the burden on the courts (read: judges) as well as on the plaintiffs.

In response to complaints about its overuse (read: misuse), it is now proposed that such failure would, henceforth, not result in patent invalidity or unenforceability. In our view, a crime without a penalty is no longer a crime, but so be it.

Summary

Congress has been working toward an overhaul of the U.S. patent system for years, in the Patent Reform Acts of 2007, 2009 and, at the time of this writing, 2010. This chapter discussed some of the areas of patent law that are currently before Congress, as well as some reforms that have been discussed in the past and others that are not in the Patent Reform Act of the moment but which may be soon.

Some of the reforms that are in the current Patent Reform Act, are being discussed as possible elements of a future Patent Reform Act, or have been included in past Patent Reform Acts include:

- *Venue*. Limiting venue to a court where the defendant has its offices or is incorporated, or where most of the acts of infringement have occurred, would prevent patent owners (especially nonpracticing entities) from choosing a patent-friendly court. This would essentially give the infringer the home court advantage.

- *Damages*. Rejecting the EMV rule would limit the basis for damages calculation to the percent of sales actually lost because of the infringing component or feature—which is sometimes a minuscule part of the whole. Proving lost sales (and thus being awarded adequate damages) would thus become more difficult for the patent owner.

- *First-to-file*. Under the current U.S. patent system, if two inventors develop the same invention simultaneously, the patent goes to the one who can prove that he invented it first. If this element of patent reform passes into law, the patent would be awarded to the first inventor to win the race to the Patent Office—to the detriment of small inventors and small businesses with limited resources to spend on patent prosecution.

- *Post-grant review*. Though the process to be used for post-grant review is unclear, and it may simply replace the *inter partes* reexamination, post-grant review would still likely be an expensive, time-consuming problem for patent owners and a disincentive to file for patent protection.

- *Willful infringement.* This proposed reform would limit damages by making it more difficult for patent owners to prove willfulness on the part of the infringer in patent infringement trials.

- *Best mode.* Currently, "failure to disclose best mode" is among almost every infringer's bag of tricks when accused of patent infringement, though it is not often true or even all that effective as a defense. This reform, which was removed from the current versions of the patent reform legislation but may yet reappear in a future version, would remove the penalty from the crime: Failure to disclose best mode would no longer result in the patent being found invalid.

- *False marking.* One area of discussion that actually could use some reform but is not yet in an official patent reform bill as of this writing, is that of patent marking—specifically, the standing required to bring suit against a patent owner for false patent marking. The statute against false marking was meant to prevent acts that would stifle competition, such as marking a product as patented when it is not (or when the patent has expired). But with the recent surge in *qui tam* patent marking lawsuits filed by opportunists, limiting potential plaintiffs in such lawsuits to those who are actual competitors of the accused mismarker is necessary to protect businesses from marking trolls who have suffered no actual damages.

Appendixes

Trademark and Service Mark Application

The following form is for informational purposes only. If you think you may need to apply for a trademark, the U.S. Patent and Trademark Office encourages the use of its online application and other services at www.uspto.gov/teas/eTEASpageA.htm. However, if you'd rather file for your trademark the old-fashioned way, you can call the Trademark Assistance Center at 800-786-9199 or 571-272-9250 to request a paper form.

Applicant Information	
☆ Name	

Entity Type: Click on the **one** appropriate circle to indicate the applicant's entity type and enter the corresponding information.

☐ Individual	Country of Citizenship	
☐ Corporation	State or Country of Incorporation	
☐ Partnership	State or Country Where Organized	
	Name and Citizenship of all General Partners	
☐ Other	Specify Entity Type	
	State or Country Where Organized	
	☆ Street Address	
	☆ City	
	State	Select State ▼ If not listed above, please select 'OTHER' and specify here:
	☆ Country	Select Country ▼ If not listed above, please select 'OTHER' and specify here:
	Zip/Postal Code	
Phone Number		
Fax Number		
Internet E-Mail Address	☐ Check here to authorize the USPTO to communicate with the applicant or its representative via e-mail. NOTE: While the application may list an e-mail address for the applicant, applicant's attorney, and/or applicant's domestic representative, **only one** e-mail address may be used for correspondence, in accordance with Office policy. The applicant must keep this address current in the Office's records.	

Mark Information

Before the USPTO can register your mark, we must know exactly what it is. You can display a mark in one of two formats: (1) typed; or (2) stylized or design. When you click on one of the two circles below, and follow the relevant instructions, the program will create a separate page that displays your mark once you validate the application (using the Validate Form button at the end of this form). You must print out and submit this separate page with the application form (even if you have listed the "mark" in the body of the application). If you have a stylized mark or design, but either you do NOT have a GIF or JPG image file or your browser does not permit this function, check the box to indicate you do NOT have the image in a GIF or JPG image file (and then see the special help instructions).

WARNING: AFTER SEARCHING THE USPTO DATABASE, EVEN IF YOU THINK THE RESULTS ARE "O.K.," DO NOT ASSUME THAT YOUR MARK CAN BE REGISTERED AT THE USPTO. AFTER YOU FILE AN APPLICATION, THE USPTO MUST DO ITS OWN SEARCH AND OTHER REVIEW, AND MIGHT REFUSE TO REGISTER YOUR MARK.

* Mark	**Typed Format** ◯	Click on this circle if you wish to register a word(s), letter(s), and/or number(s) in a format that can be reproduced using a typewriter. Also, only the following common punctuation marks and symbols are acceptable in a typed drawing (any other symbol, including a foreign diacritical mark, requires a stylized format): . ? " - ; ( ) % $ @ + , ! ' : / & # * = [ ] Enter the mark here: NOTE: The mark **must** be entered in ALL upper case letters, regardless of how you actually use the mark. E.g., MONEYWISE, **not** MoneyWise.
	Stylized or Design Format ◯	Click on this circle if you wish to register a stylized word(s), letter(s), number(s), and/or a design. Click on the 'Browse' button to select GIF or JPG image file from your local drive that shows the complete, overall mark (i.e., the stylized representation of the words, e.g., or if a design that also includes words, the image of the "composite" mark, NOT just the design element). Do NOT submit a color image. ☐ Check this box if you do NOT have the image in a GIF or JPG image file. For a stylized word(s) or letter(s), or a design that also includes a word(s), enter the LITERAL element only of the mark here:
Additional Statement	This section is for the entry of various statements that may pertain to the mark. In no case must you enter any of these statements for the application to be accepted for filing (although you may be required to add a statement(s) to the record during the actual prosecution of the application). To select a statement, check the box and enter the specific information relevant to your mark. The following are the texts of the most commonly asserted statements:	
	☐ **DISCLAIMER:** "No claim is made to the exclusive right to use _____ apart from the mark as shown."	
	☐ **STIPPLING AS A FEATURE OF THE MARK:** "The stippling is a feature of the mark."	
	☐ **STIPPLING FOR SHADING:** "The stippling is for shading purposes only."	
	☐ **PRIOR REGISTRATION(S):** "Applicant claims ownership of U.S. Registration Number(s) _____ ."	

DESCRIPTION OF THE MARK: "The mark consists of ____ ."

TRANSLATION: "The foreign wording in the mark translates into English as ____ ."

TRANSLITERATION: "The non-Latin character(s) in the mark transliterate into ____ , and this means ____ in English."

§2(f), based on Use: "The mark has become distinctive of the goods/services through the applicant's substantially exclusive and continuous use in commerce for at least the five years immediately before the date of this statement."

§2(f), based on Prior Registration(s): "The mark has become distinctive of the goods/services as evidenced by the ownership on the Principal Register for the same mark for related goods or services of U.S. Registration No(s). ____ "

§2(f), IN PART, based on Use: "____ has become distinctive of the goods/services through the applicant's substantially exclusive and continuous use in commerce for at least the five years immediately before the date of this statement."

§2(f), IN PART, based on Prior Registration(s): "____ has become distinctive of the goods/services as evidenced by the ownership on the Principal Register for the same mark for related goods or services of U.S. Registration No(s). ____ ."

NAME(S), PORTRAIT(S), SIGNATURE(S) OF INDIVIDUAL(S):

☐ "The name(s), portrait(s), and/or signature(s) shown in the mark identifies ____ , whose consent(s) to register will be submitted."

☐ "The name(s), portrait(s), and/or signature(s) shown in the mark does not identify a particular living individual."

USE OF THE MARK IN ANOTHER FORM: "The mark was first used anywhere in a different form other than that sought to be registered on ____ , and in commerce on ____ ."

CONCURRENT USE: Enter the appropriate concurrent use information, e.g., specify the goods and the geographic area for which registration is sought.

BASIS FOR FILING AND GOODS AND/OR SERVICES INFORMATION

Applicant requests registration of the trademark/service mark identified above with the Patent and Trademark Office on the Principal Register established by the Act of July 5, 1946 (15 U.S.C. §1051 et seq.) for the following Class(es) and Goods and/or Services, and checks the basis that covers those specific Goods or Services. More than one basis may be selected, but do **NOT** claim both §§1(a) and 1(b) for the identical goods or services in one application.

☐ **Section 1(a), Use in Commerce:** Applicant is using or is using through a related company the mark in commerce on or in connection with the below identified goods and/or services. 15 U.S.C. § 1051(a), as amended. Applicant attaches or will submit one specimen for *each class* showing the mark as used in commerce on or in connection with any item in the class of listed goods and/or services. If filing electronically, applicant must attach a JPG or GIF specimen image file for each international class, regardless of whether the mark itself is in a typed drawing format or is in a stylized format or a design. Unlike the mark image file, a specimen image file may be in color (i.e., if color is being claimed as a feature of the mark, then the specimen image should show use of the actual color(s) claimed).

Describe what the specimen submitted consists of:

International Class	If known, enter class number 001 – 042, A, B, or 200.
* Listing of Goods and/or Services *USPTO Goods/Services Manual*	
Date of First Use of Mark Anywhere	at least as early as: MM/DD/YYYY
Date of First Use of the Mark in Commerce	at least as early as: MM/DD/YYYY

Section 1(b), Intent to Use: Applicant has a bona fide intention to use or use through a related company the mark in commerce on or in connection with the goods and/or services identified below (15 U.S.C. §1051(b)).

International Class	If known, enter class number 001 – 042, A, B, or 200.
* Listing of Goods and/or Services *USPTO Goods/Services Manual*	

	Section 44(d), Priority Based on Foreign Filing: Applicant has a bona fide intention to use the mark in commerce on or in connection with the goods and/or services identified below, and asserts a claim of priority based upon a foreign application in accordance with 15 U.S.C. §1126(d).	
	International Class	If known, enter class number 001 – 042, A, B, or 200.
	* Listing of Goods and/or Services **USPTO Goods/Services Manual**	
	Country of Foreign Filing	Select Country ▼ If not listed above, please select 'OTHER' and specify here:
	Foreign Application Number	NOTE: If possible, enter no more than 12 characters. Eliminate all spaces and non-alphanumeric characters.
	Date of Foreign Filing	MM/DD/YYYY

	Section 44(e), Based on Foreign Registration: Applicant has a bona fide intention to use the mark in commerce on or in connection with the above identified goods and/or services, and submits or will submit a certification or certified copy of the foreign registration before the application may proceed to registration, in accordance with 15 U.S.C. 1126(e), as amended.	
	International Class	If known, enter class number 001 – 042, A, B, or 200.
	* Listing of Goods and/or Services **USPTO Goods/Services Manual**	
	Country of Foreign Registration	Select Country ▼ If not listed above, please select 'OTHER' and specify here:

Foreign Registration Number	NOTE: If possible, enter no more than 12 characters. Eliminate all spaces and non-alphanumeric characters.	
Foreign Registration Date	MM/DD/YYYY	
Renewal Date for Foreign Registration	MM/DD/YYYY	
Expiration Date of Foreign Registration	MM/DD/YYYY	

☐ Check here if an attorney is filing this application on behalf of applicant(s). Otherwise, click on Domestic Representative to continue.

Attorney Information

Correspondent Attorney Name		
Individual Attorney Docket/Reference Number		
Other Appointed Attorney(s)		
Attorney Address	Street Address	
	City	
	State	Select State ▾
		If not listed above, please select 'OTHER' and specify here:
	Country	Select Country ▾
		If not listed above, please select 'OTHER' and specify here:
	Zip/Postal Code	
Firm Name		
Phone Number		
FAX Number		
Internet E-Mail Address	☐ Check here to authorize the USPTO to communicate with the applicant or its representative via e-mail. NOTE: While the application may list an e-mail address for the applicant, applicant's attorney, and/or applicant's domestic representative, **only one** e-mail address may be used for correspondence, in accordance with Office policy. The applicant must keep this address current in the Office's records.	

☐ Check here if the applicant has appointed a Domestic Representative. **A Domestic Representative is** REQUIRED **if the applicant's address is outside the United States.**

Domestic Representative

The applicant must appoint a Domestic Representative if the applicant's address is outside the United States. The following is hereby appointed applicant's representative upon whom notice or process in the proceedings affecting the mark may be served.

Representative's Name		
Address	Street Address	
	City	
	State	Select State ▾ If not listed above, please select 'OTHER' and specify here:
	Zip Code	
Firm Name		
Phone Number		
FAX Number		
Internet E-Mail Address		☐ Check here to authorize the USPTO to communicate with the applicant or its representative via e-mail. NOTE: While the application may list an e-mail address for the applicant, applicant's attorney, and/or applicant's domestic representative, **only one** e-mail address may be used for correspondence, in accordance with Office policy. The applicant must keep this address current in the Office's records.

Fee Information

Number of Classes Paid   1 ▾

Note: The total fee is computed based on the Number of Classes in which the goods and/or services associated with the mark are classified.

$ 325 = **Number of Classes Paid x $325 (per class)**

* Amount $

Payment

☐ Deposit Account Number
(If checked, please enter six numbers with no space or hyphen)

The U.S. Patent and Trademark Office is hereby authorized to charge any fees or credit any overpayments to the deposit account listed above.

Name of Person authorizing account activity

Company/Firm Name

Declaration

The undersigned, being hereby warned that willful false statements and the like so made are punishable by fine or imprisonment, or both, under 18 U.S.C. §1001, and that such willful false statements may jeopardize the validity of the application or any resulting registration, declares that he/she is properly authorized to execute this application on behalf of the applicant; he/she believes the applicant to be the owner of the trademark/service mark sought to be registered, or, if the application is being filed under 15 U.S.C. §1051(b), he/she believes applicant to be entitled to use such mark in commerce; to the best of his/her knowledge and belief no other person, firm, corporation, or association has the right to use the mark in commerce, either in the identical form thereof or in such near resemblance thereto as to be likely, when used on or in connection with the goods/services of such other person, to cause confusion, or to cause mistake, or to deceive; and that all statements made of his/her own knowledge are true; and that all statements made on information and belief are believed to be true.

1

Signature _____   Date Signed _____

Signatory's Name

Signatory's Position

Copyright Application

F orm CO and many other copyright forms, along with instructions for their use, are available at the U.S. Copyright Office web site (www.copyright.gov).

The new fill-in Form CO replaces Forms TX, VA, PA, SE, and SR. The graphic we have included here is a sample of the new form. It uses 2-D barcode scanning technology, so users should visit the Copyright Office web site and complete the e-form from their personal computer, print it out, and mail it along with their check or money order and deposit. Please read the Form CO Instructions, available at www .copyright.gov/forms/, for more information.

UNITED STATES COPYRIGHT OFFICE
Form CO · Application for Copyright Registration

THIS APPLICATION IS INCOMPLETE
AND CAN NOT BE SUBMITTED

APPLICATION FOR COPYRIGHT REGISTRATION

* Designates Required Fields

1 WORK BEING REGISTERED

1a. * Type of work being registered *(Fill in one only)*

☐ Literary work ☐ Performing arts work
☐ Visual arts work ☐ Motion picture/audiovisual work
☐ Sound recording ☐ Single serial issue

ApplicationForCopyrightRegistration

1b. * Title of this work *(one title per space)*

WorkTitles

1c. For a serial issue: Volume ⬚ Number ⬚ Issue ⬚ ISSN ⬚

Frequency of publication: ⬚

1d. Previous or alternative title

1e. * Year of completion ⬚

Publication *(If this work has not been published, skip to section 2)*

1f. Date of publication ⬚ *(mm/dd/yyyy)* **1g.** ISBN ⬚

1h. Nation of publication ☐ United States ☐ Other

UNITED STATES COPYRIGHT OFFICE
Form CO · Application for Copyright Registration

1i. Published as a contribution in a larger work entitled

1j. If line 1i above names a serial issue   Volume   Number   Issue

On pages

1k. If work was preregistered   Number PRE-

For Office Use Only

WorkBeingRegistered

---

2 AUTHOR INFORMATION

2a. Personal name   *complete either 2a or 2b*

First Name   Middle   Last

2b. Organization name

2c. Doing business as

2d. Year of birth   **2e.** Year of death

2f. *   ☐ Citizenship
              ☐ Domicile

2g. Author's contribution: ☐ Made for hire   ☐ Anonymous
                                 ☐ Pseudonymous

Continuation of Author Information

2h. * This author created *(Fill in only the authorship that applies to this author)*

☐ Text/poetry   ☐ Compilation   ☐ Map/technical drawing   ☐ Music
☐ Editing   ☐ Sculpture   ☐ Architectural work   ☐ Lyrics
☐ Computer program   ☐ Jewelry design   ☐ Photography   ☐ Motion picture/audiovisual
☐ Collective work   ☐ 2-dimensional artwork ☐ Script/play/screenplay ☐ Sound recording/performance

Other:

UNITED STATES COPYRIGHT OFFICE
Form CO · Application for Copyright Registration

For Office Use Only	

AuthorInformation

3 COPYRIGHT CLAIMANT INFORMATION

Claimant   *complete either 3a or 3b* - If you do not know the address for a claimant, enter "not known" in the Street address and City fields.

3a. Personal name

First Name	Middle	Last

3b. Organization name

3c. Doing business as

3d. Street address *

Street address (line 2)

City *	State	ZIP / Postal code	Country

Email   Phone number
          (Add "+" and country code for foreign numbers)

3e. If claimant is **not** an author, copyright ownership acquired by: ☐ Written agreement ☐ Will or inheritance ☐ Other

For Office Use Only	

CopyrightClaimantInformation

Page 3 of 7

UNITED STATES COPYRIGHT OFFICE
Form CO · Application for Copyright Registration

4 LIMITATION OF COPYRIGHT CLAIM

Skip section 4 if this work is all new.

4a. Material excluded from this claim *(Material previously registered, previously published, or not owned by this claimant)*

☐ Text   ☐ Artwork   ☐ Music   ☐ Sound recording/performance   ☐ Motion picture/audiovisual

Other: _____

4b. Previous registration(s)   Number _____   Year ☐☐☐☐

Number _____   Year ☐☐☐☐

4c. New material included in this claim *(This work contains new, additional, or revised material)*

☐ Text   ☐ Compilation   ☐ Map/technical drawing   ☐ Music
☐ Poetry   ☐ Sculpture   ☐ Architectural work   ☐ Lyrics
☐ Computer program   ☐ Jewelry design   ☐ Photography   ☐ Motion picture/audiovisual
☐ Editing   ☐ 2-dimensional artwork ☐ Script/play/screenplay   ☐ Sound recording/performance

Other: _____

For Office Use Only

LimitationOfCopyrightClaim

5 RIGHTS AND PERMISSIONS CONTACT

☐ Check if information below should be copied from the **first** copyright claimant

First Name _____   Middle _____   Last _____

Name of organization _____

Street address _____

Street address (line 2) _____

City _____   State _____   ZIP / Postal code _____   Country _____

UNITED STATES COPYRIGHT OFFICE
Form CO · Application for Copyright Registration

Email	Phone number
	(Add "+" and country code for foreign numbers)

For Office Use Only

RightsAndPermissionsContact

6 CORRESPONDENCE CONTACT

☐ Copy from **first** copyright claimant   ☐ Copy from rights and permissions contact

First name *	Middle	Last *

Name of organization

Street address *

Street address (line 2)

City *	State	ZIP / Postal code	Country

Email *	Daytime phone number
	(Add "+" and country code for foreign numbers)

For Office Use Only

CorrespondenceContact

7 MAIL CERTIFICATE TO:

* Complete either 7a, 7b, or both

☐ Copy from **first** copyright claimant   ☐ Copy from rights and permissions contact   ☐ Copy from correspondence contact

Form CO · Application for Copyright Registration

UNITED STATES COPYRIGHT OFFICE

7a. First Name	Middle	Last

7b. Name of organization

7c. Street address *

Street address (line 2)

City *	State	ZIP / Postal code	Country

For Office Use Only

MailCertificateTo

8 CERTIFICATION

17 U.S.C. § 506(e): Any person who knowingly makes a false representation of a material fact in the application for copyright registration provided for by section 409, or in any written statement filed in connection with the application, shall be fined not more than $2,500.

I certify that I am the author, copyright claimant, or owner of exclusive rights, or the authorized agent of the author, copyright claimant, or owner of exclusive rights, of this work, and that the information given in this application is correct to the best of my knowledge.

8a. Handwritten signature

9/3/2010

8b. Printed name

8c. Date signed

8d. Deposit account number   Account holder

8e. Applicant's internal tracking number (optional)

UNITED STATES COPYRIGHT OFFICE

Form CO · Application for Copyright Registration

For Office Use Only

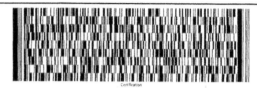

Certification

Confidentiality and Nondisclosure Agreement

THIS AGREEMENT is made the ___ day of ___, 20___, by and between _____, a _____[company type, e.g., a corporation] organized and existing under the laws of the State of _____, having a principal place of business at _____ ("Disclosing Party"), and _____, [company type, if applicable] [organized and existing under the laws of the State of _____, if applicable], having a principal place of business at [if business, or] with offices at _____ ("Recipient").

WHEREAS, Disclosing Party is the proprietor of information concerning _____ (the "Information"); and

WHEREAS, Recipient is interested to learn the Information so as to be able to determine their interest in the use of the Information [or, in connection with _____ project].

NOW, THEREFORE, in consideration of mutual premises and covenants it is mutually agreed as follows.

1. Disclosing Party agrees to divulge to Recipient sufficient details of the Information to enable Recipient to understand the substance thereof. It is mutually understood that, unless otherwise specifically indicated in writing, any information so communicated by

Disclosing Party to Recipient is confidential and constitutes valuable trade secrets of Disclosing Party.

2. In order to induce Disclosing Party to divulge the Information, Recipient covenants and warrants (i) to use the Information only for the purposes hereinabove stated, (ii) not to use any of the Information for Recipient's own benefit, and (iii) not to disclose any of it to third parties without the prior written permission of Disclosing Party.

3. Excluded from the above restriction is any part of Disclosing Party's disclosure that:

a. can be demonstrated to have been in the public domain prior to the date hereof;

b. can be demonstrated to have been in Recipient's possession prior to the date hereof;

c. becomes part of the public domain by publication or otherwise, not due to any unauthorized act or omission on Recipient's part; or

d. is supplied to Recipient by any third party as a matter of right insofar as the Information had been obtained by such third party lawfully.

4. The rights and obligations herein are personal to Disclosing Party and Recipient and cannot be assigned without the prior written permission of the other party. This Agreement contains the entire understanding of the parties relating to the matters referred to herein, and can only be amended by a written instrument duly executed on behalf of Disclosing Party and Recipient.

IN WITNESS WHEREOF, the parties hereto have caused this Agreement to be duly executed as of the date hereinabove set forth.

[Disclosing Party]

_____ By:

Name   [Title, if applicable]

_____

[Recipient]

_____ By:

Name   [Title, if applicable]

Invention Assignment Form

(*Note*: This assignment may not provide an assignee the right to sue for and recover damages for acts of infringement occurring prior to the date of the assignment.)

Practitioner's Docket No. _____ *PATENT*

For:

☐ U.S. and/or

☐ Foreign Rights

For:

☐ U.S. Application or

☐ U.S. Provisional Application

For:

☐ U.S. Patent

For:

☐ PCT Application

By:

☐ Inventor(s) or

☐ Present Owner

ASSIGNMENT OF INVENTION

In consideration of the payment by ASSIGNEE to ASSIGNOR of the sum of One Dollar ($1.00), the receipt of which is hereby acknowledged, and for other good and valuable consideration,

ASSIGNOR:

Inventor(s) or person(s) or entity(ies) who own the invention

_____

(Type or print name(s) of ASSIGNOR(S).)

_____

_____

Address

_____

Nationality

(If assignment is by person or entity to whom invention was previously assigned and this was recorded in PTO, add the following.)

Recorded on_____ **Reel**_____

hereby sells, assigns, and transfers to

ASSIGNEE:

_____

(Type or print name(s) of ASSIGNEE(S).)

_____

_____

Address

_____

Nationality

and the successors, assigns, and legal representatives of the ASSIGNEE

(Complete one of the following.)

☐ the entire right, title, and interest

☐ an undivided _____ percent (_____ %) interest

for the United States and its territorial possessions

(Check the following box, if foreign rights are also to be assigned.)

☐ and in all foreign countries, including all rights to claim priority,

in and to any and all improvements which are disclosed in the invention entitled:

_____

Name of inventor(s) _____

(Check and complete (a), (b), (c), (d), (e), (f), or (g).)

and which is found in (37 C.F.R. § 3.21)

☐ (a) U.S. patent application executed on even date herewith

☐ (b) U.S. patent application executed on _____

☐ (c) U.S. provisional application naming the above inventor(s) for the above-entitled invention

☐ Express mail label no.: _____

Mailed:_____

☐ To comply with 37 CFR 3.21 for recordal of this assignment, I, an ASSIGNOR signing below, hereby authorize and request my attorney to insert below the filing date and application number when they become known.

☐ (d) U.S. application no.   /_____ filed on _____

☐ (e) International application no. PCT   /_____

/_____ filed on _____

☐ (f) U.S. patent no. _____issued _____

☐ A change of address to which correspondence is to be sent regarding patent maintenance fees is being sent separately.

(Also check (g), if foreign application(s) is also being assigned.)

☐ (g) and any legal equivalent thereof in a foreign country, including the right to claim priority

and, in and to, all Letters Patent to be obtained for said invention by the above application or any continuation, division, renewal, or substitute thereof, and as to letters patent any reissue or reexamination thereof.

ASSIGNOR hereby covenants that no assignment, sale, agreement, or encumbrance has been or will be made or entered into which would conflict with this assignment.

ASSIGNOR further covenants that ASSIGNEE will, upon its request, be provided promptly with all pertinent facts and documents relating to said invention and said Letters Patent and legal equivalents as may be known and accessible to ASSIGNOR and will testify as to the same in any interference, litigation, or proceeding related thereto and will promptly execute and deliver to ASSIGNEE or its legal representatives any and all papers, instruments, or affidavits required to apply for, obtain, maintain, issue, and enforce said application, said invention, and said Letters Patent and said equivalents thereof which may be necessary or desirable to carry out the purposes thereof.

IN WITNESS WHEREOF, I/We have hereunto set hand and seal this _____ day of _____.

Date of signing

WARNING: *The date of signing must be the same as the date of execution of the application, if item (a) was checked above.*

Date:

_____

Signature of ASSIGNOR(S)
Date:

_____

Date:

_____

Date:

_____

(If ASSIGNOR is a legal entity, complete the following information.)

_____

(Type or print the name of the above person authorized to sign on behalf of ASSIGNOR.)

_____

Title

NOTE: No witnessing, notarization, or legalization is necessary. If the assignment is notarized or legalized, then it will only be prima facie evidence of execution. 35 USC 261. Use next page if notarization is desired.

☐ Notarization or Legalization Page Added.

Basic IP Audit Questionnaire

1. List all patents and pending patent applications, domestic and foreign. Verify that:

   a. All patents and patent applications are properly assigned.

   b. All maintenance fees have been paid, and future payments have been docketed.

   c. Prosecution of all pending patent applications is current.

2. Does the organization have a procedure for recording and disclosing new inventions? If "no," institute invention disclosure procedure; if "yes," obtain list of all disclosed inventions.

3. List all trademark and service mark registrations and pending applications for registration, domestic and foreign. Verify that:

   a. All registrations and applications for registration are in the name of the organization or have been properly assigned.

   b. All affidavits of use and renewal applications have been filed.

   c. Prosecution of all pending applications is current.

4. List all unregistered trademarks and service marks used by the organization.

5. Collect and catalog copies of all publications, including catalogues, advertising and promotional materials, shareholder reports, and so forth. Check for:

   a. Unlisted trademarks and service marks.

   b. Proper trademark and service mark usage.

   c. Proper copyright notices.

6. List all copyright registrations. Verify that all registrations are in the name of the organization or have been properly assigned.

7. List all mask works.

8. List all registered designs.

9. Does the organization possess any information that provides a competitive advantage with respect to its competitors? If "yes," verify that the information is marked "confidential," that access to such information is restricted, and that it is otherwise properly protected.

10. Have all employees executed appropriate invention assignment and confidentiality agreements? If "no," secure necessary agreements.

11. Are all consultants and independent contractors required to execute appropriate invention assignment and confidentiality agreements? If "no," institute appropriate procedure.

12. Obtain copies of all licenses of intellectual property in which the organization is a licensor or licensee.

13. List all lawsuits pertaining to intellectual property in which the organization is or was a party.

Patent Valuation

Portfolio Valuation

What is a patent worth? The answer depends on who is asking the question. Two things, however, should be apparent: The true nature of intellectual property is the additional or incremental value it brings to its owner, and the incremental value is dependent upon the manner in which the property is used. There are essentially four scenarios in which a valuation of intellectual property is commonly sought:

1. The intellectual property may be owned by an individual or an enterprise that utilizes the property to maintain a monopoly with respect to a product it makes and/or sells, or a service it provides.

2. The intellectual property may be owned by an individual or an enterprise that does not utilize the property directly but is willing to sell or license it to others.

3. An individual or enterprise may purchase intellectual property or take an exclusive license thereunder to avail itself of a patent monopoly afforded thereby.

4. An individual or enterprise may take a nonexclusive license of the intellectual property so as to be able to offer a new product or service in a competitive environment.

Let us consider each category separately.

Consider, for example, a pharmaceutical company selling a patented blockbuster drug. While the patent is active, the company enjoys a large market share and can charge for its drug whatever the market will bear. Once the patent expires (or is invalidated in court), a score of generic drug manufacturers enter the scene and the maker of the blockbuster drug inevitably suffers from price and market share erosion.

Thus, to such a company, a patent protecting a particular product or process[1] would be worth exactly the net present value of the difference between the revenues derived from the sales of this product or service under the monopoly afforded by the patent and the corresponding revenues in an unpatented, freely competitive environment. There is an additional value in a patent, which is an option to license the patent to a non–competitor who may use it in another market. Such a license can be nonexclusive or exclusive in a specific field of use. This additional revenue can be valued using real options theory or, simply, a discount cash flow analysis. For the purposes of this analysis, we will disregard this additional value.

Calculating this difference on an annual basis, we have

$$V(P) = <PR> - PR \qquad (1)$$

where $V(P)$ is the annual value of the patent P; $<PR>$ is the profit generated by the patented product or process in a given year under the assumption of a patent monopoly; and PR is the hypothetical profit generated by the same product or service without the benefit of patent protection—that is, in a freely competitive environment.

To obtain the total value of the patent over its statutory life, we need to sum the expression by years—from the year the patent was issued (one can only enjoy patent protection from the date it is issued[2]) until it

---

[1] Assuming that this product or process does not infringe the patents of others.
[2] Pursuant to the American Inventors Protection Act of 1999, a patent application published 18 months after the date of application filing will enjoy provisional rights as of the date of application publication.

expires. Assuming that an active patent has l years remaining in its term, we have

$$V(P) = \sum_{i=1}^{l} (<PR_i> - PR_i) \qquad (2)$$

where $<PR_i>$, and PR_i are values as in equation (1) taken in a year i and summed by i from the year the patent issued until it expires in year l.

Thus, the patent value is the sum of the incremental values of the patent monopoly on an annual basis over the life of the patent. Written in another way,

$$V(P) = \sum_{i=1}^{l} \Delta_i \qquad (3)$$

where

$$\Delta_i = <PR_i> - PR_i \qquad (4)$$

Suppose the patent application had been pending in the Patent Office for four years before it issued as a U.S. utility patent. Since the patent term is 20 years from the filing date, this patent (during its term) will afford its owner 16 years of patent monopoly. In this case, equation (3) will look like

$$V(P) = (<PR_1> - PR_1) + (<PR_2> - PR_2) \\ + \ldots + (<PR_{16}>) - PR_{16} \qquad (5)$$

or

$$V(P) = \Delta_1 + \Delta_2 + \ldots + \Delta_{16} \qquad (6)$$

In reality, the economic life of a product is often significantly shorter than the statutory term of the patent. Technological obsolescence, changing tastes, and other factors may shorten the economic life of the product. The average economic life of a patent (before the underlying technology becomes obsolete) is only about five years from the date of issue. In this case, equation (5) will have fewer terms as the sales volume eventually dwindles to zero.

It is important to note that the annual incremental values Δ_i change over the life of the patent. Such changes may result, for example, from product promotion, the availability (and cost) of substitute products, and general economic conditions. All such factors must be taken into account when forecasting values for equation (3), and it must be done on an annual basis, as the relative impact of each of these factors may change from year to year.

The previous formulas define the value (i.e., the incremental revenues) of a patent over its entire statutory (or economic) life. In order to obtain the present value of the patent, we must discount the future incremental values Δ_i:

$$PV(P) = \sum_{i=1}^{l} \frac{\Delta_i}{(1 + I_i)^i} \tag{7}$$

where I_i is the discount interest rate in the year i.

In a simplified case similar to an ordinary annuity, where the incremental annual value of a patent monopoly Δ_i and the annual discount rate I_i remain constant ($\Delta_i = \Delta$ and $I_i = I$) throughout the life of the patent, equation (7) can be written as

$$PV(P) = \Delta \left[\frac{1 - \dfrac{1}{(1 + I)^l}}{I} \right] \tag{8}$$

For example, the present value of a patent that secures a patent monopoly yielding a constant incremental annual value Δ, with a remaining life of 17 years ($l = 17$) and a discount rate of 10 percent ($I = 0.10$), is

$$PV(P) = \Delta \left[\frac{1 - \dfrac{1}{(1 + 0.1)^{17}}}{0.1} \right] = 8.02 \times \Delta \tag{9}$$

Thus, for $\Delta = \$10,000,000$, the present value of the patent is $\$80,215,533.$[3] Since a possibility of future design around may render the

---

[3] We assumed here that the incremental revenues Δ_i are received at the end of the annual period.

patent moot, the discount rate of 10 percent may not be realistic when we consider such a long time horizon. A more realistic discount rate may be 25 percent. For the discount rate of 25 percent the equation (8) yields 3.9Δ. Even if the patent portfolio has only 10 years of life left (i.e., the last patent will expire in 10 years), the value of this portfolio is 3.5Δ (assuming the discount rate of 25 percent).

Equation (2) and the subsequent expressions have been derived under the assumption that the patented product is protected by one, and only one, patent. Nevertheless, these formulas also describe the value of an entire patent portfolio protecting a patented product or service. (A patent portfolio represents a group of patents protecting a revenue stream. This stream may be generated by a single product, a product line, or by the enterprise as a whole.) Note that the value of the patent portfolio protecting a single product or service does not depend on the number of patents in the portfolio.

Thus, the value of a patent portfolio $V(PP)$ can be calculated as:

$$V(PP) = \sum_{i=1}^{l} (<PR_i> - PR_i) \tag{10}$$

or

$$V(PP) = \sum_{i=1}^{l} \Delta_i \tag{11}$$

The present value is given by

$$PV(PP) = \sum_{i=1}^{l} \frac{<PR_i> - PR_i}{(1 + I_i)^i} \tag{12}$$

or

$$PV(PP) = \sum_{i=1}^{l} \frac{\Delta_i}{(1 + I_i)^i} \tag{13}$$

Individual Patent Valuation

Let us assume that there are n patents in the portfolio. One might think that the value of any patent in this portfolio is its *pro rata* share:

$$V(P) = \frac{1}{n} V(PP) \tag{14}$$

This, however, can only be true when all patents in the portfolio were issued on the same date and will expire on the same date in the future, and all patents are of equal value. In real life this rarely happens.

To overcome this problem, we first note that

$$V(PP) = \sum_{j=1}^{n} V(P_j) \tag{15}$$

where the value of a portfolio of n patents is described as the sum of values of each individual patent P_j in the portfolio. To account for the fact that the patents may be obtained and expire at different times, we have to consider the situation on an annual basis (with the simplifying assumption that all patents are obtained on the first day of a year and they expire on the last day of a year[4]). Thus, in any given year i the annual value of the patent monopoly, and therefore the annual value of the patent portfolio, is

$$\sum_{j=1}^{n} V(P_i^j) = <PR_i> - PR_i \tag{16}$$

The total value of the portfolio over its entire life is

$$\sum_{i=1}^{l} \sum_{j=1}^{n} V(P_i^j) = \sum_{i=1}^{l} (<PR_i> - PR_i) \tag{17}$$

where l is the total number of years of the portfolio until the expiration of the last to expire patent.

---

[4] This assumption may be refined by further breaking down the summation periods into semiannual, quarterly, and monthly periods.

Since addition is a commutative operation, equation (17) can be rewritten as

$$\sum_{i=1}^{l}\sum_{j=1}^{n} V(P_i^j) = \sum_{i=1}^{l}(<PR_i> -PR_i) \qquad (18)$$

or

$$\sum_{j=1}^{n} V(P_j) = \sum_{i=1}^{l}(<PR_i> -PR_i) \qquad (19)$$

where $V(P_j)$ is the value of the j-th patent, P_j, over its life. Equation (19) gives the sum of values V of all portfolio patents P_j. We must solve this equation for $V(P_j)$. Let us begin by assuming that all active (issued and nonexpired) patents contribute equal value to the portfolio. We need to account for the fact that some of the patents may have been issued later than others and will expire later (or be invalidated earlier) than others. To do that, we introduce a matrix P (if the mathematical term *matrix* is unfamiliar to you, think of a table), where rows correspond to years of the portfolio's life and columns correspond to the individual patents in the portfolio. If a particular patent is active in a particular year, we write into a corresponding cell of the matrix a positive number greater than zero and less than or equal to one; if the patent has not been issued yet or has already expired, we write a zero. In other words, the matrix element p_j^i is positive $(0 < p_j^i \leq 1)$ when, and only when, the patent j is active in the year i; otherwise it is zero. Since the value of a patent portfolio does not depend on the number of its constituent patents, the values assigned to the individual cells of the matrix must satisfy a simple rule: The sum of all elements in any row of the matrix must be equal to one. We shall call this matrix P a *patent portfolio weight matrix*.

Let us, for example, consider a patent portfolio consisting of three patents over a period of four years. Let us assume that, during the first year, the portfolio consisted of only one patent, P_1; during the second year, it consisted of two patents, P_1 and P_2 (the second patent was just

issued); during the third year, there is only one patent, P_2 (the first patent expired at the end of the second year); and during the fourth year
there are two patents, P_2 and P_3. Let us insert these facts into the table:

	Patent 1	Patent 2	Patent 3
Year 1	1	0	0
Year 2	0.5	0.5	0
Year 3	0	1	0
Year 4	0	0.5	0.5

Note that we have apportioned the values pro rata to the number of
patents active each year. In years 2 and 4, there were two patents active,
and we therefore assigned values of 0.5 to each patent in those years so as
to satisfy our rule that the sum of row elements must be equal to 1. In
other words, the value in a given cell is $1/n$, where n is the number of
patents active that year.

Alternatively, in mathematical notation, the patent portfolio weight
matrix P looks, in this case, as follows:

$$P = \begin{pmatrix} 1 & 0 & 0 \\ 0.5 & 0.5 & 0 \\ 0 & 1 & 0 \\ 0 & 0.5 & 0.5 \end{pmatrix} \tag{20}$$

Generally, the patent portfolio weight matrix P gives a complete picture
of what patents are active in any given year over the life of the portfolio.

We have assumed here that all patents in the portfolio were active
throughout the entire year. This is an oversimplification, as patents may
issue and expire at any time during the year. To account for this reality,
instead of $1/n$, we can assign to an active patent a number weighted pro
rata according to the number of months the patent was (or will be) active that year. For example, suppose that in the patent portfolio weight
matrix (equation 20) the second patent was issued in the beginning of

July. Then, instead of 0.5, we assign a weighted number 0.25. This automatically raises the value of the first patent:

$$P = \begin{pmatrix} 1 & 0 & 0 \\ 0.75 & 0.25 & 0 \\ 0 & 1 & 0 \\ 0 & 0.5 & 0.5 \end{pmatrix} \tag{21}$$

Our other assumption, that all of the patents contribute equally to the
portfolio, led us to assign the same value to each patent active for a given
number of months during that particular year. This need not be so. Patents
may have different values. One would not, for example, assign the same
value to a broad patent on a basic technology as one would assign to a
narrow patent on a relatively minor improvement in the technology.

The litmus test in determining the relative values of the patents in a
portfolio is to ask the following question: How much of the monopoly
will be lost if this particular patent is removed from the portfolio (sold,
abandoned, expired, or invalidated)? The broader the scope of the patent claims, the broader the monopoly secured by the patent and, therefore, the larger the relative value of this patent to the portfolio. We
always need to remember that the patent is a legal instrument and its
value is strictly proportional to the legal protection it affords (i.e., the
scope of the patent claims).

However, individual patents may change in value during their terms
as well. For example, a patent that emerges untarnished from Patent Office reexamination with its presumption of validity enhanced is now
worth more than before. A patent that is ruled to be valid and enforceable (actually not *invalid* or *unenforceable*) in a court of law may grow in
value even more. Conversely, a patent whose validity is challenged (e.g.,
by third-party initiation of *ex parte* reexamination proceedings) is worth
less for as long as its validity is in doubt.

The patent portfolio weight matrix allows us to account both for
individual patents having different values, relative to each other, and for

patents having a relative value that varies over the patent's life. To account for these differences, one needs to weigh or assess each patent
during each year and to assign different numbers, slightly higher or
lower values, to corresponding cells in the matrix P. In doing so, one
must follow the same simple rule: *The sum of all values in every row must
be equal to 1.* For example, if, during the second year, the first patent
accounted for only 40 percent of the portfolio value that year, while the
second patent accounted for the remaining 60 percent, we would rewrite the matrix in equation (20) as

$$P = \begin{pmatrix} 1 & 0 & 0 \\ 0.4 & 0.6 & 0 \\ 0 & 1 & 0 \\ 0 & 0.5 & 0.5 \end{pmatrix} \qquad (22)$$

or, if the second patent only issues in July as in equation (21), we would
have

$$P = \begin{pmatrix} 1 & 0 & 0 \\ 0.7 & 0.3 & 0 \\ 0 & 1 & 0 \\ 0 & 0.5 & 0.5 \end{pmatrix} \qquad (23)$$

Equation (23) describes a patent portfolio weight matrix P weighted
with respect to individual patent contribution to the portfolio value,
both over time and in relative value. Thus, the patent portfolio weight
matrix P gives a complete picture of which patents are active in any
given year over the life of the portfolio, as well as their relative value or
weight.

Since the sum of all elements in any row is 1, the sum of all elements
of the matrix is equal to the number of rows—the total number of years
in the life of the portfolio (commencing with the issuance of the first
patent and terminating at the end of the term of the last patent to
expire). We will call this number a *portfolio statutory life, L.* Generally, L is
the sum of all elements p_i^j (or, simply, the number of the rows) of the

matrix P:

$$L = \sum_j \sum_i p_i^j \tag{24}$$

We will also introduce here a patent weight index p^j defined as the sum of the values in a j-th column of the matrix P:

$$p^j = \sum_i^l p_i^j \tag{25}$$

Patent weight index p^j is the sum of all weighted values for a given patent throughout the life of the portfolio. It is a weighted contribution of the individual patent to the portfolio.

The portfolio is a sum of its constituent patents and, therefore, the annual value of a portfolio PP is the sum of the annual values of the individual patents:

$$AV_i(PP) = \sum_{j=1}^n AV_i(P^j) \tag{26}$$

where $AV_i(PP)$ is the annual value of the portfolio in year i; $AV_i(P^j)$ is the annual value of the j-th patent, P^j, in year i; and n is the number of patents in the portfolio.

Since the sum of all matrix elements in one row is always equal to 1, we can multiply the left side of the equation by such a sum without changing the equation:

$$AV_i(PP) \times \sum_{j=1}^n p_i^j = \sum_{j=1}^n AV_i(P^j) \tag{27}$$

We can rewrite this equation as:

$$\sum_{j=1}^n AV_i(PP) \times p_i^j = \sum_{j=1}^n AV_i(P^j) \tag{28}$$

Since, by definition, patent portfolio matrix values p_i^j represent relative values of the constituent patents in the portfolio, it follows that all additive members on both sides of the equation must be equal:

$$AV_i(PP) \times p_i^j = AV_i(P^j) \tag{29}$$

Since the annual value of the patent portfolio is, by definition, the annual value of the patent monopoly, we have:

$$AV_i(P^j) = p_i^j \times \Delta_i \tag{30}$$

Once we know the annual values of the patent P^j, it is easy to discount them to the present value:

$$PV(P^j) = \sum_{i=1}^{I} \frac{p_i^j \times \Delta_i}{(1 + I_i)^i} \tag{31}$$

This expression allows one to calculate the present value $PV(P^j)$ of a constituent patent P^j based on the patent portfolio matrix $P = \{p_i^j\}$ and the annual values of the patent monopoly. Equation (31) for the present value of a constituent patent differs from equation (3) for the present value of the portfolio to the extent that, in equation (31), the annual value of the patent monopoly is weighted for the relative contribution of a constituent patent to the overall value of the portfolio.

In the Real World

The formulas presented thus far describe the present value of patents in an ideal world in which competitors respect the intellectual property rights of each other and do not infringe each other's patents. In the real world, where patent infringement is a commonplace reality, we must assume that patents will be challenged by infringing competitors and will need to be enforced in a court of law.

To adjust our formulas to this more realistic situation, we need to consider at least two additional factors: (1) the probability E that the patent owner will, in the event of infringement, enforce its patent rights; and (2) the probability F that the patent owner will prevail in court. With this in mind, we can now rewrite equations (3) and (8) as follows:

$$V(PP) = E \times F \times \sum_{i=1}^{l} \Delta_i \qquad (32)$$

and

$$PV(PP) = E \times F \times \sum_{i=1}^{l} \frac{\Delta_i}{(1 + I_i)^i} \qquad (33)$$

The probability E that the patent owner, in the event of infringement, will enforce its patents depends mainly on two factors: one's willingness, E_w, and one's ability, E_a, to do so. Needless to say, a patent portfolio owned by a company that is unlikely or unable to enforce it is worth considerably less (if anything at all) than a similar portfolio owned by a company that vigorously enforces its patents, all other things being equal. Both these factors of willingness E_w and ability E_a must be taken into account when estimating the probability of patent enforcement E. Assuming, for simplicity, that these two factors are independent, the total probability of enforcement E is the product of these two factors:

$$E = E_w \times E_a \qquad (34)$$

The probability F of prevailing at trial is also composed of several factors, which include:

1. the probability F_{inf} that at least one of the patents in the portfolio will be found to be infringed;

2. the probability F_{val} that at least one of the infringed patent(s) will be found valid (strictly speaking, will not be found invalid as patents enjoy presumption of validity); and

3. the probability F_{enf} that at least one of the infringed and valid patent(s) will be found enforceable (strictly speaking, will not be found unenforceable).

Based on our statistical analysis performed on the data set for the past decade (2000–2009) published by the Institute for Intellectual Property

& Information Law (IPIL) at the University of Houston Law Center,[5] the probabilities of these values are as follows: The probability F_{inf} that a given patent will be found infringed is 28 percent (down dramatically from 66 percent in the previous decade). The probability F_{val} that a given patent will be found valid is 56 percent (down from 67 percent). The probability F_{enf} that a given patent will be found enforceable is 72 percent (down from 88 percent).

In the real world, the value of a patent portfolio increases with its size; since all asserted patents must be found invalid to avoid infringement on validity grounds, the probability that at least one patent in an n-patent portfolio will survive the validity challenge is

$$F_{val} = 1 - \prod_{j=1}^{n} \left(1 - F_{val}^{j}\right) \tag{35}$$

where the Greek symbol Π (the capital letter Π, pronounced "pi") denotes multiplication by each patent P^{j} in an n-patent portfolio. This formula is shorthand for

$$F_{val} = 1 - \left(1 - F_{val}^{1}\right) \times \left(1 - F_{val}^{2}\right) \times \ldots \times \left(1 - F_{val}^{n}\right) \tag{36}$$

where F_{val}^{1}, F_{val}^{2}, and F_{val}^{n} are respective probabilities for each of the patents P^{1}, P^{2}, and P^{n} not to be invalidated (i.e., to survive the validity challenge). Equations (35) and (36) assume that the probability of invalidating any particular patent in the portfolio is independent of the probability of invalidating any other patent in the same portfolio. This is how it should be in theory as each patent stands on its own merits. In reality, however, particularly in jury trials, often all asserted patents stand or fall together. More on this point later.

Let's assume, for example, that we have a two-patent portfolio $\{P^{1}, P^{2}\}$ with the confidence level about the validity of each of these two patents being respectively $F_{val}^{1} = 60$ percent and $F_{val}^{2} = 55\%$. This

---

[5] See: www.patstats.org

means that there is a 40 percent chance $(1 - 0.60)$ to invalidate the first patent and there is a 45 percent chance $(1 - 0.55)$ to invalidate the second patent. To calculate the probability to invalidate both patents we must multiply the respective probabilities to invalidate each of them, that is, $F_{val} = (1 - 0.60) \times (1 - 0.55) = 0.40 \times 0.45 = 0.18$. Thus, the probability that both patents in our example will be invalidated is 18 percent. In other words, the probability that at least one of our two patents will survive the validity challenge is 82 percent $(1 - 0.18)$. This is what equations (35) or (36) generalize for a multi-patent portfolio.

Assuming, for simplicity, that all individual probabilities are equal $(F_{val}^j = F_{val}^1)$, we have

$$F_{val} = 1 - \left(1 - F_{val}^1\right)^n \tag{37}$$

where n is the number of patents in the portfolio. Since the probability of invalidating an individual patent is always less than 1, the probability of invalidating more than one patent falls off geometrically as the number of patents increases. For example, if the probability of invalidating an individual patent is 44 percent, the probability of invalidating both patents of a two-patent portfolio is $0.44 \times 0.44 = 0.19$ (i.e., 19 percent); the probability of invalidating all three patents of a three-patent portfolio is $0.44^3 = 0.08$ (i.e., 8 percent); and the probability of invalidating all the patents in a 10-patent portfolio is entirely negligible at $0.44^{10} = 0.00025$ (meaning 0.02 percent!).

A similar situation is true with respect to the enforceability of patents. We have, therefore,

$$F_{enf} = 1 - \prod_{j=1}^{n} \left(1 - F_{enf}^j\right) \tag{38}$$

and, assuming for simplicity that all individual probabilities are equal $(F_{enf}^j = F_{enf}^1)$, we have

$$F_{enf} = 1 - \left(1 - F_{enf}^1\right)^n \tag{39}$$

If the probability F^1_{enf} that a patent will be found enforceable is 72 percent, the probability that more than one patent will be declared unenforceable vanishes very rapidly as the number of patents increases. In a portfolio of just three patents, this probability is only 2.2 percent. We must remember, however, that if the inventor is found to be guilty of inequitable conduct before the Patent Office (an act that used to be called a fraud on the Patent Office) or if the patent owner is found to be guilty of antitrust violation involving patent misuse, the judge may (and often does) declare the whole family of related patents or even the entire portfolio of patents-in-suit unenforceable. In view of this fact, the enforceability analysis may not be appropriate on a patent-by-patent basis and a single probability F_{enf} of surviving the enforceability challenge may be estimated.

With respect to infringement, it is sufficient to prove that any one of the patents in the portfolio (even a single claim of a single patent) is infringed to establish liability. Therefore, to avoid liability for infringement, the defendant would need to successfully defend against each asserted patent (strictly speaking, each asserted claim of each asserted patent). Thus, the probability of noninfringement is the product of non-infringement probabilities for each individual patent:

$$F_{inf} = 1 - \prod_{j=1}^{n} \left(1 - F^j_{inf}\right) \tag{40}$$

and, again, assuming for simplicity that all individual probabilities are equal ($F^j_{inf} = F^1_{inf}$), we have

$$F_{inf} = 1 - \left(1 - F^1_{inf}\right)^n \tag{41}$$

When a patentee asserts only one patent, the chances of success in proving infringement are 28 percent; for two patents, the chances improve to 47.5 percent; and for five patents, the chances jump to 80 percent because the plaintiff only needs to prove the infringement of at least one patent.

The previous calculations are all based on the assumption of event independence: In accordance with the patent law, the questions of validity, enforceability, and infringement are decided independently for each patent (moreover, validity and infringement are decided on a claim-by-claim basis). It is important to remember that, in reality, human psychology plays a role equally important to (or even more important than) the law during jury deliberations. Thus, juries (and, at times, even judges) tend to lump patents together, which destroys the assumption of statistical event independence. In fact, judges rule in favor of the same party on both validity and infringement in 74 percent of the cases.[6] Juries rule in favor of the same party in 86 percent of the cases.[7]

For a plaintiff to prevail in a patent infringement trial, at least one patent must be found infringed, valid (not invalid), and enforceable (not unenforceable). The probability of such an event is the product of probabilities that a given patent is infringed F_{inf}, that it is valid F_{val}, and that it is enforceable F_{enf}:

$$F^j = F^j_{inf} \times F^j_{val} \times F^j_{enf} \qquad (42)$$

To calculate the total probability to win at trial we need to recall that when event A and B are not mutually exclusive, the probability of either is given by the formula:

$$\Pr(A \text{ or } B) = \Pr(A) + \Pr(B) - \Pr(A \text{ and } B)$$

where $\Pr(A)$ is the probability of the event A, $\Pr(B)$ is the probability of the event (B), and $\Pr(A \text{ and } B)$ is the probability of both events occurring.

If we have a two-patent portfolio, the total probability F of prevailing at trial is the sum of probabilities that at least one of two patents will

[6] Kimberly A. Moore, "Judges, Juries, and Patent Cases: An Empirical Peek Inside the Black Box," *Michigan Law Review* 99 (2001).
[7] Ibid.

be found valid, enforceable, and infringed less the probability that both patents will be found valid, enforceable, and infringed:

$$F = F^1 + F^2 - F^1 \times F^2 \tag{43}$$

or

$$F = \left(F^1_{inf} \times F^1_{val} \times F^1_{enf} \right) + \left(F^2_{inf} \times F^2_{val} \times F^2_{enf} \right)$$
$$- \left(F^1_{inf} \times F^1_{val} \times F^1_{enf} \right) \times \left(F^2_{inf} \times F^2_{val} \times F^2_{enf} \right) \tag{43*}$$

If all respective probabilities F^j_{inf}, F^j_{val}, and F^j_{enf} can be assumed to be the same for each patent in the portfolio, so that $F^j_{inf} = F_{inf}$, $F^j_{val} = F_{val}$, and $F^j_{enf} = F_{enf}$, equation (44) is simplified:

$$F = 2 \times F_{inf} \times F_{val} \times F_{enf} - \left(F_{inf} \times F_{val} \times F_{enf} \right)^2 \tag{44}$$

In a three-patent portfolio, things get slightly more complicated. The formula for the probability of the union of three events, A, B, and C is given by:

$$\Pr(A \cup B \cup C) = \Pr(A) + \Pr(B) + \Pr(C) -$$
$$\Pr(A \cap B) - \Pr(A \cap C) - \Pr(B \cap C) + \Pr(A \cap B \cap C)$$

where the symbol $\cup$ means "or" and the symbol $\cap$ means "and."

If we have a three-patent portfolio, the total probability F of prevailing at trial is:

$$F = \left(F^1 + F^2 + F^3 \right) - \left(F^1 \times F^2 \right) - \left(F^1 \times F^3 \right)$$
$$- \left(F^2 \times F^3 \right) + \left(F^1 \times F^2 \times F^3 \right) \tag{43}$$

Since, as mentioned before, the determination of unenforceability of one patent usually renders the entire portfolio unenforceable, it is not enough to prove that at least one patent in the portfolio is valid, enforceable, and infringed; the plaintiff also needs to avoid the finding of unenforceability for any of the patents in the portfolio. Therefore, we have:

$$
\begin{aligned}
F = {} & [(F^1_{inf} \times F^1_{val} + F^2_{inf} \times F^2_{val} + F^3_{inf} \times F^3_{val}) \\
& - (F^1_{inf} \times F^1_{val} \times F^2_{inf} \times F^2_{val}) - (F^1_{inf} \times F^1_{val} \times F^3_{inf} \times F^3_{val}) \\
& - (F^2_{inf} \times F^2_{val} \times F^3_{inf} \times F^3_{val}) \\
& + (F^1_{inf} \times F^1_{val} \times F^2_{inf} \times F^2_{val} \times F^3_{inf} \times F^3_{val})] \\
& \times F^1_{enf} \times F^2_{enf} \times F^3_{enf}
\end{aligned}
$$

As could be expected, the complexity of the analysis increases with the size of the portfolio. At some point, it becomes impractical to do this on a patent by patent basis for large patent portfolios. A single empirical estimate can be used instead for the probability F in equation (32).

Portfolio Net Present Value and Yield (IRR)

Let us now consider an important economic indicator of a patent portfolio: its yield or internal rate of return (IRR).

It is well known that the yield, or IRR, on an investment that produces annual cash flow C_i is the interest rate that satisfies the equation

$$
p = \sum_{i=1}^{n} \frac{C_i}{(1+y)^i} \tag{45}
$$

where p is the price paid (or investment made), C_i is the annual cash flow, y is the yield, and n is the number of years. Yield is determined by a trial-and-error procedure.

In the case of a patent portfolio, the cash flow C_i is equivalent to the annual value of the patent monopoly secured by the portfolio:

$$
C_i = AV_i(PP) \tag{46}
$$

Let us turn our attention now to the price (or investment) p. Traditionally, the cost of a patent, p, is thought to be the sum of the cost of prosecution (including the costs of drafting and filing the patent application), p_{pros}, and the cost of maintenance (including payment of USPTO filing and issue fees), p_{main}:

$$p = p_{pros} + p_{main} \qquad (47)$$

These numbers are well known. The cost of patent prosecution is between $8,000 and $15,000 (lower for a patent on a mechanical invention, higher for a biotechnology patent). Over the life of the patent, the minimum filing, issue, and maintenance fees are $9,410 for a so-called large entity U.S. patent and $4,622 for a small entity U.S. patent. Patents filed internationally may, over the course of their lives, cost over $100,000.

However, it is a mistake to think that the cost of a patent is simply the cost of patent prosecution and maintenance. The true price paid for a patent includes disclosure of the invention. An inventor has a choice: Keep the invention secret or disclose it in the hopes of obtaining a patent. An undisclosed invention, if kept confidential, is intellectual property, too, protected as a trade secret.

Valuation techniques for trade secrets lie outside the scope of this appendix. What is important for our present discussion is understanding that the value of the trade secret is a part of the price paid for obtaining a patent. Thus, we rewrite equation (47) as

$$p = PV(TS) + p_{pros} + p_{main} \qquad (48)$$

where $PV(TS)$ is the present value of the trade secrets TS, forfeited in exchange for the constituent patents of the portfolio. Equation (49) now takes form:

$$PV(TS) + p_{pros} + p_{main} = \sum_{i=1}^{n} \frac{C_i}{(1+y)^i} \qquad (49)$$

The interest rate y that satisfies this equation gives us the yield or the IRR of the patent portfolio.

Value in the Event of a Known Infringement

When patent infringement occurs, the patent monopoly is violated, and the methodology developed here may no longer be applicable unless a permanent injunction restoring monopoly is obtained. In the event injunction is not available as a remedy, a patent or patent portfolio may only be worth as much as one expects to recover in damages through litigation less the cost of litigation.

The cost of litigation may be forecasted based on well-known statistics. The average cost of patent litigation in the United States is $2.5 million for small cases with damages between $1 and $25 million. For larger cases with damages over $25 million, the median cost of litigation is $5.5 million.[8] Such statistics are available by state as well.

---

[8] See www.patstats.org.

Invention Disclosure Form

1. Full name, address, and telephone number of each person who conceived the invention.

2. General subject matter and purpose of the invention, including an explanation of the problem(s) to be solved and the deficiencies in the existing technology.

3. A description of the invention, including, if available.

   a. Drawings, photographs, charts, test results, and so forth.

   b. Identification of each novel feature.

   c. An explanation of how the novel features provide advantages over the existing technology.

   d. A description of any presently contemplated modifications, alterations, improvements, or extensions of the invention.

4. A description of the closest known prior art (attach copies of prior art documents if available).

Attach additional, consecutively numbered pages as needed, each having the signatures of the inventors and witnesses as indicated below:

Inventor Signature(s) and Date:

_____   _____

Name   Date

_____   _____

Name   Date

Read and Understood by Witnesses:

_____   _____

Name   Date

_____   _____

Name   Date

License Agreements

This template can be used for either a running royalty agreement or a paid-up license agreement. Only Section 3, "Payments," will change depending on the type of agreement used.

NONEXCLUSIVE LIMITED PATENT LICENSE AGREEMENT

THIS AGREEMENT (hereinafter referred to as the "Agreement") is made by and between Licensor Company (hereinafter referred to as "Licensor"), a _____[form of organization] with principal offices at _____, and _____, a _____ corporation with principal offices at _____ (hereinafter referred to as "Licensee").

<u>WITNESSETH</u>:

WHEREAS, Licensor is the owner of all right, title, and interest in United States Patent Nos. _____ (which patents are hereinafter collectively referred to as the "Licensed Patents");

WHEREAS, Licensee is in the business of making and selling _____, and desires to obtain a nonexclusive license to make, use, and sell products and to practice the inventions covered by the Licensed Patents;

WHEREAS, Licensee has made and sold certain _____ [if applicable];

WHEREAS, Licensee consents that the Licensed Patents are valid and enforceable [if applicable];

WHEREAS, Licensee consents that the Licensed Patents have been infringed by certain products made, sold, and/or offered for sale by Licensee [if applicable];

WHEREAS, Licensor and Licensee desire to enter into a license agreement covering the Licensed Patents; and

WHEREAS, Licensor has the right to grant a nonexclusive license to Licensee under the Licensed Patents and is willing to do so on the terms and conditions recited in this Agreement.

NOW, THEREFORE, in consideration of the preceding and the mutual covenants recited below, and for other good and valuable consideration, receipt and sufficiency of which is hereby acknowledged, the parties agree as follows:

1. DEFINITIONS.

1.1 Licensed Patents. "Licensed Patents" as used in this Agreement shall mean the _____, collectively, and any patent issued in the future from any reissue, reexamination, divisional, continuation, and/or continuation-in-part of the Licensed Patents, including any foreign counterpart thereof.

1.2 Territory. "Territory" as used in this Agreement shall mean the United States and its territories and possessions. [If foreign patents are licensed, include respective countries.]

1.3 Effective Date. "Effective Date" shall mean _____, _____.

1.4 Term. "Term" as used in this Agreement shall mean the period beginning on the Effective Date and ending with the expiration of the last to expire of the Licensed Patents or the termination of this Agreement, whichever occurs first. This Agreement shall, if not terminated sooner, terminate at the end of the Term.

1.5 Licensed Product. "Licensed Product" as used in this Agreement shall mean certain _____ made, used, imported, sold, or offered for sale by Licensee, including, but not limited to: _____.

1.6 Past Products. "Past Products" as used in this Agreement shall mean the Licensed Products made or sold by Licensee before the Effective Date of this Agreement.

2. LICENSE.

2.1 License Grant. Subject to the terms and conditions of this Agreement and the due performance by Licensee of Licensee's obligations under this Agreement and in reliance on Licensee's representations and warranties set forth in this Agreement, Licensor hereby grants to Licensee a personal, nonexclusive, nontransferable limited license under the Licensed Patents for the Term in the Territory to make, use, import, offer to sell, and sell Licensed Products and Past Products, with no right to sublicense. This license shall not extend to any third party, subsidiary, division, or any entity acquired after the Effective Date.

2.2 Basis. The foregoing license is granted solely under the Licensed Patents. No license under any other patents or intellectual property of Licensor is granted, either expressly or by implication.

2.3 Marking. During the Term of this Agreement, Licensee shall affix to Licensed Products a statement in substantially the form: "U.S. Patent Nos. _____." The Licensee shall provide Licensor with the samples of its Licensed Products evidencing proper marking as required hereunder. From time to time, and within a reasonable time after written notice from Licensor, Licensor shall have the right to inspect Licensee's Licensed Products to determine if Licensee is marking in accordance with this paragraph.

2.4 Past Sales. Subject to the terms and conditions of this Agreement and the due performance by Licensee of its obligation to make the payment required by Paragraph 3.1, Licensor hereby grants to Licensee a nonexclusive limited license under the Licensed Patents on all Past Products.

3. PAYMENTS. [*For running royalty license agreement*]

3.1 Past Products. For the rights granted in this Agreement relating to Licensee's Past Products, Licensee shall pay Licensor a past license fee of _____ percent (___%) of Licensee's net sales (defined as gross sales less returns and allowances) for each Past Product sold during the last six years from the Effective Date hereof, which shall be due and payable immediately upon the Effective Date hereof.

3.2 Running Royalty.

3.2.1 Royalty Payment. For the rights granted in this Agreement, and subject to Paragraph 3.2.2 hereinbelow, Licensee shall pay Licensor a royalty of _____ percent (___%) of Licensee's selling price for each Licensed Product manufactured, used, or sold by Licensee in the Territory or imported by Licensee into the Territory.

3.2.2 Termination of Royalty on Invalidity or Unenforceability. The royalty payments shall terminate if all of the Licensed Patents are held invalid or unenforceable. A Licensed Patent shall be deemed invalid or unenforceable under this Agreement if a court or tribunal of competent jurisdiction makes such a determination, and the determination becomes final in that it is not further reviewable through appeal or exhaustion of all permissible petitions or applications for rehearing or review.

3.3 Accrual. A running royalty as to a unit of Licensed Product shall accrue on the day the unit is shipped or invoiced to a Licensee customer, whichever occurs first.

3.4 Payment. All royalty payments to Licensor shall be made quarterly by Licensee, with the first quarter being defined as January 1 through March 31, the second quarter as April 1 through June 30, the third quarter as July 1 through September 30, and the fourth quarter as October 1 through December 31. Payment of royalties shall be made to Licensor not later than the thirtieth (30th) day (the "Due Date") after the end of the period to which the payment relates. Each royalty payment as defined hereinabove shall be subject to and be no less than a minimum royalty of _____ ($_____) dollars per quarter.

3.5 Accounting Statements. Licensee shall provide Licensor with a statement of royalties due Licensor under this Agreement quarterly (as that term is defined in Paragraph 3.4) on or before the Due Date, setting forth the amount due to Licensor for the period and, in reasonable detail, the factual basis for calculating the amount.

3.6 Interest. Subject to the limits imposed by any applicable usury law, interest shall accrue on payments made more than ten (10) days after they are due at the rate of _____ percent (___%) per annum, compounded daily, from the due date until paid.

3.7 Books and Records and Audit. Licensee shall keep full, complete, and accurate books of account and records covering all transactions relating to this Agreement. Licensee shall preserve such books and records for a period of three (3) years after the Due Date to which the material relates. Acceptance by Licensor of an accounting statement or payment hereunder will not preclude Licensor from challenging or questioning the accuracy thereof. During the Term and for a period of one (1) year thereafter, Licensor may, upon reasonable notice in writing to Licensee, cause an independent audit to be made of the books and records of Licensee in order to verify the statements rendered under this Agreement, and prompt adjustment shall be made by the proper party to compensate for any errors disclosed by the audit. The audit shall be conducted only by an independent accountant during regular business hours and in a reasonable manner so as not to interfere with normal business activities. Audits shall be made hereunder no more frequently than annually. Before any audit may be conducted, the auditor must represent that the auditor's fee will in no manner be determined by the results of the audit and must agree to maintain the confidentiality of all confidential material to which the auditor is given access. Licensor will bear all expenses and fees of the audit, but if the audit reveals an underpayment for any quarter of more than five percent (5%), Licensee shall pay all such expenses and fees. Licensee shall provide samples of any new _____, and/or a complete written description thereof, sufficient to enable Licensor to determine whether such product is covered by any of the claims of any of the Licensed Patents.

3.8 Patent Validity and Infringement. Licensee acknowledges and consents that the Licensed Patents are valid and enforceable. [*If applicable*: Licensee further acknowledges that the Licensed Products infringe the Licensed Patents. Licensee admits that it has been infringing the Licensed Patents and this infringement shall be cured by the License granted hereunder.]

3.9 Nonaggression. Licensee shall not at any time, directly or indirectly, oppose the grant of, nor dispute the validity or enforceability of, nor cooperate in any suit, claim, counterclaim, or defense against any patent or claim included in the Licensed Patents.

3.10 Confidentiality. Licensor and Licensee acknowledge that the amount of Licensee's payments actually made to Licensor under this Agreement are confidential and proprietary information relating to this Agreement and the business of Licensor and Licensee. Accordingly, the parties agree that each of them shall keep that information confidential and shall not disclose it, or permit it to be disclosed, to any third party (other than to agents or representatives who need to know such information). Licensor shall have the right, however, to disclose that Licensor and Licensee have entered into this Agreement, the royalty rate(s) set forth in this Agreement, that Licensee is paying for Past Products, and that Licensee has consented to the validity, enforceability, and infringement of the Licensed Patents.

3. PAYMENTS. [*For paid-up license agreement*]

3.1 Paid-up License. For the rights granted in this Agreement, Licensee shall unconditionally pay Licensor a one-time license fee of _____ and 00/100 dollars ($_____.00), which shall be due immediately upon the Effective Date and payable within three (3) days of the Effective Date.

3.2 Patent Validity and Infringement. Licensee acknowledges and consents that the Licensed Patents are valid and enforceable. [*If applicable:* Licensee further acknowledges that the Licensed Products infringe the Licensed Patents. Licensee admits that it has been infringing the Licensed Patents and that this infringement shall be cured by the license granted hereunder.]

3.3 Nonaggression. Licensee shall not at any time, directly or indirectly, oppose the grant of, nor dispute the validity or enforceability of, nor cooperate in any suit, claim, counterclaim, or defense against any patent or claim including in the Licensed Patents.

3.4 Confidentiality. Licensor and Licensee acknowledge that the amount of Licensee's payments actually made to Licensor under this Agreement are confidential and proprietary information relating to this Agreement and the business of Licensor and Licensee. Accordingly, the parties agree that each of them shall keep that information confidential and shall not disclose it, or permit it to be disclosed, to any third party (other than to agents or representatives who need to know such information). Licensor shall have the right, however, to disclose that Licensor and Licensee have entered into this Agreement, that Licensee is paying for Past Products, and that Licensee has consented to the validity, enforceability, and infringement of the Licensed Patents.

4. INDEMNIFICATION.

4.1 Licensee Indemnification. Licensee shall at all times during the Term of this Agreement and thereafter, indemnify, defend, and hold Licensor, its directors, officers, employees, and affiliates, harmless against all claims, proceedings, demands, and liabilities of any kind whatsoever, including legal expenses and reasonable attorneys' fees, arising out of the death of or injury to any person or out of any damage to property, or resulting from the production, manufacture, sale, use, lease, or advertisement of Licensed Products or Past Products, or arising from any obligation of Licensee under this Agreement.

4.2 Licensor Indemnification. Licensor shall at all times during the Term of this Agreement and thereafter, indemnify, defend, and hold Licensee, its directors, officers, employees, and affiliates, harmless against all claims, proceedings, demands, and liabilities of any kind whatsoever, including legal expenses and reasonable attorneys' fees, arising out of any breach of any representation, warranty, or covenant expressly made by Licensor in this Agreement.

5. TERMINATION.

5.1 Termination by Licensor. In addition to all other remedies Licensor may have, Licensor may terminate this Agreement and the licenses granted in this Agreement in the event that:

a. Licensee defaults in its payment to Licensor and such default continues unremedied for a period of thirty (30) days after the Effective Date of this Agreement;

b. Licensee fails to perform any material obligation, warranty, duty, or responsibility or is in default with respect to any term or condition undertaken by Licensee hereunder, and such failure or default continues unremedied for a period of thirty (30) days after written notice thereof to Licensee by Licensor;

c. Licensee is liquidated or dissolved;

d. Any assignment is made of Licensee's business for the benefit of creditors;

e. Licensee liquidates a substantial portion of its business or engages in a distress sale of substantially all of its assets;

f. A receiver, or similar officer, is appointed to take charge of a substantial part of Licensee's assets;

g. Licensee is unable to pay its debts as they mature; or

h. Any petition in bankruptcy is filed by or against Licensee that remains undischarged for sixty (60) days.

5.2 Termination by Licensee. If all the Licensed Patents are determined to be invalid or unenforceable by any court or tribunal of competent jurisdiction, and the determination becomes final in that it is not further reviewable through appeal or exhaustion of all permissible petitions or applications for rehearing or review, Licensee may terminate this Agreement at will and shall have no further obligations hereunder.

5.3 Effect of Termination. After the termination of this Agreement, Licensee shall have no rights under the Licensed Patents.

5.4 No Discharge on Termination. No termination of this Agreement for any reason shall relieve or discharge either Licensor or Licensee from any duty, obligation, or liability that was accrued as of the date of the termination (including, without limitation, the obligation to indemnify or to pay any amounts owing as of the date of termination).

6.   REPRESENTATIONS   AND   WARRANTIES   OF LICENSOR.

6.1 Right to Grant License. Licensor represents and warrants that Licensor has the right and authority to grant the licenses granted to Licensee in this Agreement and that this Agreement and the licenses granted in this Agreement do not and will not conflict with the terms of any agreement to which Licensor is a party.

6.2 Disclaimers. Except as otherwise expressly set forth in this Agreement, Licensor, its directors, officers, employees, and agents make no representations and extend no warranties of any kind, either express or implied. In particular, and without limitation, nothing in this Agreement shall be construed as:

a. a warranty or representation by Licensor as to the validity or scope of the Licensed Patents;

b. a warranty or representation by Licensor that anything made, used, sold, or otherwise disposed of under any license granted in this Agreement is or will be free from infringement of patents of third parties;

c. an obligation on the part of Licensor to bring or prosecute actions against third parties for infringement of the Licensed Patents or other proprietary rights;

d. an obligation on the part of Licensor to furnish any manufacturing or technical information;

e. the granting by implication, estoppel, or otherwise of any licenses or rights under patents other than the Licensed Patents; or

f. the assumption by Licensor of any responsibilities whatever with respect to use, sale, or other disposition by Licensee or its vendees or transferees of Licensed Products.

6.3 Limitation of Liability. In no event shall Licensor, its directors, officers, employees, and affiliates be liable for incidental or consequential damages of any kind, including economic damage or injury to property and lost profits, regardless of whether Licensor shall be advised, shall have other reason to know, or in fact shall know of the possibility.

7. REPRESENTATIONS AND WARRANTIES OF LICENSEE.

Licensee represents and warrants that Licensee has the right and authority to enter into this Agreement and that this Agreement and the exercise of the licenses granted hereunder does not and will not conflict with the terms of any agreement to which Licensee is a party. Except as otherwise expressly set forth in this Agreement, Licensee, its directors, officers, employees, and agents make no representations and extend no warranties of any kind, either express or implied. In particular, and without limitation, nothing in this Agreement shall be construed as an obligation on the part of Licensee to furnish any manufacturing or technical information.

8. RELATIONSHIP OF THE PARTIES.

Nothing in this Agreement will be construed to constitute the parties as partners or joint ventures or constitute either party as agent of the other, nor will any similar relationship be deemed to exist between them. Neither party shall hold itself out contrary to the terms of this paragraph and neither party shall become liable by reason of any representation, act, or omission of the other contrary to the provisions of this paragraph. This Agreement is not for the benefit of any third party and shall not be deemed to give any right or remedy to any such party, whether referred to in this Agreement or not.

9. ASSIGNMENT.

9.1 No Assignment. This Agreement, the rights granted to Licensee, and the duties and obligations of Licensee are all personal to Licensee and Licensee agrees not to sell, assign, transfer, mortgage, pledge, or hypothecate any such rights in whole or in part, or delegate any of its duties or obligations under this Agreement; nor shall any of Licensee's rights or duties be assigned, transferred, or delegated by Licensee to any third party by operation of law. Any purported transfer, assignment, or delegation in violation of the foregoing sentence shall be void and without effect, and this Agreement shall thereupon become terminable without further notice by Licensor. In the context of this provision, "assignment" shall include the transfer of substantially all of the assets of Licensee, or of a majority interest in the voting stock of Licensee, or the merger, consolidation, or reorganization of Licensee with one or more third parties.

9.2 Binding on Successors. This Agreement will inure to the benefit of and be binding upon Licensor, its successors, and assigns.

10. DISPUTE RESOLUTION.

10.1 Arbitration of Royalty Disputes.

a. Any dispute between Licensor and Licensee concerning the amount of royalties payable to Licensor under this Agreement shall be submitted for binding arbitration in accordance with the provisions of this Section 10 and the then–applicable rules of the American Arbitration Association (the "Association"). Judgment upon the arbitration award may be entered in any court of competent jurisdiction.

b. The power of the arbitrators shall be limited to resolving the specific issues stated by determining the royalties Licensee owes or should receive credit for, if any, under this Agreement. The power of the arbitrators shall not extend to any other matters. All other disputes shall be subject to litigation in a court of competent jurisdiction.

c. The arbitration panel or tribunal shall consist solely of neutral arbitrators.

d. The parties agree that arbitration proceedings under this Agreement shall not be stayed on the ground of pending litigation to which either or both of them is a party.

10.2 Remedies. Except as expressly provided herein, all specific remedies provided for in this Agreement are cumulative and are not exclusive of one another or of any other remedies available in law or equity.

11. LIMITATIONS OF RIGHTS AND AUTHORITY

11.1 Limitation of Rights. No right or title whatsoever in the Licensed Patents is granted by Licensor to Licensee, or shall be taken or assumed by Licensee, except as is specifically set forth in this Agreement.

11.2 Limitation of Authority. Neither party shall, in any respect whatsoever, be taken to be the agent or representative of the other party, and neither party shall have any authority to assume any obligation for the other party, or to commit the other party in any way.

12. MISCELLANEOUS

12.1 Computation of Time. The time in which any act provided in this Agreement is to be done shall be computed by excluding the first day and including the last day, unless the last day is a Saturday, Sunday, or legal holiday, and then it shall also be excluded.

12.2 Notices. All notices given in connection with this Agreement shall be in writing and shall be deemed given upon actual receipt by the addressee. Notices shall be personally delivered or sent by telex or facsimile (with prompt confirmation by registered or certified air mail, postage prepaid) or by registered or certified air mail, postage prepaid, addressed to the party to be notified at the following address, or at such other address as the party may designate by notice:

Licensor:

_____

_____

_____

Attention: _____

Phone: _____

Facsimile: _____

Licensee:

_____

_____

_____

Attention: _____

Phone: _____

Facsimile: _____

12.3 Survival. The provisions of this Agreement relating to payment obligations, confidentiality, indemnification, remedies, and arbitration shall survive the expiration or termination of this Agreement.

12.4 Severability. If any provision of this Agreement is declared by a court of competent jurisdiction to be invalid, illegal, unenforceable, or void then both parties shall be relieved of all obligations arising under such provision, but only to the extent that such provision is invalid, illegal, unenforceable, or void. If the remainder of this Agreement is capable of substantial performance, then each provision not so affected shall be enforced to the extent permitted by law.

12.5 Waiver and Modification. No modification of any of the terms of this Agreement will be valid unless in writing and signed by both parties. No waiver by either party of a breach of this Agreement will be deemed a waiver by such party of any subsequent breach.

12.6 Headings. The headings in this Agreement are for reference only and shall not in any way control the meaning or interpretation of this Agreement.

12.7 Interpretation. No provision of this Agreement is to be interpreted for or against any party because that party or its attorney drafted the provision.

12.8 Governing Law. This Agreement shall be construed, governed, interpreted, and applied in accordance with the laws of the State of _____.

12.9 No Other Agreement. The parties each represent that in entering into this Agreement, they rely on no promise, inducement, or other agreement not expressly contained in this Agreement; that they have read this Agreement and discussed it thoroughly with their respective legal counsel; that they understand all of the provisions of this Agreement and intend to be bound by them; and that they enter into this Agreement voluntarily.

12.10 Entire Agreement. This Agreement constitutes the complete and exclusive statement of the terms and conditions between the parties, which supersedes and merges all prior proposals, understandings, and all other agreements, oral and written, between the parties relating to the subject of this Agreement.

12.11 Counterparts. This Agreement may be executed in counterparts, which taken together shall constitute one document.

IN WITNESS WHEREOF, the parties have executed this Agreement by their duly authorized representatives.

For and on behalf of

_____

Date: _____, 20_____

By: _____

Title: _____

For and on behalf of [Licensee]

_____

Date: _____, 20_____

By: _____

Title: _____

Bibliography

Moore, Kimberly A. "Judges, Juries, and Patent Cases: An Empirical Peek Inside the Black Box." *Mich. L. Rev.* 99 (2001).

Quinn, Eugene R., Jr. "Using Alternative Dispute Resolution to Resolve Patent Litigation: A Survey of Patent Litigators." *Marquette Intell. Prop. L. Rev.* 3 (1999): 77.

Smith, Gordon V., and Russell L. Parr. *Valuation of Intellectual Property and Intangible Assets.* New York: John Wiley & Sons, 1989.

Stewart, Thomas A. *Intellectual Capital: The New Wealth of Organizations.* New York: Doubleday/Currency, 1997.

Vermont, Samson. "Business Risk Analysis: The Economics of Patent Litigation." In *From Ideas to Assets: Investing Wisely in Intellectual Property*, edited by Bruce Berman. New York: John Wiley & Sons, 2001.

Further Reading

Berman, Bruce, ed. *From Ideas to Assets: Investing Wisely in Intellectual Property*. New York: John Wiley & Sons, 2001.

Chisum, Donald S., Craig Allen Nard, Herbert F. Schwartz, Pauline Newman, and F. Scott Kieff. *Principles of Patent Law*. New York: Foundation Press, 1998.

Davis, Julie L., and Suzanne S. Harrison. *Edison in the Boardroom*. New York: John Wiley & Sons, 2000.

Rivette, Kevin G., and David Kline. *Rembrandts in the Attic*. Boston: Harvard Business School Press, 2000.

Shulman, Seth. *Owning the Future*. New York: Houghton Mifflin, 1999.

Smith, Gordon V., and Russell L. Parr. *Valuation of Intellectual Property and Intangible Assets*. New York: John Wiley & Sons, 1989.

Stewart, Thomas A. *Intellectual Capital: The New Wealth of Organizations*. New York: Doubleday/Currency, 1997.

Sullivan, Patrick H. *Profiting from Intellectual Capital: Extracting Value from Innovation*. New York: John Wiley & Sons, 1998.

Index